RIVERS RUNNING FREE

RIVERS RUNNING FREE

Canoeing Stories
by Adventurous Women

edited by Judith Niemi & Barbara Wieser

SEAL PRESS

First published by Bergamot Books, 1987
First Seal Press edition, 1992

Cover art by Kris Wiltse
Cover design by Clare Conrad
Book design and typesetting: Annie Graham Publishing Services, Iowa City, Iowa
Maps by Elizabeth Barnard

Photos on pages 20, 82, 173 and 174 courtesy of the Minnesota Historical Society

Library of Congress Cataloging-in-Publication Data

Rivers running free.

Includes bibliographical references.
1. Canoes and canoeing. 2. Women canoeists—United States—Biography. I. Niemi, Judith. II. Wieser, Barb.
GV783.R5115   1992   796.1'22   92-23108
ISBN 1-878067-22-2

Printed in the United States of America

10   9   8   7   6   5   4   3   2

Foreign Distribution:
In Great Britain and Europe: Airlift Book Company, London

CONTENTS

Part Three
Urban Wilds

Part Four
The Very Poetry of Travel

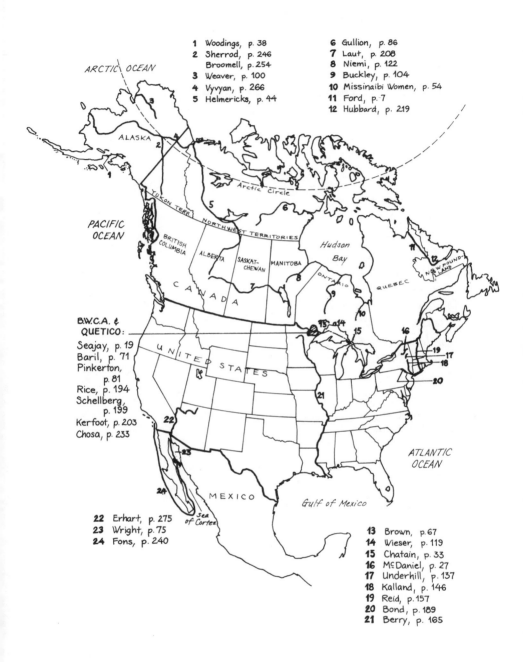

PREFACE

This is a book about adventurous and exploring impulses in women, about travelling in wild places by canoe. Many of these women have travelled great distances, but the real stories are the journeys of mind and spirit. Here's why and how they all got together in this book.

In the summer of 1980 editor Barb Wieser was setting out with a woman friend on her first long canoe trip, and was plenty scared. There would be just the two of them, quite inexperienced, alone for six weeks as they made their way to the Winisk River and Hudson Bay, for reasons they couldn't quite explain. They happened to find and bring along a copy of Judith Niemi's "Hudson Bay Journal," which Barb read, on the road and on the river, with excitement and relief—so there *were* other women doing things like this! That October Judith was teaching a women's log cabin building course, where a friend of Barb's appeared, bringing along the journal Barb had kept on her Winisk trip. "No kidding!" thought Judith, "other women who are as fanatic as I am. I've got to meet them."

It had been so important to each of us to find our realities in print that almost as soon as we met we began talking about collecting other women's canoe stories. Stories about canoeing as a way women have found their most adventurous, most free selves. Stories about the joy and changes that happen when we step out of our everyday lives into a world where we can feel more powerful, where our days are shaped by our skills and knowledge and spirit.

Compiling the book was a natural idea, since both canoes and books have been central to each of us for many years. Barb was a founder of Iowa City Women's Press and Aunt Lute Book Company, has written an auto mechanics book for women and has been involved in editing and publishing several other feminist books. For eight years, no matter what else has been going on in her life, she's made time every summer to spend several weeks canoeing Canadian wild rivers; more recently she's also started

1

guiding women's trips. It seemed like time to put the two interests together, and she founded Bergamot Books to publish this book and other outdoor women's writings.

Judith has been canoeing for twenty-five years, and since 1976 has made a career of teaching canoeing and guiding adult women's trips, as a founder of Woodswomen and now director of Women in the Wilderness. She's has canoed with women in Arctic Alaska, Labrador, Florida and the Minnesota-Ontario woods. From a former life as a literature teacher, she knows the fun of detective work in libraries and dusty old bookstores, and for many years has been teaching classes at various Minnesota colleges in the history of women and wilderness adventure.

Obviously canoe trips and wilderness life has meant a lot more to us than healthy exercise and nice vacations. We thought about moments from past trips. A Brooklyn woman who carefully gathered wood, lit and nurtured her first campfire, saying quietly, "I feel like I'm remembering all this." A circle of women on a rocky shore in the moonlight, remembering that back in the city our friends were at a Take Back the Night march, and realizing how much safer we felt in our dark woods than on a city street. Meeting in the supermarket, but not quite recognizing, a woman who a few months ago had been drinking hot soup and drying out clothes after a dunk in an October river. "It changed my life," she said. "I figured if I could do that, I could do anything. I've gotten a lot happier, and next week I'm moving to the Ozarks with my new lover and buying a farm."

We wanted women like these in the book, women who found a different way of being in the woods. Some general ideas about the book were clear from the beginning. It should include the romance, the emotion invested in wilderness travel. Women who can't recall one other moment from their fifteenth year remember in vivid detail their camp canoe trip. Years afterwards a woman may remember each campsite on the river, the pattern of the moonlight through the trees, what was said around the fire. There is, after all, some reason why women who never write another word often keep detailed trip journals, sometimes just recording the daily activities, but often trying hard to articulate what the experience *feels* like. We also wanted the writing to be down to earth and realistic, with mosquitoes as well as sunsets, close to the daily experience of canoe trips. We wanted to include not only arduous and impressive "expeditions" but the more common kinds of trips accessible to more people. And especially we hoped to find writers who would reflect on what being women had to do with their canoeing experiences, and how canoeing has influenced their lives.

In 1984 we began sending out requests for writing to women's bookstores, outdoor magazines and organizations, friends and acquaintances. We said that women didn't have to consider themselves writers to send us work, and that submissions could be in any form. What came back was a great pile of 50,000-word manuscripts, essays, long journals, letters, and introductions to other women we should meet. Out of all that we tried to select pieces from a wide variety of experiences – week-end trips, months in the Arctic, first experiences, solo travel and trips in big groups, and a few trips by sea kayak and raft. Relatively few of the manuscripts we received were about trips made with men; women most often wrote about women's experience on trips made with other women or alone. The writers vary greatly in age, in outdoor experience, in lifestyle, and in their reasons for writing. Many would probably never meet each other in the city, but we think would get along fine out on the river.

To the contemporary writings we've added older writings from Judith's growing collection of articles and books.* Many of these are not segregated in this book from the "modern" writings – a few generations is actually a pretty short span of time, and while writing styles change quite a bit, it doesn't seem to us that canoeing women have changed all that much. And we were especially happy to get letters and contributions from several women who were canoeing fifty or sixty years ago, and who are still canoeing today.

Chapter Four is arranged to include some historical perspective – on how canoeing has developed as a leisure activity, the ways women have learned canoeing, the changing styles, and the sheer impressive scope of some of the trips made by women in past generations. The other chapters follow some of the major themes that appear in women's writing about canoe trips: the joy of companionship; the valuable process of learning skills and learning to feel at home in the natural world; the interesting water-level angle from which the urban canoeist views life; the interior journeys that are a part of wilderness travel.

Canoes have been essential in the history of this continent. The native people designed them for food-gathering, for long-distance travel, for transportation of goods. The fur trade and major explorations were carried out by canoe travel. Most canoes are now intended for play, but it is still a craft well suited for serious travel, between our everyday lives and other parts of ourselves, other ways of being.

---

*A note about how we edited previously published writings when the authors are no longer among us to voice their opinions: We've freely omitted repetitions, obsolete technical information and sections of less interest. It soon became clear that if we marked every omission with ellipses (. . .), it would be very distracting, the page looking like an Arctic traveller's journal crawling with black flies. So we put academic prejudice aside and have used ellipses very rarely. Aside from unmarked omissions, pieces are exactly as they were first published, except in several places where words that were commonly used in past generations are not acceptable; even if the writers intended no offense, "savage," "squaw" or "primitive" have been replaced by more appropriate words, e.g., "Indian."

ACKNOWLEDGMENTS

Thank you to the following authors and publishers for permission to reprint their work:

Helen Broomell for excerpts from *Solo on the Yukon and Other Alaskan Adventures* and *Solo on the Yukon Again,* published by her in 1982 and 1984

Valerie Fons for excerpts from *Keep It Moving: Baja by Canoe* (Seattle: The Mountaineers, 1986)

Constance Helmericks for excerpts from Chapter 5 of *Down the Wild River North* (Boston: Little & Brown Co, 1968)

Justine Kerfoot for excerpts from *Woman of the Boundary Waters: Canoeing, Guiding, Mushing and Surviving* (Grand Marais, MN: Women's Times Publishing, 1986)

Peter Owen Ltd, London, for excerpts from *Arctic Adventure* by Lady C. C. Vyvyan

The University Press of Hawaii, Honolulu for excerpts from *Paddling My Own Canoe* by Audrey Sutherland

⋆   ⋆   ⋆

We wish to thank very much all of the contributors: those included in the book, who were very gracious and patient about the blue pencilling and revision suggestions, and the many more who sent manuscripts that we weren't able to include. We enjoyed reading every bit you sent us.

Special thanks to: Carol Iwata for the depth of her patience and understanding while living with this project for a long time, and for bringing a computer onto the scene and unravelling the mysteries of using it; Pamela Mittlefehldt for her friendship, faith in the book, and astute critical reading; Lisa Schoenfielder for her initial encouragement to start this project; Joan Pinkvoss and Sherry Thomas of Spinsters/Aunt Lute for their advice, support, and publishing help; Marcia Teal for her continuing encouragement and midnight xeroxing.

Thanks also to many members of Women in the Wilderness classes who have shared their enthusiasm and ideas and helped dig up new books and articles. Thanks to our gang of meticulous proofreaders: Ellen Brinkman, Beth Dalby, Vicki Dunevitz, Amy Lytton, Julie McGarry, Laurie Schroeder, Caroline Scully, Kathleen Remund, Jane Reynolds, Ann Wilder.

And thanks to all the women we've gone canoeing with over the years, especially the Sturdy Girls of Minnesota and Iowa, with whom we've shared wet feet, rowdy and quiet times, and life stories. You've given us a lot.

PART ONE:
The Companions of Her Days

Singing in the rain, Noatak River, Alaska, 1984 (Judith Niemi)

"We were two middle-aged women travelling for pleasure, disheveled and unwashed, with tired feet and tired bodies, but I think as we stood on the shores of that lake, listening to the silence that was almost audible, we must have experienced what the Saints describe as ecstasy."

—Lady C. C. Vyvyan, *Arctic Adventure,* 1961

"ALL THE INSTINCT OF REVOLT bubbles forth as I paddle away from civilization," wrote Isobel Knowles in 1905, and from her time on, one of the joys of canoeing for women has been getting away from the rules and the selves we're supposed to be in society. Especially when our canoeing companions are other women, we get to make up the rules, new ways to be. "You get to act out in the woods what we theorize about in classes," said a professor of women's studies. These chapters are by women enjoying canoe trip society—mothers or camp counselors sharing the outdoor life with kids, girls finding camping friendships and their own possibilities, older women being rowdy and relaxed—and about women finding joy and strength in each other.

"What did flies matter when you were free?"

JESSE FORD

Jesse Ford is a scientist and academician whose primary academic goal is to live in a cabin in the woods. She is an ecologist, teacher, traveler and writer who likes bogs, wetlands, long winters and lots of light in summer—also, all manner of wilderness travel and dancing. She maintains her Gemini credentials by living in New York, Minnesota, and Alaska.

Jesse made this 31-day trip on the George River in Labrador in 1982 with six other women from Minnesota. They were following a route explored by Mina Benson Hubbard in 1905. (For a description of Mrs. Hubbard's travels, see Judith Niemi's "Following Mina Hubbard Through Labrador" in Part Four.)

I dreamed this river before I went, but it was a static thing, an immense area of blue cutting diagonally across the topographic sheet, filling a quarter of the quadrangle. In my dream we flew down into this immensity, and I thought: it's so big! How could we not have known it was so big?

Later, back again, or partway back, I woke one night in the second story bedroom, warm from my lover's arms but feeling only the cool, cool river; the river, the water, and all the caribou. There was a restlessness to it, the endless shallow rapids, the caribou swimming, swimming. That restlessness stays with me still in all the places where straight lines cut across the natural contours of the land, bleeding the energy down.

It didn't take me very long to feel that I lived there. First, we stayed still a day, fresh from flying an hour across a maze of land threaded through water that all looked alike. We needed to work out the strangeness of finally being deposited in a place we'd all spent the last two years wondering about. Kristin and I danced off the pontoons, the last to arrive, and we all

7

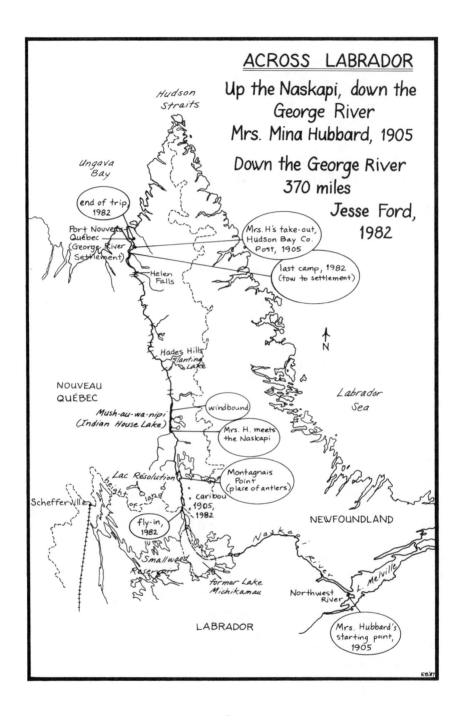

ACROSS LABRADOR

Up the Naskapi, down the
George River
Mrs. Mina Hubbard, 1905

Down the George River
370 miles
Jesse Ford,
1982

Hudson Straits

Ungava Bay

end of trip 1982

Port Nouveau Québec (George River Settlement)

Mrs. H's take-out, Hudson Bay Co. Post, 1905

last camp, 1982 (tow to settlement)

Helen Falls

N

Hades Hills Slanting Lake

NOUVEAU QUÉBEC

Labrador Sea

Mush-au-wa-nipi (Indian House Lake)

windbound

Mrs. H. meets the Naskapi

Lac Résolution

height of land

caribou 1905, 1982

Montagnais Point (place of antlers)

Schefferville

fly-in, 1982

NEWFOUNDLAND

Naskapi River

Smallwood Reservoir

former Lake Michikamau

Melville

Northwest River

L. Melville

LABRADOR

Mrs. Hubbard's starting point, 1905

EB'87

8

pitched gear and the last canoe off the Beaver. It flew off, tipping its wings goodbye, and the silence gathered in the wind, and reality started seeping upward, from underneath my boots. The very real feel of this solid place. The wind. The wind across the water. Blue sky. Tundra underfoot. A windswept hilltop somewhere in Labrador.

That morning Jean caught three northern pike in quick succession, so we ate breakfast. After breakfast one more casual cast brought in a huge fourth, so we made stew. Before this one became stew, though, her nine pounds of toothy pike broke our net. Thus I began mending – as we'd often do – while Judith read what Mrs. Hubbard, who had travelled here 77 years before us almost to the day, had to say about the northern end of Lake Michikamau in mid-August.

The thing of it was, it was so simple. On only the third day, I was already sore-muscled from many portages through impassable boulder gardens, through muskeg scattered with the first ripe cloudberries, portages with four or five weeks' gear for seven women . . . but it was so simple. My paddle cut across my field of view in a steady rhythm, once every two seconds, for weeks. We had food, fire gear, shelter, clothes, and mending stuff. Every night we unpacked the part we needed and every morning we packed it all back up again. The ritual of Stuffing. Stuffing socks into ziplocs into stuff sacks into plastic liners into Duluth packs into canoes under spray skirts. By the time we got to the snaps on the spray skirts most of us were generally on the verge of either giggles or grumpiness. Which it was depended on things like the ratio of last night's dreams to how much sand had worked its way into the long succession of snaps, zippers, and other fasteners. Also, how many caribou had wandered curiously through camp that morning, and what the berrying was like. Many levels of reality existed comfortably together.

Each morning I had the same dilemma. I'd brought too much. My stuff kept . . . expanding. Each morning my despair about the volume of my belongings deepened. Stuff stuff stuff stuff stash stash stash stash . . . this is keeping it simple? But in the afternoons, gear safely snugged up in canoe with only the lunch on top, paddles cutting the still waters, I couldn't remember why it had taken us two years to plan this trip. What in these packs could eat up two years? There were, after all, only eleven of them. It was and is a mystery to me still how living so simply can be so complicated to plan.

Later, there was much wind, always in our faces, and the temperature dropped, and it rained, and rained, and rained. There were many days filled with the kind of constant exaggerated attention to detail that helps keep wet camps dry and cozy. Lying in the tent one morning, listening to the wind and chilly rain for the third or fourth or fifth day in a row, it took me awhile to figure out that the peculiar burning sensation on the backs of my hands was actually sunburn. Relic of another reality several days ago on Adelaide Lake, when the water was still and the sun hot and high, and the land and water dropped away in all directions from this place just a few hundred yards from the continental divide. Or maybe it was from the day we had lunch at the Gull Rock Lunch Stop Cafe, where all seven of us perched precariously on a very small and pointy rock bedecked with guano, but in the wind and therefore free of Small Winged Companions. The five members of the Chocolate Committee were absorbed in Higher Mathematics, figuring out how to divide 7 Tobler bars by 5 travellers by 31 days. This kept most of us amused, while Connie and Jean enjoyed the peace of knowing they didn't have to figure out anything at all except how to get comfortable on this small, pointy, unappealing rock. Later, reloading the canoes, I almost capsized ours, but it was actually all Judith's fault for humming *all* the verses of the "Volga Boatman" while I tried to heave the three packs into precise appropriate locations, one foot on rock, one in the canoe, between convulsions of laughter at yet another verse.

But all that was several days ago, before the rain and consequent continuous meticulous attention to detail set in. After awhile it was very tiring, all this constant exaggerated attention. We did laugh, as we dried the evening's clothes around smoky fires, about seven women in all the hundreds of miles of wilderness, always and forever shoulder to shoulder under a smoky tarp. Still later we were more damp than dry, more claustrophobic than cozy. But that was much further on, because for many days almost every time we finished paying attention to paddling in the headwinds, or tarping up for lunch, there were amazing things about, everywhere. Rainbows. Double rainbows. Triple rainbows. Rainbows with both feet clearly visible. Rainbows lying on the land. Northern lights that joined us for dinner, rippling the cold subarctic sky with the dance of the universe. Alpenglow on a long sinuous esker, the highway of the caribou. Their restlessness in them still, and in their trails. It was possible to wander on their trails, and to start wanting to migrate. More than one of us had this tendency. Others watched closely for signs of hoof and antlers.

Once we made camp in a place of antlers, where the Montaignais used to live. It was hard, slow work to get to the top of the hill, bushwhacking through willow and alder, but the views were immense, and there was a glorious sunset. In the purpling night several were too tired to eat, too worn from the days of wind to want to talk. Some of us took antlers from that place. I cut a small piece, to hold my fishing line. I look at that piece now, and wonder how it was I didn't know then that this was somehow like desecration. Inappropriate. Those antlers were there for a reason, which was not to hold fishing line. It was so that the caribou would know to return to that place, so that the Montaignais could live. Well, the caribou did know, even though the Montaignais are no longer there. The caribou were there on that very day. Connie saw them, fifteen or so. They shared their camp with us, and were as curious about us as we were about them. I wondered if they explained to the little ones that we sometimes shed our Duluth packs like antlers, but several times a day. The natural history of canoe people.

The same small claw end of antlers wrapped in trolling line sits on my kitchen shelf, reminding me to think, and to listen.

After awhile, the days always seemed to begin with a certain dread about wetsuits. A word about wetsuits. One-piece wetsuits are not unlike oversized rubber bands. They hold one together, upright. I sprang as I walked. We all did. Certainly the suits did seem to change us from a normal band of generally dissimilar people into a chorus of small, tidy, effective women, giggling our way through the early days of small rapids and excellent pranks. At first all we needed to wear in addition to our wetsuits were a wool shirt, a life vest, and a wool hat. Up to the waist in rapids, lining, no problem. Later, when the temperature dropped, these svelte one-piece suits would cause dismay among many of us, for in order to follow the logical consequences of eating and drinking, one had to remove all her clothes: raingear, jackets, sweaters, shirts, more shirts, pants, and wetsuit. Naked midst a pile of steaming clothes in all that wind and rain. Now, what order did those plaid shirts go back in? We often followed the chilling experience with hot soup, to warm up. This seemed to sum up a certain sort of paradox about this journey.

We tried to think of ways to detect the approach of hypothermia. Anyone who couldn't rattle off the names of our five staple berries was suspect. After all, how could we forget the ever-present blueberries, the crowberries that cooked up so well in pancakes, or the cranberries, sauce for the bannock? Or the hairy gooseberries, called, of course, porcupine berries? Or, most amazing of all, the cloudberries? The first time I saw cloudberries on a portage was early on, after several hard short portages and puddle jumps. Packing canoes and unpacking canoes and carrying gear and canoes. Packing canoes and unpacking canoes and carrying gear and canoes. Somewhere in the middle of a carry I stopped dead in my tracks, grinning at the first patch of pale yellow cloudberries, ripe for eating. Judith, scooting along behind me with a 90-lb Mad River canoe, dropped it. Cloudberries take precedence.

The naming of the berries wasn't always enough to catch cold-induced sluggish brains, however. One day we stopped for lunch in the cold drizzle and tried for an hour, unsuccessfully, to make a fire from wet green willow wood so we could have hot drinks to warm up – and then discovered it was 6 P.M. and why hadn't we used a stove anyway? Carol and I invented a sort of a dance that revived us a little – face your partner and jump up and down in a short-legged sort of way, energetically slapping your partner's clothing-padded shoulders. When you start giggling, you know you're on the road to recovery. And we did giggle. Two short bulky female forms, in ritual garb of modest neoprene undergarments covered with fourteen layers of outerwear, hopping around the soggy willow break.

Caribou often swam the river. Our first encounter with any number of them began on a day of ferocious headwinds. Getting back in the canoe again after a hot tea break, Fisher and I had an odd sensation, looking at the rocks in the shallows ahead. Everything had that peculiar disorienting look of a successful ferry traverse in fast-moving water, yet we weren't ferrying. Each of us held our peace, trying to shake the hallucination, until we both realized at once that the "rocks" were moving – and that they weren't rocks, but a mama caribou and her calf! We saw them for many days, then, in bands of three or eight or twenty or more, on the move, until we crossed the invisible but apparently well-known border of legal hunting country. After that the only caribou we saw for awhile was the one that swam steadily across the wide expanse where the George River widens into Indian House Lake. We watched it for a long time, swimming and swimming and swimming as patiently as we paddled and paddled and paddled, in the headwinds. As it neared the west shore, engines cut the air, and when four hooves found shore the rifles spoke and the world had one less caribou. It's one thing to live with the caribou, and subsist on them. It's another thing, and one I don't understand, to spend what some people make in a year to come to this wild place for a few weeks and kill those who live here, in the name of recreation.

One cold windy afternoon, a helicopter dropped out of the wild sky, and we met the game wardens who were posted on the river to keep an eye on the hunt. None of our French speakers were in the front canoe, but the uneasy message generally seemed to be that Connie's eighteen-year-old son Christian had been hurt. In his leg. He was in the hospital . . . but no need for her to return.

On our hurried way down the long lake to the game warden's hut to radio for more news, we spent a day weathered in, windbound in winds that rose so high, so suddenly in the night, that our tentpoles bent and one tent collapsed, corner by corner. There's something unnerving about having your house fall down around your ears in the middle of the night. It wasn't until the third corner fell at about 3 A.M. that three of us reached unanimity about turning the tent to face in this hour's wind direction.

12

We'd spent a lot of time talking about the pros and cons of trying this maneuver in winds so cold and heavy it was hard to stand, never mind produce such a delicate operation, and in the dark, too. For some reason the main issue seemed to be how long this would all take. ("It'll take forever!" "No, it won't take very long at all." "In the dark?" "Well, it'll take some time but not too long.") So we placed bets. Forever bet an hour and Hardly Any Time At All bet 30 minutes. Jean and Connie turned the tent, corner by corner, and I played movable ballast, and dawn came on us in the process. Diving back into the sleeping bags Connie, who had guessed 40 minutes, was proclaimed the winner, because the entire body-and soul-numbing operation took exactly 48 minutes.

After many more hours of wild screechy weather Judith's voice arrived, followed shortly by Judith herself, serving Lavendar Lines Tempest Special—a bit of anything one might care to eat, including blueberries (yes, they're local, Ma'am). The poles on all tents were still bowing at precarious angles and the tents themselves seemed restless as caribou to be off and running across the tundra. We passed the daylight hours repositioning tents off into the timber, whittling new tent stakes, eating a great deal, and staying warm. We read Mrs. Hubbard's account of her 1905 journey down this river from the old original edition, the red hardbacked one with the gold letters on the cover. And we sang. Much singing, with Carol's lovely tenor guiding us through Peace of the River, followed by a new song concerning Sarah Lou the Caribou, the Lily of the North ("Her stately rack, her velvet lips, my affections did call forth . . .").

Still, the next day dawned as windy as ever. After packing up everything but one tent and the cook pack, we ate dozens of potato pancakes slathered in butter and rehydrated sour cream. When, and if, to leave might have been a problem, but the most conservative (that day) got together with the most adventurous (that day) and appointed themselves the Committee on Leavetaking. We finally left sometime in the afternoon, paddling off into whitecaps with rainbows behind us lying flat and brilliant against the forested hills. It was such a joy to be out again, paddling into the wind and held together by wetsuits and pancakes, after a day of ordinary tent fever spiked by anxiety over Christian. At dusk, having paddled steadily into headwinds for many hours, we chose to have a floating dinner and keep going as long as possible into the peaceful moonlit night, northern lights flashing behind the clouds. There weren't many words about it, but we wanted to get to the wardens' hut and radio for more information as soon as possible.

We did make the hut that night, stumbling and lurching up to the door on feet numb with cold and legs accustomed only to the dance of the water, not hard, solid ground. The crew made us welcome in a quiet way, and tried to radio out the next morning, but weather made radio communications impossible. What to do. We finally arranged with the helicopter mechanic to call Christian directly on his next flight into Schefferville and relay Connie's messages and questions, and to find us later on the river to deliver the answers.

Although it was only two days before Donald and the helicopter brought reassuring news for Connie, there were to be many adventures, including our hours at the Culos' fish camp. It felt odd to be eating lunch indoors, stuffy and windless and not at all luxurious. The sports at the camp took Carol, who is Japanese, to be our "Indian guide." She said it gave her a good chance to look inscrutable and pass up the small talk. One Texan wanted to take our picture. Jean and Connie spent much time with Madame Culos in the kitchen, washing containers and measuring out new supplies. Madame Culos was pleased to see us, and Connie allowed as how it must be nice to see other women. Yes, she replied, it is. You know, she said, all the men in the fish camps below are waiting for you. Well, said Connie, we're not waiting for them! Gales of laughter all around. Madame Culos was still chuckling as we left, rich in flour and butter and peanut butter and all the chocolate in the Culos' camp.

The guests at the camp had told us many stories with much knowing laughter about the upcoming rapids. Much heavier than anything you've done yet, they said. It sounded menacing. A mist of apprehension blew through and was gone. Rapids are our thing.

After lunch we paddled out slowly. Judith and Jean took an enormous amount of time scouting one set of rapids. Must be some kind of water down there, the rest of us reasoned, too generally satisfied with our recent hot lunch and life in general to want to move much. Eventually they came back. It's *very* big, hug the left shore. Stay just to the right of the enormous boulder, between it and the huge standing waves just to its right.

Duffer canoe, heavy laden, went first, and Kristin and I watched Carol, Fisher, and Connie high sign about their good run as they disappeared around the corner. Then we go. It is . . . huge! But with a clear, small passageway just as described. In the bow, dwarfed by green and froth and roar on all sides, time slowed so much that the timing was easy. Backpaddle, draw left, draw right a hair, a hard left, and paddle out. We hooted all the way into the eddy, heady with the precision of it. Jean and Judith followed us in, grinning and excited.

Later, we asked about how they'd decided, in this very long scout, to treat it the way they did, and Judith and Jean recreated the entire scouting conversation for us. Big, sez Jean. Yep, sez Judith. Runnable, sez Jean. But nine out of ten times? sez Judith. Small channel here, sez Jean. Yep, sez Judith, small. Yep, sez Jean.

14

We were not an excessively wordy crew.

The days spun on and the river got bigger, and bigger, and bigger. Some days we'd have hours of rapids, sometimes running them in headwinds, sometimes in the snow. One long set just above Wedge Hills became known as Crabby Rapids because the headwinds were so fierce we had to fight our way through them. Even though we could see the land dropping away in front of us, if we stopped paddling our hearts out for even one instant, we got blown back upriver, uphill. Learning to live even more in the very present moment, one roller to the next, keep the bow up, catch the crests. Painful progress. Stay sensitive to slight changes in the wind, and when it lets up for even a second, go even HARDER. Feels like no progress at all. I select markers on the shore about ten meters apart, and it takes minutes to fight from one to the next. Blackface rock, double leader spruce, whale rock. Finally the wind died a little, the river turned a little, and we ended the run in tailwinds.

In these days Mrs. Hubbard was strongly with us. We read her account of the final days of her Race to Ungava. "A toboggan slide," she said, tumultuous rapids. Watching boulders reaching up like jagged teeth as she duffed her way through the foam and churn of the white, white water, consigned by chivalry to a permanent position as non-paddler in her group of four Indian guides and herself. There is an art to duffing, especially when sitting immobile in fierce headwinds when it's in the mid-40's and raining. The duffer's job is to be cheery, alert, and steady—and to keep her body core temperature somewhere above critical. Under these circumstances, isometrics take on survival value. The duffer's partners also have a job, which is to KEEP THE DUFFER DRY. We each tried to explore the gentle art of duffing as little as possible, and marveled at Mrs. Hubbard's good humor.

As the rapids continued our rowdiness grew. The morning it hit 26 degrees and we had to thaw out our wetsuits before we put them on, we decided to place an ad in the personals when we got home: "Do you consider yourself 'far out'?? Seven resolute canoeists, average age 38, seek likeminded others for fun and adventure. We are into: neoprene, mushroom bulgar, Sousa marches, and stuffing. Only serious inquiries invited."

By the time we arrived at the three-mile portage around Helen's Falls, it had been weeks since our last portage. It was a slow business, unpacking the canoes and getting ready to be land beasts again, probably made slower by the realization that we were getting near the end of our trip. Slowly we packed and slowly we portaged. This was a place of a confusion of trails, some human, many caribou, wandering everywhere. The woods were much used and trampled, and sparse with deadfall, full of shed antlers. Parts appeared to have been burned, and these places were the only ones in which a second species of blueberry commonly joined the ever-familiar *Vaccinium uliginosum* that we'd feasted on for weeks. We portaged about half the gear halfway, and collapsed into camp for an early dinner. That night in the firelight I looked around our quiet circle of faces and saw strangers, strong faces, haunting and unfamiliar. Poised, in this place, and full with the spirits of the night. Slowly and of its own accord, the image slipped back into recognizability, my friends, my tribe. For a moment I'm overcome by the power of this silent circle flickering in the firelight.

The next morning began with an act of true heroism, as two members of the Coffee Affinity Group (whose membership, of course, overlapped exactly with that of the Chocolate Committee), raced out for an early morning portage. This was not about Aerobics or Fitness or even Feeling So Terrific We Couldn't Be Restrained. No, this was, instead, about Frantic. Unbelievably, after all these weeks of incredible organization and meticulous attention to all kinds of arcane details, *all* the coffee, the several separate stashes of precious, fine-ground, St. Paul, Extra Delicious, heat-sealed, ziplocked, zealously guarded coffee, had already been portaged a mile and a half past camp. By the time these heroic, exhausted women returned, most of the rest of the Affinity Group had somehow managed to make it into their wetsuits, an event which all by itself called for a coffee break.

We had followed this river, now, since before it was a river, had come upon it from the other side of the height of land, in this flat topography merely a scraggly wet ribbon of spruce threaded through the flat still lakes and large sky. We'd paddled and portaged hundreds of miles, from tiny puddles through shallow rapids and around steep-sided canyons of granite pink in the afternoon sun, carried gear and canoes along caribou trails, through the reindeer moss and berries, around boulder gardens of rock so strongly metamorphosed that the patterns in the bouldery beaches curled and danced with a life of their own, an art gallery in pinks and greys and blacks and reds. We'd paddled in the swell and surge of the growing river, into the afternoon winds, through whitecaps, under a sun like weak tea, and deeply grey and changeable skies, ever-shifting light, and rainbows. We'd kept company with caribou and porcupines, loons and osprey, trout and char, purple harebells, white lichens, deep red *Sphagnum* moss, dark green spruce. Not long into the journey I thought of how people say things like, "Why do you want to go off in the middle of nowhere?", as if a place without settlements has no identity. And yet this is the most immediate, most tangible, most *where* place I've ever been.

On the river it was not often what one would call easy, but it was so simple that it often felt easy. There were only simple sets of situations. Rain. Wind. Wet sand in the zippers. Cold. Strong challenges, with single strong threads. Shortly after returning, I found myself in the middle of a bewilderment of traffic, papers everywhere, emotional turmoil and random entropy. I left again to guide a canoe trip in northern Minnesota with a friend. It poured rain for three days, and my sense of relief at having to deal only with such manageable things as rain (which would eventually stop), wet tents (which would eventually dry), a small band of open and humorous women, and the incredible beauty of dense fog parting to give glimpses of spectacular cliffs along Vern Lake, was profound and tangible. The delights of complexity began to wane for me, that August in Labrador.

The days were hard and simple and free, and we cared for each other in simple, individual ways. One turned another's shoes by the campfire. Another caught fish to eat. One turned our cracker crumbs into croutons, and someone else gathered dwarf fireweed to add to it. One secured the tarps at night, often, when others were too tired. One or two almost always rose the earliest to wake the camp, and someone else cooked breakfast. Two picked berries all the time, and one often made fires first thing, to warm us when we stopped. One had a talent for finding portage paths, and another for finding beautiful campsites.

One conquered her uneasiness in groups; another her dislike of cold. Someone taught someone else the best way to keep her shoe tied. One, believe it or not, helped another on with her wet suit. This is far more easily said than done. Everyone looked like elves by the third week. Two cultivated this look. One became incredibly handsome shortly after we began. One, who doesn't speak much, drew her partner's attention to many rainbows, vistas, and swimming caribou. Three discussed glacial geology.

One asked for a quiet camp and seven spent a silent evening, afterwards thanking her. One measured our miles, another our drop to the sea. A third took the temperature a lot. One heard a woman's voice, not ours; two heard a hum, and, later, singing. One ate a lot all the time. So, quite soon, did all the others. And everyone drank that wonderful river water all the time.

On the last morning, windbound again, each found her own way to patience. A large Peterborough canoe came across the river under power from the Inuit fish camp and offered us a tow through the high winds and waves and tidal rapids to the settlement where our bush flight would meet us. As we began to make our way across to the camp, the first canoe had no sooner gotten their paddles in the water when the skies opened one final time in a sudden, drenching deluge of rain, sending most of us into a fit of helpless giggles. Later, fortified by hot tea and bannock and quiet, funny conversation with the women of the fish camp, we joined them in the rain under orange and blue tarps in their boats, and watched our own canoes, now dwarfed, bounce along under many horsepower tow. We arrived at the settlement just before the tides turned, and watched alpenglow paint the mile of suddenly exposed mudflats. By now it was mid-September with tundra plants turning a brilliance of color: scarlet alpine bearberry, pink and purple blueberries, brilliant yellow dwarf birch, rich orange Labrador tea.

The next few days were quiet, or seemed quiet. Maybe we just talked less. Or maybe it was just that, for the first time in five weeks, we were neither travelling, nor deciding about travelling. Living indoors again was peculiar and confusing, but warm in a way we hadn't been for awhile. Even the noise of friendly settlement life was a lot to deal with. We flew our kite, went for walks, and tried to adjust to life beyond our own tribal existence.

The immediate shock of returning to life in the U.S. was the most difficult of all, even if it was Minnesota. But, after awhile, I found that somewhere along the line I had discovered a long-forgotten connection with my own calm and competent self. Suddenly, things seemed possible. Paddling the whitewater of my life, I let my relationship go, sold my house, acquired a Siberian husky, accepted a job in a Far Distant Land (upstate New York), and completed, at long last, my doctoral dissertation.

Although I didn't end up, as Connie suggested, moving to Alaska, I do have a research program up there, and trips to guide. All this is in the way of health management, because it seems that I, like many travelers in the North, have contracted that incurable disease: Arctic Fever. So, for those of you that travel, let this be a warning. The large skies and stark beauty of these northern places can move and challenge you as gently, as insistently, as completely as the warmest and most profound of lovers. It truly becomes possible to have a love affair with the land. As for us, we all had a difficult time returning, and part of each of us probably never will.

Becoming a Canada Tripper, 1965

CAROL (HEENAN) SEAJAY

Carol Seajay has lived in the San Francisco Bay area for fifteen years. She was a founder of Old Wives' Tales, one of the largest feminist bookstores, and she is the editor and publisher of the trade magazine, Feminist Bookstore News. *She is also a writer, and loves being outdoors. She used to camp out secretly within Bay area parks, likes heading into the Sierras for skiing.*

Carol hadn't been canoeing for ten years when Barb moved to California and started looking for paddling partners. Carol writes, "I was broke and didn't have my rent money and didn't know what to do with my life. Barb called me up and said, 'Let's go canoeing.' So we took off to the Eel River for four days. When I got back everything just fell into place. It was the best thing I could have done."

While out canoeing, Carol started telling enthusiastic stories of her Girl Scout camp days. So we asked her to write her memories of camp and canoeing.

Maybe the rest of the campers were at Crafts. Maybe I was headed back to my tent for something I'd forgotten. I don't know where I was supposed to be, but I wasn't intended to be walking up the path alone. I heard the sharp crack first, then looked up to see the counselor pick up another length of wood, set it on the stump, swing the ax high and bring it down. The wood split neatly in two, flying away from the ax as the clean crack filled my ears. She reached for one of the pieces, balanced it on the stump again as she freed the ax from the home it found in the stump. She held the ax in front of her, looking at the wood for a moment, then once again lifted her hands in a fluid movement, bringing the ax high over her head and down again with a sharp crack.

I had never seen anything like it. I'd never seen anyone split wood; I'd certainly never seen a *woman* split wood—or do anything as bold as pick up an ax and use it. Washing machines and vacuum cleaners, yes. And the

Canoe lesson, Chisago, Minnesota, 1948 (Gene Becker)

endless round of canning all summer. But nothing like this tall lean woman stretching her body, lifting her arms, swinging the ax high and splitting the wood so cleanly.

I stood there in the path watching while she split the rest of the wood and stacked it away. Then I still stood there, staring into the clearing as if I could see in the pattern of trees or the pattern of the light in the air, how the future had just changed for me.

I didn't mean to become a canoeist; I hadn't wanted to go to Girl Scout camp at all. The other kids in the neighborhood were going to Van Buren County Youth camp, a subsidized program for city kids. My brother had gone the year before and came home with exciting, terrifying tales of stealing girls' panties, running bathing suits up the flag pole. All the kids were going, it was the thing to do. Maybe my mother wanted something different for me. As the years passed, I came to see that she wanted something better for all of us than just getting by, than fear, than the early pregnancy and early marriages that grade school sexuality promised. Whatever her reasons, she pounced on the Girl Scout camp flier she found in my coat pocket and campaigned for my willingness to try "this other camp." I wanted to go where my friends were going. I didn't want to go away for two whole weeks—one was enough! But I must have nodded my head at a wrong moment one sleepy night, because by the time I got up in the morning, she had already mailed the deposit to the Girl Scout camp. I never did remember agreeing to go.

But I did go. And at nine I fell in love with trees, with the out-of-doors, with something I later called community—living and working together, sharing projects and goals, succeeding at firebuilding, outdoor cooking, scavenger hunts. When the other girls complained of being homesick, I'd say that I wasn't homesick but that when I got home I would be "camp-sick." I'd carry on about how I'd be "Mac-sick" ("Mac" being the graceful ax-wielding counselor) until my tent-mates would tell me to shut up.

Back home, I raved about camp until my mother made me a deal: if I could save half of the fee for next summer, she and my dad would come up with the rest. How they expected a nine year old on a ten cent a week allowance to come up with $22, I never knew. Perhaps the point was that I wouldn't be able to. But that fall we moved to a rural school district with new adventures like school busses and hot lunch programs. I found that if I bought a carton of milk with the sack lunch kids, and mooched a piece of bread or peanut butter sandwich from a kid who did buy the hot lunches, I could save up as much as 25 cents a day. I made my $22 easily.

There was no stopping me. As a non-scout I had to wait until after a certain date to apply, but I went every summer. Being tiny, I called myself

21

"Shrimp" and after the first couple of years, all the returning staff knew me by name, would greet me when I arrived. I fell in love, again and again, with camp, with the counselors, with the particular quality of energy, with sharing, with acceptance, with having a place and knowing what to do in it.

Home again after the third summer, I sat on the back porch and thought intently, comparing the world I lived in at camp—the ease and joy I felt there—with the awkwardness since I'd returned to my folks. I thought about boarding school kids (I'd just seen *The Parent Trap*) and how they lived in one place all winter, and then went away to summer camps, but still called "home" the place they went at Christmas and for a week here and there. I decided that if they could call "home" someplace they only spent a few weeks a year, then I could call Girl Scout camp my real home, and know that I was just "staying" at this other place the rest of the time.

I had a regular summer gang of girls who went to the same session year after year, and ended up in the same units. At fourteen we were finally old enough to sign up for the canoeing units. Somehow I missed the word that we were all going to sign up for the intermediate trip. I carefully followed the rules and signed up for the beginner trip, and ended up with no one I knew. There was one girl from my school, though, and she and I became tent and canoeing partners. Dot didn't *get* canoeing. Didn't get why, if you paddled on this side, the canoe went the other way. So even though I was far smaller, I ended up in the stern, learning to guide the canoe, to compensate for her odd and erratic strokes, and to load the canoe to make up for the weight disparity.

We had the classic worst trip possible. We were an odd group of girls who never did click together. It stormed the entire time we were actually out on the river, and we had to get off the river any time the lightning was at all close. Our clothing and gear were soaked and we camped in farmers' barns both nights. We probably canoed a total of eight miles in three days. Describing the trip afterwards to my friends, I told about the excitement of being on a real river, about the intensity of the lightning and about dragging the canoes over downed trees in the river. They were skeptical and asked about being cold and wet, about soggy peanut butter and jelly sandwiches, about whether we'd seen any whitewater *at all?*

They came home from their trip later in the summer radiant and sparkling, full of tales of Pooh, the canoeing counselor, doing headstands on the bow as they floated lazily downriver on hot sunny days. They heard tales from the counselors of our ill-fated trip and laughed at and with me. "Shrimp is so into canoeing that she has a good time even when it's awful!" was the word. "Next year," they said. Next year they wanted to go on a canoe trip to *Canada.* They'd heard that the camp had run a trip to Canada a few years earlier and decided that it could happen again, for us. By hook or by crook. And I was going. Forget the progression of trips. If I could canoe with Dot through the rain, I must be ready for Canada.

Most of the gang went to the Catholic girls' school, located conveniently across the street from the Girl Scout office and very handy for lobbying for a special trip. "You aren't even Girl Scouts," they said in the office. We all promptly found troops and joined up. "It costs too much," they said. We agreed to pay a higher camp fee. "We have no way to know the trip will fill." We called everyone we knew who had ever gone on a canoe trip and guaranteed eight of the twelve places. I think we wore them down with our sheer persistence. They didn't know where in Canada to take us. They couldn't find staff with enough whitewater skills. Finally they came up with the Boundary Waters Canoe Area on the Canadian border above Minnesota, where we could do an eight-day lake trip in real wilderness. We wanted a river trip. BWCA was their final offer. We agreed jubilantly. We were going to Canada!

As the Canada Trippers we were the elite of the camp. Each session, all the campers gathered to wave the current group of "Trippers" off. When the canoers returned to camp, the dinner bell was rung, and everyone gathered from all over the camp to greet them. Only the Counselors-in-Training ranked higher. But that summer we Canada Trippers out-ranked even the CIT's. Canada was exotic. Going on the trip was brave. Very few in the entire camp had been in a real wilderness before. It was a two-day drive, including a four-hour ferry trip across Lake Michigan, just to get there. The few days in camp before the trip were heady. We did canoe drills, paddled hour after hour to build up strength; we practiced portaging. This was going to be no easy downriver ride. And at last we set out.

We drove across Michigan and Wisconsin, into Minnesota, farther away from home than I'd ever been before. On the drive we spent hours planning chore-charts and a rotation of tasks so that everything would go smoothly. We camped in the woods near the outfitter's parking lot, and it wasn't until the next morning as we were loading gear into the canoes that I realized we were going to *canoe* into Canada.

This was like no place I'd ever been before. We were a gang of young women, mostly fifteen, our counselors barely twenty-one. No one had offered us this trip—we'd thought of it, lobbied for it, planned and prac-ticed for it. Suddenly there we were: pushing off into the wilderness, the lake and the vast sky stretching out before us in welcome and invitation. We were on our own, with stars and sun, compass and map to guide us.

On this trip, we couldn't simply follow the current downstream—every direction was a real possibility in the maze of lakes. Someone turned out to be good at reading the maps and compass. I think it was actually a committee of three or four who watched the contour lines and the compass, who compared the islands and shorelines to the map to determine where we were, and where we should head next. I was content to follow their lead, paddling back and forth cheerfully looking for a portage, only to have it turn out to be around the next bend. I didn't care if we went on a side trip to see the Indian Rock Paintings or which route we chose to get to the next chain of lakes. We were *here*. Everywhere was here. Sky and water, trees and waves. Loons laughing and calling, diving and surfacing. Our silver canoes glinting in the sun. I had, in those moments, everything I had ever wanted in my entire life.

We saw a bear on the shore that first day. A small, unconcerned black bear, but very exciting to us. None of us had ever seen a wild bear before, so we decided to camp on an island. It seemed safer. Others had done that before us, and after we had unloaded all our gear we realized there was no firewood on the entire island. Four of us took a look at the driftwood on the opposite shore and set out in empty canoes to bring it back.

Only later did we realize that we had blown the careful pre-trip plan of patrols and chore-charts that organized all of us into "fair" and rotating divisions of camp chores. By the time we got back with the firewood, the tents were set up and dinner was ready for the quickly built fire. Someone had initiated an inventory of the food and gear packs from the outfitter and re-packed them to distribute the weight evenly. (It had taken two of us to even lift the one filled with canned goods and four of us to get it over the first portage.) Someone else had started thinking out menus.

After that first night we wordlessly dropped our carefully made chore-charts and began another system of simply pitching in to do the work at hand, each one following her own inclinations but mindful of all that needed to be done. I loved (and still do) building fires more than almost anything. So did a lot of us, so I did a lot of tent staking to share it around. Skills were shared informally. Someone always had a new and better idea for pitching the tents, for stringing up the food at night. "That works, but try it this way," was the approach. Any three of us could get a fire going no matter how much it had rained. I knew almost nothing about cooking, but others did and the rest of us were there to chop and stir and keep the fire below the pots burning steadily. If you saw something that needed to be done, you did it. If you were too busy, you mentioned it to someone else and she did it. Even after all these years I'm still amazed if I find myself in a group of women that *doesn't* function on this model.

I'm sure it wasn't always golden – it rained a lot, and we suffered some anxiety before we realized it was a weather pattern, that it would sprinkle every afternoon and clear off about four. The nights were the coldest I'd ever known and few of us had sleeping bags built to accommodate them. We tried every combination of doubling up and tripling up under sleeping bags. The only night I recall being warm was when I snuggled up to Minnie's broad and warm back. She didn't want to do it again, though, and I didn't understand why.

The days were filled with paddling, with gazing into the trees, with watching the wildlife. We saw a mother bear with two cubs. I watched loons diving and flying, landing on water and taking off. We paddled on and on, in the solitude, in the beauty, day after day, as if we were the first people there.

We rarely saw other people, but the night we decided to go skinny dipping in the pool beneath a waterfall we were invaded by a troop of Boy Scouts who camped noisily on the other side of the small lake. We hated them. But the next day, when Ruth slipped on a portage and twisted her ankle, we were glad enough to have the Boy Scout leaders nearby. Even collectively, our first-aid skills were theoretical. They knew how to set the broken (we thought) leg, how to make splints from tree branches and pad them for comfort. I was strangely embarrassed by our ignorance and never wanted to be vulnerable and dependent like that again.

Ruth's fall came two days from the end of the trip. Despite the splint – or because of it – she was in considerable pain. When it became clear that a couple of aspirin weren't going to help enough, we decided to do two days of paddling in one, and try to get her back to the outpost that night for real medical attention. We were now much stronger than when we set out. We made our strokes deep and powerful, singing all the canoeing songs we knew to keep our rhythm steady and our spirits high. We finished the last portage by late afternoon. Motorboats were allowed on the US side of the border, and we flagged one down, asking them to tell our outfitter that we'd had an injury, that we were trying to get in that night, and to please send the pontoon boat out for us. Then we paddled on, eating another lunch for dinner, paddling through the sunset, into the long northern twilight and into the darkness.

I think we would have paddled all night if we'd had to, but finally a beam of light and the roar of an outboard motor invaded the stillness. We flagged them down with the flashlights we'd steered by. There was an hour of unloading, tying the canoes all over the edges and the top, and fitting fourteen tired scouts in somehow. Then the pontoon boat turned around and roared us slowly, but much faster than our tired arms could take us, back to civilization.

We did other trips after this one, including a senior scout trip with no adult supervision and a canoe trip on the fastest river in lower Michigan. But eventually we began going our separate ways into adulthood. I felt myself pulled towards college, and for me that meant paying jobs all summer and on weekends, a necessity that interfered mightily with my camping.

I always meant to return to the Boundary Waters, the place that more than anywhere else gave me the ability to envision and bring my dreams into reality. I'm amazed that twenty years have gone by and I've been too busy with all my other dreams to go back.

Scouts on the Saranac

JUDITH McDANIEL

Judith McDaniel grew up with the Girl Scouts. She was in a troop from the time she was old enough to join the Brownies until she was a senior in high school and went to International Scout Camps in Germany, England, and Denmark. As an adult she has served on the Board of Directors of the Adirondack Girl Scouts, led a Scout troop of 4th graders for a number of years, and from 1980–82 guided canoe trips of Scouts on the Saranac and other rivers and lakes in upstate New York.

She is also a political activist and writer, the author of two books of poems and a novel. In the spring of 1987, Firebrand Books published Sanctuary, *a book of essays and poems which includes her experience of being captured by contra forces in Nicaragua in 1985.*

"I hope you like this story," said her note accompanying Scouts on the Saranac. *"I think it may be the most wholesome piece I've ever written."*

"You're going to do what?" my friends asked when I announced my summer recreation. "With how many Girl Scouts?" And, "What do *you* know about canoeing?"

Not a lot, I had to admit. I hadn't been in a canoe for ten years when I went on the spring trial run with others who had also agreed to lead a short canoe trip on the Saranac River. I am more often behind a desk or at my typewriter, but my canoeing muscles hadn't been *too* out of shape, I remind myself as I stand looking at the piles of gear stacked around the first two girls to arrive. Another car pulls up and deposits two more girls. As Mary's mother gets back in the car, Mary pulls out a huge portable radio and starts to tune it in. I signal her mother to wait and edge toward Mary.

"Gee, Mary, I don't think you'll have much time to listen to that. And we wouldn't want it to fall out of a canoe, would we, hmmm?" I maneuver her toward the car and she very reluctantly deposits the radio with mother.

So does her friend Julie, to Mary's distress.

"Oh, Julie, why'd you have to tell them you have one?" Mary pouts. "You know I can't sleep without a radio on."

As I wave goodbye to the departing mother, I hear Beth's undertone, "Never mind. I brought mine with me and my mother is already gone." They all look relieved. I file the information for later. At 10 A.M. our sixth canoer arrives and we heft our gear and set off down the path to the tents we will occupy for this one night before our outing. By 10:30 the girls are out in canoes on Hidden Lake, getting checked out by the resident canoe staff on how much they remember about their strokes and canoe safety from last year's lessons. I take half an hour to reconnoitre.

Checking through the gear, I realize that most of it is borrowed from the other volunteers. This is an all-volunteer camp, sponsored by the Adirondack Girl Scout Council. The staff has run the camp for three years now, more elaborate each time. This year the girls who were trained in camp last year are eligible for an out-of-camp canoe trip, which is why I'm here.

At noon the girls troop up to the boat house where I've laid out peanut butter and jelly for sandwiches. Mary tells me she doesn't eat peanut butter. I explain that it is all we will have for lunch for the trip, since it doesn't spoil. I'm irritated with her already because of the radio incident, because she seems so lethargic and whiney.

"What's for dinner, then?" she asks, looking with distaste at the sandwich counter.

"Barbecue chicken," I tell them enthusiastically, "won't that be good?" But Mary doesn't eat chicken either. "What do you eat?" I inquire with some rancour.

"Oh, steak," she replies languidly, then more animatedly, "and pizza." I grind my teeth. It is time for the food statement.

"Look," I tell the group as we sit on the dock for lunch, "the food for this trip was planned for nutrition and easy preparation over a campfire. There will always be plenty to eat. If you don't like some things, eat what you do like. The main thing is, I don't want to hear complaints. O.K.?" They say O.K. Mary eats two stale Girl Scout cookies in silence.

After a rest, I put them in the water for swim tests. They are all water rats. They love the water and undergo instant and complete personality changes when they're soaking wet. Mary and Beth want to learn the butterfly so they can try out for the swim team when they start ninth grade. Julie is a gymnast and takes her lithe young body through a marvelous series of contorted dives, then asks, "Can I do a cartwheel dive off the end of the dock?" I suggest it might be a little narrow and unsteady. She settles for a handstand backflip. I feel stiff just watching her.

Sally arrives in the late afternoon. She is the other adult who is going with us. The girls come up from the lake, tired, but less cranky, it seems to me. Sitting around a table in the kitchen area, I try to set a few rules for the next three days, just a few so we can all relax. Buddies at all times. No swimming without the lifeguard (that's me) present. Camp jobs get traded off — fire, cook, cleanup. When I get out the map, they begin to believe we are really going. I trace our path from the put-in at Second Pond, up the Saranac River to Oseetah Lake, then through the inlet to Kiawasa and the lean-to there.

It's dinner time and they cook. We all eat chicken, even Mary. After dinner I go through the gear each girl wants to take. We leave home Mary's seven extra t-shirts, Elaine's five pair of blue jeans and Beth's radio. She gives it up with good grace. I am looking forward to our trip.

The next morning we are up at six, packed and canoes loaded by eight. The girls sleep most of the drive north, but start to wake up as we drive by the Lake Placid Winter Olympic sites and are ready to go when we pull into the unloading ramp. I let the girls untie the canoes and start carrying them down to the water, while I worry to myself about how to pack and tie down our gear in each canoe, something I'd thought a lot about, but never done before. It seems to me to be common sense — a canoe trip's gear has to stay dry and with the canoe — but the practice makes me feel all thumbs and the end result was not the neat packaging I had imagined. Nonetheless, we stow all of our gear and shove off into Second Pond.

Sun is hot, humidity high as we paddle up Second Pond to the lily pads where we take a right and meander over to Cold Brook. One of the canoes is making a crisscross rather than a straight path, as Mary's stroke is so strong in the bow, Beth can't hold a course. It looks like they are canoeing twice as far as the rest of us! After lunch we canoe through dead tree lake and down to the state locks, the highlight of Mary's day. The iron gates clang shut behind our four canoes and the floodgates in the front open.

As the water pours out and our canoes begin to descend, Mary asks longingly, "Oh, wow, can we come back this way when we go home?"

"Why?" I ask. "Now you've already seen it?"

"I know, I know," she said, "but I want to go the other way. I want to know what it's like to be elevated." We all agree that may not be possible for Mary and paddle on laughing.

We come out of the locks into the marsh of Oseetah Lake, lily pads and purple-spiked flowers. The sun is even hotter than at noon and our heavily loaded canoes move slowly around the point to the creek into Kiawasa. In midafternoon we reach the lean-to, find it uninhabited, and even, Sandy tells us all proudly, find a roll of toilet paper in the latrine. General rejoicing. I promise them a swim as soon as camp is set up. Tents spring up miraculously. I check the swim area with mask and snorkel and then we spend the next hour jumping and diving off a large rock.

Out here the girls seem to me very independent and capable. They fix and eat dinner with no complaints and little direction from Sally and me. They are considerate of one another. Although four of the more lively girls bond instantly, the other two are never left out, or teased, but given room to enter in as they wish. They all seem to be slowly sloughing off bits of that "civilized" behavior I found so irritating back in camp.

At dusk I sit writing in my journal, resting under the pines on this beautiful and silent lake. The girls are fixing popcorn around the fire up at the lean-to.

I wake at dawn to hear a single white-throated sparrow greet the first light and wake the other birds. I lie for a half hour listening to each separate chorus enter the cacophony. The last of the night's rainfall drips on the tent fly.

Elaine and Sandy rise with the birds. I suggest that it *is* their one morning to sleep in, if they want. But Elaine is practicing with the hatchet, to her sister's disapproving, "Elaine, not now, go somewhere else, you're such a *twerp!*" from inside the tent. Sandy is washing out the pillowcase that got muddy when she used it in the canoe as a kneeling pad. She is the only girl on the trip I have not yet seen laugh.

After cold cereal and hot cocoa we head to Pine Pond. The morning is grey, but still. I am afraid of a storm, though it is more overcast than threatening.

We beach the canoes in marsh mud and walk into the woods carrying our paddles, lunches, raincoats and watermelon. Paddles are hidden behind a log and we quickly walk the half mile to the pond. As we come over a rise and look down at the water, we are all amazed. This incredibly pure and beautiful pond with a natural sand bottom and beach is breathtaking. The morning is still grey, and we are hungry after the canoeing, but we swim for nearly an hour before I insist on a lunch break. I feel totally relaxed, at ease, and sense the girls feeling a new freedom. After lunch we slice the watermelon and Sally starts a vigorous watermelon pit spit. They are all easily roused, love the attention and the forbidden pleasure of spitting their watermelon seeds at one another.

I wake from a catnap on the beach to see Elaine covered with sand from her shoulders to her feet, the five other girls gravely smoothing the wet sand over her entire body, admonishing her not to breathe too hard or she'll cause an earthquake. They decide she will be Dolly Parton and I watch as they mold her enormous breasts, smoothing each fondly, placing a nipple on top, consulting about whether they are lopsided or not. "Can you see your toes, Elaine?" Beth asks, "Cause if you can, they're not big enough yet." Sandy giggles with embarrassment and glee behind her hand.

I go over and suggest Dolly needs a belly button, craft one carefully in the appropriate zone, but Beth chides me, "Judith, Dolly Parton wouldn't have an inny belly button, hers is an outty," and she corrects my sculpture accordingly. Elaine decides she has to breathe and an earthquake finishes off Dolly.

I have to flog them out of Pine Pond. No one wants to leave, but it is late afternoon and the sun is gone again. I am afraid to take more of a chance with the weather. But it is too late. When we pull away from the cove, out past the protective point, a gusty wind hits our canoes broadside. An enormous thunderhead lowers in front of us, the wind is picking up even more, but I see no lightning, hear no thunder. I decide to head for home and turn to see how the girls are. They are paddling ferociously, putting their shoulders and backs into the effort as I have never seen them before, and I lead us out across the choppy lake toward our inlet. Virginia is in the bow of my canoe and in my anxiety I shout directions at her: "Pull right, Virginia, now left. Virginia, put your shoulders into it," screaming at her in frustration. "Feather your paddle, it will help me." As a gust of rain hits us, I catch a glimpse of her face. She is grinning with exhilaration.

The rain comes harder, but no one thinks of rain gear. We are all soaked and if we stopped we'd be blown clear back to Pine Pond. Still I hear no thunder. When we make the narrow channel a fisherman calls out to offer us shelter in his camp. We are only half a mile from camp now, so we shout no and head for home. As we beach the canoes at our lean-to, the rain comes down in sheets and I hear the first thunder blowing across the lake.

"They loved it," Sally says in amazement as we flop into our tent to dry off after drying off the girls and giving them hot chocolate. "They weren't scared. Just Mary. She kept asking me, what will Judith do if there's lightning?" She pauses, then turns to look at me. "What would you have done?"

"Put in," I answer emphatically. "We'd still be sitting in the rain on a shoreline somewhere waiting for this to pass. Were you scared?"

"Nervous," she allows.

"Me too," I confess, "me too."

The rain quits in the early evening while we make dinner and sit around the campfire toasting marshmallows. When it starts to pour again, we all go to bed. In the grey morning we cook french toast and start to break camp. I contemplate the peanut butter for the day's sandwiches, eye Mary, and ask, "Anyone prefer pizza for lunch today in Lake Placid Village?" Mary's whoop echoes in the trees and her enthusiasm carries us back down the trail, packs the canoes and sets us off again.

We vote to go back through the locks, retracing our steps, hoping to give Mary a real "elevation" like she'd asked for. As we start up the inlet, we all cheer to see the sun come out through the clouds, shining on just us. I know that when we get to the village Mary will start to whine and complain about her wet sleeping bag, she and Julie will point at every teenage boy we drive by, and Beth will spend fifteen minutes in the only ladies room at the pizza place combing her hair while five of us are waiting to go to the bathroom. But for now I let the girls lead the way out into the marsh, enjoying the sparkle of the water as it comes off their paddles, watching the reflection of their firm and strong strokes in the rippled water.

The Log of the African Queen

LAURA CHATAIN

Every year a group of women from Harbor Springs, Michigan, get together for a Canadian wilderness canoe trip. Different women come each year, always six for safety. Route finder-organizer Margie Graham's gone six times, Sandy Danforth (who sent us this log) and Laura (who wrote it) have gone four times. "How long do you expect to go on doing this" we asked Sandy.

"Oh . . . indefinitely. I'm a pretty urban person otherwise; I just want to keep on doing these trips."

The log excerpted here is from their five day trip in 1983 on the Wenebegon River, 100 miles north of Thessalon, Ontario. Laura Chatain is a sailor, windsurfer, canoeist, free-lance writer and entrepreneur, who now lives in Evanston, Illinois, with her husband and two children.

June 10

Three canoes, six slightly crazy women and one trailer packed with gear headed north on Rt. 129 in Canada to Aubrey Falls Gulf Station/General Store/Motel/Restaurant. We walked in and saw a hat rack on the back wall. "Cook" said one, "Concierge" said another, "Hunting Guide" yet another. One hook was empty. "Fishing Guide" said the hat worn by our friendly proprietor, who was happily regaling us with stories of extraordinary fishing, showing us pictures of Big Fish and informing us of the most sure-fire, never-miss lures to use. "These guys come in here, eh? and buy every one of those ones colored like bumblebees, eh?"

Full of easy confidence in our future fishing success we filed upstairs toward the dining room. The menu was enticing, especially after a long drive, and we knew we were in an establishment of unequalled culinary excellence when we asked the cook (our erstwhile fishing guide with a different hat) what was good. "Oh," he shrugged, "I don't know. I cook everything and it all tastes the same to me." Ordering dinner was thus our first taste of adventure in Canada.

After a very, uh, interesting dinner, we drove north towards our put-in point. Our first sign of wildlife – two skunks digging for grubs by the side of the road. Live, unmushed skunks! Up the road from our take-out point we came to Burying Creek, where we parked and camped. Black flies and mosquitoes greeted us in great clouds.

June 11

We were delighted in the morning to see a cow moose feeding by the river. Very casual. Even a car driving slowly by didn't faze her. She just ambled off into the woods. After a breakfast of coffee and dry granola, we put our canoes into the creek.

We paddled through slow water, buttercups and wild cherry lining the creek. We came to a lake, and our first portage. After scouting the rapids going into the lake, we decided not to run it and carried our canoes loaded, six to a canoe, over a very short portage. Clear slow water to our second carry, "Partridge Portage" or "Dead Man's Hill." There were moose tracks all along the trail, fresh boot prints ahead of us. The partridge was on the trail when we scouted the rapids – she (we think she was a she) was either ignorant, brave or protective, because she let us walk within six feet of her. There were low overhanging cedars of strainer potential across the river so we decided not to run it. (I use the word "we" with some poetic license. *Margie* decided *we* wouldn't run it.) We carried the canoes up a big hill, and lowered them down the other side with ropes.

Our favorite portage of the day, "Moose Poop Portage" or "Lichen Pine Portage," for those who prefer more poetic appellations, was a long, long 600-meter portage. Only the exquisite tiny lavender butterflies and lichened pines saved this portage from being unmitigated drudgery.

Back in the river to meet our first log jams. Only about six, due to the high water. One Laura and Sandy took apart log by log, one Nancy facilitated passage through by standing on a sinking, rotating log that only moments before looked as solid as your kitchen table. "Stand up, Nancy," called Kay, as Nancy, like Alice, got shorter and shorter.

"I *am* standing up!" replied Nancy, as she continued to sink. Nancy says that when confronted with a log jam or its equivalent she likes to tempt fate, which, she finds, is almost always able to be tempted. "Get out and see what happens," she says gaily. Nine times out of ten, *something* happens.

We arrived at Lake Wenebegon. Our first choice of campsites was taken, so we headed for the one on the south end by a rocky outcropping. It looked private enough from the water, and was, until our bathing activities seemed to lure the men from the north campsite out in their boats to, uh, fish.

We had paddled 11.5 miles and six inches on the map, and thoroughly enjoyed Nadine's creation of hamburger carrot onion potato stew, followed by mint tea and popcorn. During dinner preparation we were introduced to our soon-to-be favorite game.

The Bucket Game

It is a game of endless variations, for six players, time limit dictated only by the patience, diligence and desire of the players. Our version for this evening was "Find the Spices" and is played thus: Six players sit on six food buckets. One player, usually the cook, requests an item, for example, "I need the little spice container," and then chooses a bucket which *may* contain the spices. "It should be in the green bucket with the two yellow stripes." The turn then passes to the player sitting on that bucket, who can choose to stand up, pry open her bucket, dig to the bottom searching for the spices, reclose her bucket and sit down – *or* she can bluff: "No, it's not in this bucket. I saw it in the gray bucket at lunchtime." (It should be noted here that the consequences of having your bluff called – ie. the spices *are* in your bucket after the rest have been searched – can be dire indeed. Only slightly less severe are the consequences of not searching your bucket thoroughly enough.)

If the spices are not found, the turn passes to the player with the most definite opinion expressed in the loudest voice. For example, Margie, sitting on the white bucket, says "I'm *positive* I saw it in the green bucket with the W." This would override Laura, sitting on Green W saying, "But I really think it may be in the white." And so on.

Note: there should be consensus among the players before beginning as to whether the object of the game is to prolong the search as long as possible, or to find the object as quickly as possible, else confusion may result. This game obviously has endless variations. We enjoyed it so much that towards the end of the trip, as we became more familiar with the contents of the buckets, it became necessary to engage in discreet sabotage, replacing objects after use in the wrong buckets. In this way we were able to continue play right to the end of the trip.

June 12

We had lake paddling today, and so broke camp at 7:30 A.M. to get some miles done before the wind came up. Our fisherwomen caught three pike – Kay caught one by wrapping a slip knot around its nose, no hook.

Honest to great goodness, she did. And Nadine caught a whitefish — we have a picture to prove that!

We stopped for lunch, and for the day, as it turned out, at a beautiful campsite with lots of space and a wonderfully delicate pink flower nested in the rocks. Our lunch spot was furnished with a huge stone table. Exquisite fried pike and whitefish. After lunch and siesta black flies were fierce and drove us to the tents. Back to the north end for dinner to get some relief from the black flies — the wind was stronger there. We feasted on an unabashedly gourmet dinner of boiled pike in orange, pineapple, coconut and lemon sauce over rice.

June 13

Smoke from our campfire kept the bugs at bay long enough for us to enjoy our pancakes. Broke camp at 8 A.M. We decided to run Bear Falls. Margie and Nadine decided to run full, the rest of us portaged our gear. It was the Bear Falls portage that convinced us this trip would be good practice for an aspiring actress who wanted to practice for the inevitable remake of the movie *African Queen*. Slogging through mud up to our calves, head nets securely fastened, clothed wrist to foot in the sweltering heat to avoid being eaten alive by black flies was just the kind of fun stuff we all had in mind when we planned this trip.

Bear Falls was a scary looking rapids, and our muddy portage gave us plenty of time to enjoy that small terror of anticipation, with what felt like a bushel of our lovely lavender butterflies in the stomach and Sahara mouth. Exhilaration of the whitewater and the sheer exaltation of survival made for a heady and volatile mix of emotions as we gathered, giddy with relief, at the run-out to catch our breath.

June 14

After breakfast we portaged around the next falls and headed on down the river. We tried a couple of shortcuts: one worked, one took us inland to a small lake, and one was a dead end. After this we all joined Shortcuts Anonymous and if any of us was possessed of a need for a shortcut we all rallied around in support until the craving passed.

We came upon an elegant public bathing house cunningly disguised as a log jam. After luxuriating in our bug free(!) baths, we worked our way out of the jam. As Sandy and I slipped through the rapidly closing gap in the logs, a monster log broke free and began chasing us downstream. "Heads up!" I cried as we paddled furiously around the bend. "There's a log after us!" My fearless companions were not a bit impressed, even when the canoe-eating monster log did in fact round the bend and catch its huge teeth on the small loop of rope at the stern of our canoe. "Help!" I cried, and Margie grabbed my arm from shore as the log tried its crocodilian best to drag us off the beach. "Help!" I cried again in an unmistakably urgent tone as it became clear that the rest of the party thought Margie and I just enjoyed holding hands as a method of securing a canoe. It worked. Some clear-thinking, fast-acting woman grabbed a knife and cut the loop, and not a moment too soon, as only Margie's iron grip stood between us and uncertain fate at the mercy of the monster log. It drifted downstream, undoubtedly to seek easier prey, probably beaver or bear.

Moments later we were happily slogging through mud to our ankles again, dragging our canoes through buggy silt-covered bushes, relieved to be rid of that unaccustomed feeling of being clean and refreshed.

June 15

This morning Nancy while brushing her teeth spit her toothpaste through, not under, her headnet. This maneuver graphically illustrated to us all just how oblivious to our survival gear we had become by this fifth and last day on the river.

The last rapids. Kay and Nancy were doing fine until the Big Wave which filled their canoe, spinning it broadside and throwing them downstream about eight feet. Maneuvering themselves upstream of the canoe, they managed to swim it to shore.

Meanwhile, Sandy and I were making our way down the rapids, taking on significant amounts of water but still in control until we, too, were caught by the Big Wave. We swam toward the island where Margie and Nadine were waiting, and they were able to throw us a rope. Unhurt, with no significant gear losses, warm air, and a fire going, we were in high spirits as we celebrated our survival.

We paddled across to our take-out spot against an exhausting headwind. The trip had met our criteria of success—a good balance of challenge, leisure, log jams, rapids, fishing and fish dinners. And us! "There's no such thing as a negative experience," Nancy had said early on in the trip. And right she was.

It's All Old Ladies

HELEN WOODINGS

Helen Woodings came to Alaska in 1953 on her honeymoon and has lived there ever since. She taught physical education, raised three daughters, and re-modeled an old log home. When her "sidekick" Wendy moved to Alaska, they began yearly trips: backpacking, canoeing, cross country skiing, sea kayaking.

Ginny, Helen B., Helen W.; Prince William Sound, Alaska (Wendy Couch)

Exploring Prince William Sound by kayak caught her heart and she has continued this love for the past eight years, eventually turning it into a business, Alaska Sea Kayaking.

Much of her energy is now devoted to running the business, but she still finds time to get away with the "old grey gals."

In April of 1985 nine feet of snow fell on Prince William Sound in one week. So is May 10th too early for a sea kayaking excursion in Alaska? Not for this hardy group. Why May? Because Ginny and I, who organized the trip, are both wilderness guides, too busy in the summer for our own personal trips.

"It's all old ladies," I explained to Denis when he called to book the earliest possible trip. "Just my speed," he retorted. He joined, and added spice to the group. Ginny and her pals, Celia from Fairbanks and Helen B. from Wisconsin, are all 67 years old. My paddling partner Wendy and I are both in our mid fifties. Elizabeth from Anchorage and Denis from New York are in their forties.

Day 1

The gang assembled in Whittier, arriving on three different trains. A busy time: unloading gear, transporting supplies, meeting Jack, our charter boat operator.

Finally, ready to depart at 7 P.M. – it had taken all day to get this far. Somebody whispered, "Shhhh, it's snowing." We cruised past glaciers, historic landmarks, and then saw a distress flare. A small boat with a dead battery. In the dark and snow we towed the boat to a sheltered bay and set our anchor for the night. Sleep came quickly with the gentle rocking of the boat, the silence of heavy wet snow, the solitude, stillness.

Day 2

We woke to four inches of wet snow covering the Klepper kayaks in their cloth bags tied to the deck. Visibility was low as we slowly navigated out of Culross Passage. Jack took a careful bearing before attempting the long open water crossing to Knight Island. As we neared land, the clouds lifted and a pod of Orcas ("killer whales") appeared, a salute to our wilderness adventure.

While Jack put on full scuba gear to free the anchor ropes that had tangled in the props, we began unloading. "You bring more junk every trip, Helen," he teased. Three times we loaded the skiff and rowed to shore.

We tromped through snow drifts, crossed a creek, and threaded through the ruts and roots of closely spaced trees to assemble our camp high on a hill. Nothing had greened up. Trails of animals were visible, and, yes, bear scat. This is bear country, and we took every precaution in storing food, keeping a clean camp, and making noise when on the trails.

This gang had all spent years gathering confidence from life's greatest teacher, experience. They knew what to do and what to wear. What could I tell them? "Today is the first time out. Let's explore the leeward side and take it easy."

Soon we were in the unbroken expanse of ocean, no clouds, no boats, no people; just seals, otters, colorful birds. Mt. Logan and Mt. St. Elias were visible 100 miles away. The stark detail and sharp stillness gripped me. We were near enough to each other for conversation but distant enough to have uninterrupted thoughts: "I am here today and am in love with life." One never loses that feeling.

By mid-afternoon certain muscles knew they had been unused for a while. Hoping for a shortcut back, we explored a deep cove. Contrary to the pre-earthquake map, we found a 100-yard portage at low tide! What a decision. Do we paddle another two miles against the wind or carry the five kayaks across? We emptied the kayaks of the day's gear and portaged; with two people on each end of the 75-pound doubles and 55-pound singles, the job was easy. By the time we walked three or four trips each, our paddling fatigue and stiffness were gone.

Day 3

Two calm days in a row, how lucky. "How about exploring the windward side of the island today?" I suggested. Intrigued by harbor seals playfully poking their heads out of the water, we settled in our seats for another day's entertainment.

Spotting red round floats caught high above the waterline, Wendy decided to race to shore to secure three of the 18" balls. With two balanced in front of her on the bow deck and one behind on the spray cover, she looked like a big buxom babe who had just laid an egg.

That afternoon hundreds of mew gulls were feeding. Salmon jumping around us whetted our appetite for sea food. When a fishing boat came into the bay, Denis volunteered to paddle over to say hello and ask to buy a fish. They didn't want to talk to him. We should have sent a woman—at least then fishermen take notice.

Evenings around the fire were hilarious. Tales of the North and incredible stories of pioneering Alaska came so fast and humorously that we sounded like cackling hens. Denis would impersonate a hen house, which would set us off into another round of laughter and another story.

Day 4

"Let's go around the island today," I suggested. But Ginny, the backpacker, decided to hike to the highest point; her sidekick Celia accompanied her. Helen and Denis chose to stay at camp. Elizabeth borrowed Denis's single Klepper and took off with Wendy and me to explore.

The sea swells were something to pay attention to, but fun. An island created a shallow where the waves were three-foot haystacks—our apprehension turned to glee. "We must be the first people out here this year," Wendy said, as she spotted more floats washed high on the shore by winter storms. A crisp clean breeze gently blew off the snow fields. We were so all alone in that magnificent air.

It started with a song and developed into creative verse. We captured the greatest goof of each person in the group, ending with a chorus of "The ol' grey gals they ain't what they used to be, but they're doing what they want to do, being where they want to be. . . ."

Day 5

A charter boat came to transport fresh shrimp to Whittier and pick up Denis, who had made plans to attend his son's college graduation. The outfit of the day became Helly Hanson heavy duty raingear and the sprinkles of rain made our smiles glisten for the final round of photos. Genuine hugs of fond farewell showed our admiration for this big fun-loving man from New York. His final compliment: "I would not have changed any part of this trip."

The rain turned into wind. Wendy and I abandoned the plan of taking the kayak for a firewood run; we scrounged the rocky shores instead. After the pace and hilarity of the previous five days, we crashed with books and pens. The wind howled, but we had a cozy camp.

Day 6

What woke me up? Was it the sharp stillness of the intense blue sky? "Everybody up, it's a perfect day," I called to the five other women snuggled in their sleeping bags. Rested and ready to go after our day of silence, we spun into action. Our routine was well established by this time.

Our plan to circle the island would return us to base camp that night. "Only take water bottles, rain clothes, lunch, a book, camera, and, most important, sunscreen and sun glasses," I said.

"Then why are you taking all that stuff?" they asked as I gathered a sleeping bag, repair kit, first aid kit, two tarps, stove, food, emergency gear and VHF radio.

"If I bring it, we won't need it," I answered. But really, I am never without it—storms pick up fast in Prince William Sound, and extra ballast adds stability. Before we pushed off I noticed others making one more trip up the hill for additional gear.

Helen and Elizabeth took off first, enjoying those quiet moments alone. We saw them watching something over near the island and took off to see what they'd spotted. We silently approached to observe a charming otter fondling her pup on her belly. We all had a view through the binoculars before the otters felt our presence and dived. A mother merganser and her ducklings, too small to take flight, scooted off to the protection of the rocks.

In this narrow channel we remembered the pod of Orcas and hoped they would reveal themselves again. No, I don't fear the "killer" whales. They are extremely intelligent, and I think they are curious about me. We spotted shore birds and waterfowl. The lead kayaker would glide in with raised binoculars and those behind would float into position, hoping we would not spook the birds into flight. Another visitor. "This one looks like my golden Labrador retriever." The harbor seal's eyes registered peace, then disbelief, as he sank under the water.

The channel opened wide, and we swiftly stroked out into a panoramic view of azure skies contrasting with shining white sharp peaks, glistening under the sun's intense rays. Tantalizing still seas of silver water filled the expanse. "That has to be Columbia Glacier 40 miles away." To the East was Cordova and to the North Mt. Marcus Baker standing tall over Harvard Glacier. They all seemed so near. I would not have traded that moment for anything.

For two hours we sat, not paddling hard. I knew of a perfect place for a break. "This is worth waiting for," sighed Celia as she stretched her back on a sunny point and shed layers of clothing. The warmth of the mid-day sun—the first any of us had felt since last August—a full stomach, and a "live-it-up" philosophy affect a mature, older woman the same way as a young gal—strip off those clothes and breathe deeply.

Groggy after our break, it took some paddling before we fell back in tune with the sea, bluer yet from the afternoon sun. From the tallest hemlock, a bald eagle watched our procession into his land. He sat there, majestic and untouchable, but seemingly curious about these cheerful ladies. "What are you women doing out here? I see you, Helen, out here all the time." He held his perch as we rounded the point and looked back.

Someone else was watching from under our fleet of grey-bottomed boats. He waited until the fourth boat had passed before he raised his mighty head. By the splash he made plunging back under the water, we knew he was big, maybe a sea lion. Intimidating.

The lead kayaker could poke around in unknown places, and Ginny followed her curiosity through a shallow drainage into a huge circular bay. "Put an X on your map, Helen. This place has everything: fresh water, protection, a good campsite."

The afternoon sun was in our eyes and the wind picked up as we completed our circle around the island. The shrimp boat Poker and I spotted each other, so I radioed him on my hand-held VHR; he motored over to share news of the day. A spare twenty-dollar bill in my secret cache bought freshly caught shrimp, absolutely the most tasty any of us could ever remember. With the buttery glow on our faces, we nodded in agreement—a perfect end to a perfect day.

Day 7

The last day. We cleaned camp with as much energy and vigor as we gave to play and paddling. The only trace would be our packed track through the snow drifts.

To see us ready and waiting pleased Jack, who hoped to catch the last train to Whittier. He could tell at a glance we'd had a good time. Three round trips with the skiff transported our stuff to the charter boat and we took off.

Minutes out into the open seas, we looked back and there they were again, a pod of Orcas, dorsal fins high, as if to wave goodbye. Did they know where we were all along?

River Camps My Mother Used to Show Me
CONSTANCE HELMERICKS

Constance Helmericks went into the Alaska bush in 1944 as a young married woman. Her life as an amateur explorer on the Yukon, Koyukuk, and other rivers is told in her We Live in Alaska *(Boston: Little, Brown & Co., 1944), and other books written with her husband, Harmon Helmericks. In 1965, divorced, she was living "Outside." "Life stretched out, dull and endlessly worry-filled for me, a civilized adult mother, breadwinner by necessity." But she wanted to share the North with her daughters, and she believed in freedom for animals and children, "even if grown-ups don't like freedom, or at least seldom have it." When she told her daughters Jean, 14, and Ann, 12, that they were going North, Jean said, "I've been ready for years." They took off for two summers of travel by freighter canoe down the Peace, Slave and Mackenzie Rivers to the Arctic ocean.*

The three next embarked on a 50,000 mile trip by car in the back country of Australia, which Connie describes in Australian Adventure *(Englewood, NJ: Prentice-Hall, 1971). And they went on separate adventures. Like her mother before her, Jean went to the Brooks Range in Alaska, where she lived off the land for four years in a cabin 150 miles from the nearest settlement. Ann traveled in Africa and Europe. Connie explored 700 miles of remote Central American jungle rivers by raft and log canoe. "It was fun," she says, "but among the most dangerous things I've ever done in a long life filled with adventures." Constance Helmericks died in the spring of 1987 after a year's struggle with cancer. She was 69 years old.*

Down the Wild River North *(Boston: Little, Brown & Co., 1968) is the story of a great adventure of a mother and two teenage daughters. As they were packing for it, one of their neighbors was raped at knifepoint. "Through this weird 'civilization' we had wended our way for some years," Connie wrote, "and had luckily survived its many dangers. When anybody asked me later, 'How could you dare to go alone, a woman, taking your two little daughters away to the Arctic Ocean in a canoe?' I would think of this."*

In the following excerpt it is early in the first year of their river travels, and the Peace River is at dangerous flood levels.

Our first day really on our own found us motoring down the great flood feeling the keenest interest in finding out what lay ahead and the rarest exhilaration at our own audacity in finding out.

We started traveling very late in the day, after 5 P.M. It was only then that the rain clouds lifted.

"Don't stay out on the river when it gets late in the evening," the old guide had originally instructed. "Get off the river early," he had warned. Nevertheless, I felt we could count on about four hours' light today. It was eighty miles to Peace River town. At a motor speed of twelve miles per hour and a current estimated at about the same, we ought to be able to make it there before dark, with some margin. But life on a river is not that way. Nor is life any place that way, so far as I have found.

The people at Dunvegan had told us that there was another party of canoeists on the river somewhere ahead of us.

"Nobody saw them here," was the word. "They didn't stop. Very unusual this summer, two parties now, including you. Not many cares to make this trip, it seems."

Official letters, I must make clear again, had assured me months ago that the Peace River canoe trip was considered a reasonable undertaking for the experienced riverman. Here was a river! Rivers naturally all have their little ways. Anyone knows that. Officials might make recommendations that rivermen be physically fit, and that their craft should meet certain specification in size and should preferably be powered; but officials did not interfere if citizens or noncitizens decided upon any kind of expedition here—even to swim. If a person believed he could tackle the river, he had the basic right to elect himself for this undertaking. It was somewhat like a man challenging a bull in the ring in Mexico. But on the river he would experience a good many more nuances of courage and a good many more moments of truth than the bullring offers, and his dream offered beautiful scenery rather than blood. However, the individual who sets himself up to be captain of his own boat and his own life would do well to be fully aware that the authorities usually give up their search for missing persons on the river within a period of two or three days, because they never find them here.

Thinking this over, the sheltered wobbly little person who has never before faced up to such a degree of freedom wonders if he is ready for it.

"When you go out into the North," I heard many persons say both in Canada and in Alaska, "be prepared for anything. Things can happen. You never know if you're going to be out there for a day or for a year."

Connie, Jean, and Ann Helmericks, on the "Wild Rivers North," 1960s (Photo courtesy of Jean Aspen)

Quite true. Whether you travel by boat or by small airplane, in the event of power failure or some unforeseen miscalculations, you will have vanished into that wilderness, and if the northern authorities give you up for dead, you might starve to death. At one time I had become completely at home with such risks. But I now wondered how I was going to get used to them all over again.

The danger here was not just capsizing. The danger was losing your boat and dying of exposure. My big bugaboo was that somehow when we slept ashore the canoe might get away from us, and all our things in it. To overcome this fear I got rings put into each end of the canoe, and used chains with clip snaps instead of ropes. I was afraid that ropes might fray, or a beaver or porcupine might chew them — I had had that happen, once.

But the chains which arrived turned out to be cheap, flimsy things. I had asked for an eighteen-foot length of heavy-duty chain on each end. I ended up with ten-foot chains that were lightweight, and one of the nose rings was weak and wobbled during the whole trip. That's the way things go. In our civilization many people who fix things either have no imagination or don't care. I intended, therefore, always to camp in creek mouths or in eddies out of the main current. This was theoretical. Of course it did not work out that way.

Another aspect of the bugaboo was the dropping water levels. In choosing campsites, whether up some creek mouth or along the edge of the Peace, we would have to be vigilant that our heavy boat did not get so hard aground in the mud that we could never launch it again. That might be nearly as serious as losing the canoe.

And I was alert for other kinds of boat trouble. For instance, some campers have had their canoes destroyed by bears. We would therefore always take our guns ashore when we camped, and most of the spare ammunition, in an emergency pack containing a few other things to be kept right beside or even inside the sleeping bag. Bear marauders are possible but not usual. The real reason for keeping the guns right with you is for food insurance in case the canoe escapes, leaving you stranded. You should have ammunition for a half year or so. Furthermore, the big rifle might be used to signal some passing boat, in case of emergency. Since you might be camped off the main channel, it would certainly take a rifle to reach the ears of any passerby. No voice could rise above their boat's engines, even if they happened to come close to you.

Now the little motor purred softly in regular cadence, and the green-forested Alberta hills rolled by. At last I was feasting my eyes and spirit upon green. Here were the green and blue distances so loved and longed for by the longtime wilderness dweller; the feeling of freedom, the space, the golden sunlight, the clear, pure air like wine to drink in. The children

47

opened their senses to the spirit of an empty land.

From across the water came a muffled pumping sound.

It wasn't man-made. "I think it's the slough pumper, God bless him. The great northern bittern. Funny bird, he sounds like he's trying to pump the slough dry."

"He'll never make it, Mother," laughed Ann. "There's a lot of water here."

Jean was the sole boss of the motor. She had proven to be the one in the group who had nerves of steel as well as an aptitude for mastering mechanical monsters, for which I had little love. Our lives were in the hands of a fourteen-year-old girl, I thought. Jean got very tired and her back ached from sitting sideways all day crouched over her motor jealously with greasy hands. I sat in the bow to plot our channel, and to watch for dangers, weather, man, and beast. Ann lazed away the hours opening cans of food or drink to pass around, or snoozing under the "bearskin."

The bearskin was really just my old skunk coat. It looked exactly like a black bear. It wouldn't do for a woman explorer to wear this in the woods – she might get shot! – but I had brought it along from the States to use as a comforter in the boat and for a bed skin in camping. Spruce tips and balsam boughs may be all right as a supplement, but they can never take the place of animal robes.

We had filled the canoe up with spruce tips, and had put our entire load on top of the springy, water-resistant boughs. For three people there were three wooden slat seats. The seats were built high up out of water and mud which would collect in the canoe: one seat in the bow, with leg room, and two seats quite close together in the stern. That's the way I ordered it from the factory. The high seats enabled you to observe the water half a mile ahead or more, so that you could choose your channel and not get drawn into what you didn't want. Our load was covered with canvas.

"This is Burnt River on the map," I called to the expedition members, as we approached a river mouth.

"We want to see it," came the cry.

I realized then that I was going to have a hard time getting us to Great Slave Lake in just one summer, with people who wanted to stop and see every creek along the way. But we turned in. This was the beginning of a summer of endless creeks and rivers. What were we looking for? I couldn't tell you what I was looking for in the twelve years I wandered the North before the children were born. Looking into creeks and rivers can simply become a way of life.

We nosed into Burnt River's stagnant red algae and found ourselves floating in sudden primordial silence; the humming clouds of mosquitoes which met us sounded very loud. A few big fat raindrops pattered down, the hoods of our parkas went up and the bug lotion was passed quickly from hand to hand. This typical maneuver would be repeated a thousand times until the countering readjustment tactic to nature's tactic became second nature in living afloat in the wilderness. We took up our paddles to make our way slowly through swaths of timber that had accumulated where the Peace River in flood had backed up half a mile into the creek mouth.

As the canoe tunneled into the forest, the high-water mark was above our heads. Six feet above even the reach of our paddles, its heavy gray line cut across tree trunks and along the willow fringe. Vegetation was dead from mud. Branches and leaves were festooned with mud as snow may festoon a forest. Log jams sagged over seas of mud.

"Mud," I told the kids. "Not many people have seen a sight like this." We marveled at the pure havoc of nature.

Up the river we found a moraine of continuous boulders jamming the creek bed. Everything in this whole country was either jagged rocks or mud. There wasn't a square inch of conventional, tame, normal ground anywhere.

"I want to make camp and sleep here," insisted Ann.

"No," I said. "And that's final."

We had spent an hour of daylight exploring and marveling. Off we motored, then, out of Burnt River, and on down those moving, broad sheets of water of the skylit Peace. Ann took along several large flat rocks she had gathered.

"You know what, Mom? These rocks are what we need to make steps the next time we come ashore." I smiled tolerantly, hardly dreaming what genius this child possessed, as I allowed her to take her rock steps along in the canoe.

Presently the Peace became completely glassy, almost hypnotic, as night's clouds gathered. I recognized danger.

As the shadows settle the only sound is the gurgling of the swirling boils of the river, and the occasional sound of a distant bank caving in. The whirls and boils are golden in the light of the setting sun, the sun which rolls like a ball around the horizon during the night, dipping just below the rim of the world to set in the north. The fifty-foot whirls and boils merge and dissolve, and merge again; you watch them, fascinated. Now, later, they are turning red, brassy, copper, and at last purple and black. Now the black coils of water squirm into a million changing mirror facets. Gradually it becomes impossible to tell which waters are moving in which direction. You search for indented coves where you might get ashore, but each cove is veiled in shadow, and getting in close for a look is courting danger. The old guide had cautioned against getting swept down small, narrow side channels. In floodtime some of them might be spanned with log jams. As for telling which was island and which was mainland—well, that was not always readily possible, even in broad daylight, until you got in very close.

"We've got to get off the river," I kept saying aloud to Ann, who lay near me apprehensively, on top of the load with the bearskin.

"Mother, I'm praying," she said. "You pray, too."

"I'll pray with my eyes open," I concurred, as I continued to probe the twilight with the binoculars. Big rivers can make you religious very fast, if you aren't already.

It was nearly dark when we found Griffin Creek. At first I thought it was an island. I couldn't be sure whether it was a boat trap with a rushing narrow channel behind the island, or a safe creek from the mainland. "Turn in, turn in," I waved to Jean, and the canoe obediently turned toward the opening. Yes, the water in the opening was quiet water. Still frozen with fear, we went right into the purple darkness.

"You see, Mom, I prayed," whispered Ann sincerely.

It was hard to believe that Ann was the same twelve-year-old who a short time ago spent her whole life studying her reflection in the mirror, worrying about keeping up with the fashions of America. Who telephoned the U.S. Weather Bureau imperiously to determine which ensemble she would wear for the day. Who used up all my nail polish, razor blades, deodorants, eye make-up, and a full can of hair spray for one week's attendance of seventh grade.

I guess it was hard to realize that I myself was the same person, too, because I was now very much without the above beauty aids, and a few dozen more. As for Ann, she had forgotten they ever existed, and I should like to contend that this is a wholesome thing for twelve-year-old girls.

Griffin Creek, like Burnt River, was full of the backed-up waters of the Peace and half-submerged logs and mud. But it was safe, and we were thankful to have it.

After Jean cut the motor we heard the sweet chirping of baby frogs in chorus. They could have been angels. Paddling up around three bends of the creek, I still had no true idea of our whereabouts, when a beaver swam across our bow and cracked the water cheerfully in the gloom. That beaver materialized like a river pilot, as though he had come just to be our guide.

As the creek rapidly narrowed to nothing, a kingfisher rattled in alarm from the weird snags overhanging our heads. He had been sleeping. There was a pervading smell of wet raw earth and mud; the place smelled the way you would think coffins and earth and graveyards ought to smell, I thought; the smell of death and decay.

"Kind of a funny place, Mother," spoke up Jean, quavering.

50

"A rather objectionable place, dear," I agreed with trembling voice, "but we've got to make a camp here for the night somehow."

Suddenly my gaze fastened upon an object ahead in the muddy, stagnant creek bend, just as we were pushing forward, sounding with the paddles, and the hairs on the back of my neck prickled and simply stood right on end.

The object I saw ahead was the exact shape and size of a partly buried kayak.

Poling inch by inch toward the horrid object, I was certain that we had here before us the grisly remains of one of the American canoeists who had preceded us down the river. Then, just as suddenly, the object clarified itself into a perfectly ordinary, kayak-shaped white sandbar rearing out of the mists.

I groaned audibly. "Relax, Mother!" said Jean out loud. "We'll take care of you."

I had to poke at the sandbar with my paddle to make absolutely sure. Then, we turned the canoe around, retracing our way back around the bend. Somewhere in this impossible place we must make a camp tonight. We searched up and down the stagnant cut-bank channel. The only way was to cut steps up the sheer sixteen-foot raw mud walls, and choose a place that would not cave in when we did it. Then we could pitch our tent on the grassy prairie up on top.

"We can use my rocks to make our first steps," offered Ann.

We set to work stamping out steps up a traverse crack in the soft and oozy mud wall, and eventually carried all our junk up.

After some hours our little band of intrepid female explorers had accomplished the herculean task. Floundering through deep mud we got the thirty-pound tent package, the stove, the grub box, the rifles, the water bucket, and three bulky eighteen-pound sleeping bags high up on the wet but clean pasture above. Here we overlooked the depths where our canoe lay tied to small poplars. Once up on top, we tugged and hauled on the tottering tent poles, and at last hitched her fast to her stakes and to some limber willows, tying the tent fly with a neat bow knot.

"You will always find that the handiest things in life," I told my campers, "are the bow knots and large safety pins."

Of course there were a few cracks over the head with the tent poles, which had a way of collapsing; and a few yelps of rage rent the peaceful night. But the main thing is that in all these episodes, we survived.

On top we had a surprisingly cheery camp. A crackling stove inside the tent poured out its smoke from the little stovepipe, and we drank the turgid, fishy water in a nourishing, warm prepared soup mix. The prairie grass was long and filled with water. But camping right on top of such long wet herbage can give you a good camp, for if rain comes, I told my crew, it will soak right into the porous mat and there is no runoff. But you must have not only a canvas floor tarp but plenty of fur robes and eiderdown bags. Our bags had cost one hundred and twenty dollars each and were heavy duty. They were suitable for polar winter as well as summer.

It was midnight when we rolled out the three sleeping bags; but the distant sky remained pale yellow, for it was the longest day of the year.

I spread the bearskin out under my own bag, adjusted a life preserver under my head for a pillow, and crawled into my sack. All lapsed into silence.

"Thump, thump!" came mysterious sounds, close to the tent.

Jean looked out the tent flap on her hands and knees. Was it a bear? "Thump, thump, thump."

"Mother, what's that noise?"

"It's only rabbits. It will be a good rabbit year next winter."

"Mother, can I go out with the gun?"

"Not tonight, dear. For mercy sake, I haven't had a night's sleep in weeks, can't you settle down?"

"Couldn't I shoot one to eat?"

"Well, you can try, if you like. I've never been able to see one in summer."

Jean took the .22 and went outside. You could hear the dew falling. It misted onto the tent roof and saturated the long, green prairie grass. Occasionally you could hear a breeze sigh across the tent, rattling the tin safety against the little stovepipe, a breeze that spoke of our arctic prairies up north where nothing stops the wind and there is no habitation. "If only we can do this with safety!" I thought. I wouldn't want to get them into some of the tight spots I got myself into during my early life. Someday one's luck runs out.

Out in the night Jean stood silently with the little .22 rifle, surrounded by wild primroses in full bloom – Alberta's flower – and by the lovely scattered bright field lilies which were the official flower of next-door Saskatchewan. Jean's feet were wet and cold, and she had a tendency toward bronchial pneumonia; she had been hard to raise because she was allergic. She had taken years of allergy treatments. Only modern science had kept her afflictions under control and protected her from the menace of asthma.

I worried that she might shoot through the tent, what with excitement and myopia. But she never saw a rabbit – the thumping, playful varying hare or "snowshoe rabbit" which was pounding the ground with powerful hind feet. *Lepus americanus macfarlani* is rarely visible until the leaves drop.

Jean was one of those kids you see occasionally who has no visible social life – like the *Lepus americanus* in summertime. Living in the city most of her life, she saw the others of her species only dimly through smeared glasses; and the concrete streets she walked she saw not at all. She took refuge in some inner dream because, except for our pets and the tree she climbed, she hated where she was. She became an honor student in school but aside from that became absent mentally and emotionally. Walking across a room she stumbled into things, and frequently tables, lamps, and dishes collapsed into disaster.

She lost books and sweaters and sneakers, and you caught her reading books that were far, far beyond her age, and on every notebook cover and scrap of paper she drew beautiful pictures of idealized wilderness scenes containing animals. In her early years most of the animals were horses. She cared nothing for people her own age, or friends. Her friends were animals. Her dreams were of some beautiful place that she had never been but which some uncanny instinct in her soul informed her surely must be there, if she could but find it.

Jean remains graven for me at this moment of her development on one summer night, alone with our tent. There she is, gratefully breathing in the fresh mysterious scents, and trying, eager as a pup, to catch those elusive thumping rabbits throughout the subarctic summer night. In the Peace River summer Jean was getting the chance to be young out in nature, and it was helping her to grow into some kind of real person.

Missinaibi Group Journal

MISSINAIBI WOMEN

Introduction. Judith

The lower Missinaibi River flows 200 miles, unobstructed by dams or development, from the old Trans-Canada Highway to James Bay. It is generally described as "only for the experienced canoeist." As the river carves its way down through the hard rock of the Canadian Shield, through beds of limestone, into the clay of the Hudson Bay lowlands, the canoeist meets challenging rapids, spectacular waterfalls, and portages up to three miles long.

Eleven women shared this trip in 1980. Two of us were guides; four more shared the work of planning and packing. Although most were experienced campers, only a few had ever paddled in rapids. One woman had never been in a canoe, but only a week before departure talked her way into the group – "I learn physical skills fast." There were a few good friends along, but mostly we were a group that knew each other only slightly, or by letter, but came with incredibly high expectations of the trip and each other.

The Missinaibi was a late addition to our group. We had plotted out every detail and variation of another route near Lake Nipigon, but two days before we drove north a violent forest fire broke out. We quickly re-routed to the Missinaibi – a bigger river, more whitewater, harder portages. Somehow the blend of these eleven very diverse women and this particular river seemed just right for that point in many of our lives.

We've never done this before or since, but someone suggested a group journal. We drew straws to assign days, but generally women wrote whenever the mood struck. This piece is excerpted from several women's entries, filled in from my own journal and memories when we were too caught up in the experience to record it.

The Missinaibi Women: Elizabeth Barnard (E.B.), Jane Eastwood, Daphne Hall, Anne Jemas, Julie Marraccini, Mary Neikirk, and Judith Niemi

DAY 1. Mary

Starting our Missinaibi Journey. Actually, seven of us are waiting around at this bridge construction site, waiting for the drivers to take the cars and truck to Mattice and then find A Helpful Person who's going to give them a ride back.

We camped here last night with the construction cranes looming like dinosaurs over the tents, the bridge-to-be being the most level spot. A nice four-plex of tents – the walls were a little thin, but the neighborhood noise soon subsided.

Of the two-day drive I remember the scenery along Lake Superior and Lake Nipigon, catnaps, a wonderful Cris Williamson concert on the tape deck and the beautiful smiles as we talked, sharing our lives and anticipating this adventure.

Albany Rapids. Judith

Collecting information on a new river is both fun and frustrating. Besides the topo maps, I brought a route description from a whitewater magazine – rather hair-raising descriptions of derring-do and horseplay. To my relief, the women refer to the article as "Jerks on the Missinaibi."

Then in Hearst, Daphne and I had a good time talking to people. Two young men had a trap line up the Mattawichiwan River, where we planned to put in. Friendly and helpful, they insisted we shouldn't do that. Avoid Albany Rapids for sure, they said. Only *one* way through, they said, and if you miss it. . . . Said folks had been killed on the river. "It gives the North a bad name." We should start downstream at Mattice.

Then we found Daniel, who opened his office at the Ministry of Natural Resources on Sunday so we could get more copies of the route map. He was full of enthusiasm about the river, including Albany Rapids. "Not too hard," he said, "just big boulders, eh? Just follow the current left."

Our first afternoon on the river we were into the rapids, playing it very conservatively, much scouting, much instruction. Fun, very manageable. At the last pitch, rock islands divided the river into three channels, all looking pretty steep. Whoa! While people made camp on one of the islands, Janine and I waded, lined and bumped our way down, right next to shore. After scouting the main channel from below our verdict was firm: don't mess with it.

But in the evening the sun came out, and as the ominous gray waves turned blue and white, they seemed a lot smaller. I said something about how in the morning we *might* try it, although nobody should be talked into it. . . .

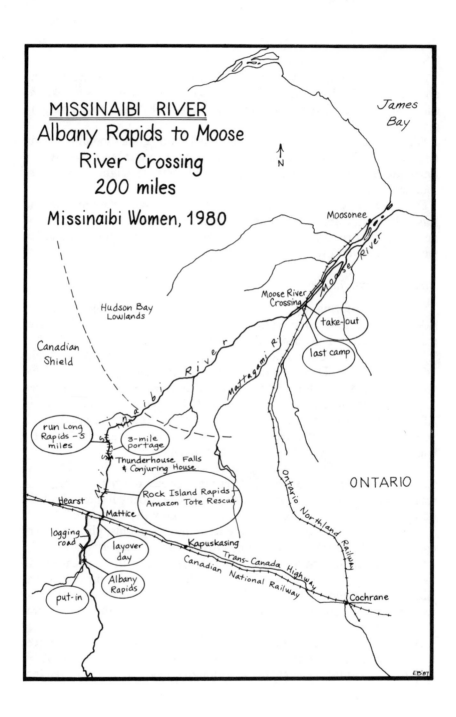

MISSINAIBI RIVER
Albany Rapids to Moose
River Crossing
200 miles

Missinaibi Women, 1980

N

James Bay

Moosonee

Hudson Bay Lowlands

Moose River Crossing

Moose River

take-out

last camp

Canadian Shield

Missinaibi River

Mattagami R.

run Long Rapids - 5 miles

3-mile portage

Thunderhouse Falls & Conjuring House

Rock Island Rapids Amazon Tote Rescue

ONTARIO

Ontario Northland Railway

Hearst

Mattice

logging road

layover day

Kapuskasing

Trans-Canada Highway

Canadian National Railway

Albany Rapids

put-in

Cochrane

EB'87

56

Albany Rapids Continued. E. B.

We woke to shorts and t-shirt weather. Judith and I had bantered about the possibility of running this drop, and a needed bit of prodding came with Daphne bouncing up asking, "Thinking of running it? I'll go!" We consulted about the best route; I got so nervous I could hardly see.

We paddled way up above the rapids for a careful entry. By then I was breathing again, and we ran it just as we had planned—and hoped. I was aware of nothing but intensely focused concentration on being where we wanted. Then below, I was suddenly conscious of the women on shore cheering us on.

Jane and Janine ran a second canoe through, hitting a rock but recovering beautifully, again with cheers and hoots from shore. Then Carol and Judith came down, ran to the wrong side of a critical rock, and swamped. Cameras clicked furiously, and a rescue canoe sped to help. After recovering their composure, and getting fortified with hugs, they hauled the canoe up for a second try, and repeated the scene exactly, frame by frame. They declared the river had won, best two out of three. On shore we got a fire going, had a round of soup and dried out lots of clothes. Exciting way to begin a day, and with so many rescuers at hand, the photographers didn't even need to feel unscrupulous. "You could hardly hear the roar of the rapids over the clicking of cameras," said Jane.

The next long stretch of river was quiet, relaxing, beautiful. "Dead water," according to the whitewater fanatic whose article we've been reading. We saw moose and beaver, tied all five canoes together for a floating lunch, then stopped to sun and swim.

Below Beaver Falls canyon we found big standing waves in one channel, rocky drops in the other, and an impossibly awful portage as the alternative. We solved the problem "elegantly" by running the easy upper portion, eddying out before the big water, and lining and hoisting the loaded canoes over sharp drops.

Tired but exhilarated, we made camp in a less-than-ideal spot, a grassy island. Grand supper of several courses and Bonaparte's gulls that gave a lovely air-dance performance.

DAY 3. Layover Day. Jane

A long night of rain and discomfort. Didn't sleep much. Strange dreams of Carol and me shopping for corporate executive wool suits in a department store full of young women in eye make-up, listening to the latest rock'n roll. Strange city dreams—at bad moments they mix with the more frightening images of *The Wanderground.* [Sally Gearhart's grim and inspiring futurist novel, 1978. Everyone we knew seemed to be reading it that year, and someone had brought a copy along, which we often read aloud.]

Today is just one of those adjustment days for me. Yesterday was both leisurely and adventurous. I got carried away in the excitement and joy and hilarity of being with women in the woods.

Then – thunk! I'm back on earth, grounded in my aching body, slightly headachy, feeling a cold coming on. Totally beyond thinking or movement. Did I over-extend yesterday? I didn't think so, but when I recount our adventures in the rapids, I have to admit it was exhausting. Felt like three or four days of excitement.

Later – I'm still in the mood of barely being capable of anything. Crouched by the river, I stare and think the best thing I can do for myself today, besides brush my teeth again, is to clean my fingernails. It's tedious and painful, with cuticles already torn from exposure to water and earth, but it pleases me to do something so simple and yet beneficial for myself.

Nails finished, I doze off, it seems, in a gaze at the water. Didn't realize I was so lost in thought until I was startled by a fish swimming by. Then I spied a dragonfly clinging to the rock in the hard wind. She wasn't the elegant kind, lacy black with midnight blue, that flew around the canoes. She was a simple green and gold one, more plain and fitting for a gray morning. I liked her. We sat together for a while in thought. I was happy to be alone. The confusion of eleven women, mostly new to each other, is so hard on the psyche and the viscera at first.

There was a phrase in *Wanderground* about coming so close that auras mixed. That fits for me as a description of the first days of an intimate adventure such as this. Our auras are mixing and blending, phases and cycles that are so different coming together for shuffling, sorting and new phasing. The blend is a good one, I believe, but time and experience will age and balance us. It's all so compressed, this living together in the wilderness. Time and simple dragonflies will help me sort it out.

Judith

I think today is not just about avoiding travel in a drenching rain, or recuperating from yesterday. I think we are resting up from the shock of adjustment, from the packing, preparing, and wrapping up of our city lives. Stopping so we can realize we're really *here*, feel in control.

Earlier I felt tense, restless, down. Partly from pain, maybe (my knees got pretty scraped back in Albany Rapids), but mostly about time and schedules. I badly want this trip not to feel rushed. And realistically, there are only two places we can end this trip on the 15th, with 150 or 200 river miles between us and there. I felt like I was the only one concerned with the real miles and real time dimension of living our fantasy.

Carol's playing the guitar settled me. I recognized that sense of alone-ness as part of an old self. A self I respect – my restlessness and stubborn-ness have been useful, are why I'm here right now. That aloneness stuff I can give up.

The tenseness left, replaced by sadness that how we are at our best, or even our middlin', isn't often how the world is – we all believe in the scari-est *Wanderground* stories for some good reasons.

It isn't easy to be writing this while laughing. We're all singing now, the new round Anne brought from St. Louis: "Cows like ice cream, they like it." A chorale fugue, in the manner of Gertrude Stein. "And rutabagas tooooooooo, cows like them. . . ."

Mary

This day has ended with such a clear blue sky after morning rains. Shar-ing and growing close. As the evening light changes and the river grows even smoother, we sit reading, writing, cat's cradling, stitching, playing classical guitar.

DAY 4. Rock Island Rapids. Judith

The river crossed under the highway at Mattice. We stopped at our cars, regretfully leaving behind the old guitar, Stella Armatrading, who had two broken strings. Then we left behind all roads until we'd catch a train back from Moose River Crossing, 150 miles downstream, or Moosonee, 50 miles farther.

Just a few miles down from Mattice we had an intense encounter with the Missinaibi at Rock Island Rapids. Just looking at the big waves in the middle gave me an adrenalin stomach ache. We talked of taking the alu-minum canoes down a sneak or "chicken" route. Some women were eager to get out into the rapids in the more nimble plastic canoes.

For Carol and Jane, it was the biggest, most exhilarating rapids they had ever done. ("No finesse at all," said Carol years later, "but a Coming of Age.") Floating alone in the quiet pool below, where they'd been assigned to be rescue canoe, flushed with heady success, they couldn't resist getting up for a congratulatory hug. Capsized, of course. The old Home Free Phenomenon. Moments later all the rest of us upriver were making the wild paddle signals that meant "Something has happened, get your bods up here to help." We couldn't read their mysterious answering gestures, which turned out to be the rescuers sheepishly wringing out their clothes.

What had happened: Bonnie and Julie had both felt the hunch that says, "Not us. Not this rapids. Not today." And we said, "Right. Pay attention to your instincts." But when three other canoes had danced through, the temptation to try was too strong. Cautious, they started down too close to shore, crashed on a hidden boulder. The women easily got ashore, but the canoe was badly pinned, the already wrinkled and patched veteran canoe Martha Martin (named for a woman who survived a winter alone in an Alaska cabin, pregnant, with a broken arm and leg).

It took all afternoon to get Martha off, wading in deep rushing water, fastening ropes. Finally Mary got us all chanting "Am-a-ZON!" (Heave!) to coordinate our pulling, and Anne, new to canoeing, figured out exactly the right pulling angle. "When that canoe finally moved," she said, "it was a spiritual experience." We floated the old canoe in shallow water and stomped her back into generally canoe shape, and painted her name on the stern in bright red letters.

DAY 5. The Morning After. Julie

Yesterday was much of a fog for me—I remember it being very tiring, and I ended the day dozing around the campfire listening to Ojibwe legends.

After Bonnie and I were so awkwardly inhibited by the river at Rock Island Rapids, and poor Martha took such a beating—and after the great rescue by Amazon Tote and a night of recuperation—we gathered for an energy circle at breakfast. It was then that some new realizations came over me (in a flood of tears). I love these women, these feet I'm looking down at, and it's time for me to be one of them too. I've always felt uncomfortable in my relationships with women in general. Now, with this receptive, gentle group, I can feel how it is to be a woman among women—something I've been striving for.

DAY 7. One More Damp Day. Daphne

I'm *not* looking forward to the end of this trip. There's something very right about being out here, travelling in this way, with these women. Even with the irritations of being bug-bitten and dirtier than I'd like, it's wonderful to be here. Things are really flowing together much better now and I'm loving it.

The day ended with the river taking her toll again. We were running some very shallow rapids near dusk when she nearly got Judith and Anne. (Anne's first day in the stern and she's doing really well.) She did get Jane and Mary, whose bow went right under. Bonnie and Julie swamped too, Bonnie nearly going down solo, but Julie managed to hold the canoe. Having watched the three Old Towns bump through, we Grummans had the choice of running the rapids *way* right or lining. E.B. and Carol chose running it, reasoning that if they were going to get wet, it might as well be glamorously. Jan and I chose lining and got very unglamorously wet.

We made our usual comfy campsite in a seemingly uninhabitable place. Although most people didn't realize it, it was well after 1 A.M. when we turned in.

Judith

We'd been paddling so late hoping to reach a campsite at a very dramatic section of the Missinaibi, Thunderhouse Falls. We were creeping along very cautiously in the shallows—Thunderhouse is *not* a place to come upon unaware.

The river here begins a swift drop of 300 feet in a few miles, down into the clay banks of Hudson Bay country. In the canyon below the three waterfalls an angular rock pillar stands in the river, the "Conjuring House," since it resembles the shaking tent used by a Cree shaman, conjuring for either good or evil purposes. "Conqueror's House" it was misnamed by the people who wrote the article that rated each drop of the falls. ("Grade V—wish I had my kayak along!") Missing the point, we thought.

DAY 8. At Conjuring House. Anne

A clear day, and everyone was moving in slow motion until Judith asked for an Estimated Time of Departure. A half hour was suggested. Jane offered that she'd begin her half hour *after* drinking her coffee.

It didn't take long to reach Thunderhouse Falls and the mile-long portage. I followed a path that led to a view of the falls and the huge stone pillar in the center of the river. The timelessness, awesomeness and sensuous beauty of this place struck me—on the way back to the beginning of the portage we walked in total silence. I felt very calm and centered—centered within myself and with all that surrounded me.

The portage was hot and buggy, but at the end a wonderful swimming hole waited. Julie suggested doing the laundry in a canoe filled with water—a sound ecological idea. By the time Janine dropped her clothes in, the water was too dark to see them as they sank to the bottom.

After lunch everyone took their own paths, Carol and Judith canoeing up the canyon in search of the sound of the sirens, others sitting and talking, taking walks, or writing. I returned to the view of the waterfalls, climbing down the rocks to be as close as possible to the powerful energy of the water and stone.

DAY 9. At Conjuring House. Mary

The energy of this place is incredible. Every time I stand on a rock look-out, facing the falls, my *ki* rises—I feel my center reach out to meet/tap/mingle with/give-to that water energy. A place of much magic. I'd like to return with these women or a similar group and stay for awhile. The power we could tap!

Right now I'd like to send some of that energy in healing form to Jane, who awoke soon after first light this morning, vomiting. She's the only one afflicted.

These women are wonderful—all of us Hags, sure to become Crones. ("If I live, I'll be great, I can hardly wait!")

I regret that we must move on—and yet I would like to see Moose Factory. We'll be pushing hard even to get to Moose River Crossing, unless we are fortunate enough to receive tailwinds from the Wind Womon.

DAY 11. Three-mile Portage and Long Rapids. Mary

It's my day to write in here "officially."

Yesterday we had that *three* mile portage around Stone Rapids. Such a lot of walking and hauling and the bugs were horrible. We did it, though, in good style (not *quite* elegant) and had "lunch" (at 7:30 P.M., Jan's time) on the rocks below the campsite.

Early to bed, for a change, with everyone agreeing to get up nicely when awakened by the first woman up. Most were fairly cordial when I said good morning.

Right now I'm duffing. This morning I paddled bow and Judith stern through about five miles of rapids in the Missinaibi Gorge. Everybody did *very* well—precision paddling! Now we have a tailwind, and we're heading as far as we can go, up to the last campsite on this stretch of map.

Late afternoon, sailing down the Missinaibi, all five canoes hooked together by arms and legs, and the orange tarp for a fine sail. Eating nuts and seeds, drinking lemonade, then the afternoon concert. "Cows Like Ice Cream." New verses to "Shady Grove": "The water is wide / The water is strong / We're moving with the river / She answers questions that we never asked / She'll stay with us forever." New verses to The Birdy Song: "It'll be a loooooooooong rapids / And WHAT will the birdies do then, the poor things? / They'll paddle like hell / At the bottom they'll bail / And TUCK their heads under their wings / The p'or things!"

DAY 12. Lower Missinaibi. Judith

Catch-up while duffing. Looks like we'll go 50 km. today, and it sure is easy from where I sit, except for the horseflies.

I have felt more content, calmer, ever since we reached Conjuring House. I climbed out on the rocks for a first not very close acquaintance with the falls, and right away I remembered—I'm *here.* I could know that any place, but it takes special places to remind me. As we walked the trail back I noticed more the sweetness of the air, and began to enjoy the leaves brushing my body.

We haven't talked much, except in twos and threes, about the power that place has. Mary said it focuses energy. My listening and watching became clearer there—I don't need to know what it is I'm listening and watching *for.* I could spend days studying the rocks, trying to read their hieroglyphics.

Yesterday in Missinaibi Gorge was deeply satisfying—watching everyone run the rapids so confidently. Playing with large forces, but with finesse and grace. A sense of fitness to it.

That's the feeling I woke with this morning. Gray dawn, a white throated sparrow piping keenly outside, and I foggily knew my dreams had been something about balance, fitness, proportion. About adventure not as the surge of energy that exhausts you (from which you have to return to "real" life), but of finding balance points, a moving equilibrium, riding our lives with care and joy.

It's getting horribly hot now. I bet I should offer to change places with one of the paddlers.

DAY 13. Beginning to Leave. Julie

I found a rock (makes a great paperweight) with a wonderful crystallized shell-fossil in it. I have it here in front of me, and I can't stop gazing at it, as if it might disintegrate in front of my eyes from exposure, and because it is so beautiful. But I know it's been lying out here for thousands of years and will stay this way for many more thousands; I will only have it for a while.

The fossil rock reminds me of this trip and these women—so wonderful-looking and yet such a seemingly fragile experience. (I can't gaze enough at these women.) I can have the experience now, a place in time, try to keep it from disintegrating from memory and meaning, knowing that women have existed this way for years and years.

Anne

I know I've said it before, but I need to say again that I feel a whole lot of love in my heart for these women, individually and as a group. I love the way we have worked together and played together, usually combining the two. The abundance of humor astounds me (sometimes it *is* a little obscure . . . nevertheless . . .) The care I see we've taken with each other and the faith and patience we've had with each other have shown me more of the ways that women can be, and given me even more faith in my own strength. Thank you all for being here.

Jane

Good morning. It's been a long time since I wrote here. Reading the last week's entries, I realize that most of the time has become a blur. I don't remember many times in the past when I was so unconscious of events and thoughts. I've been almost non-verbal. Not in my day-to-day interactions—I'm sure I appear to be functioning quite normally. But on another level, the voices of my rational mind have been stilled. The power and the calm of the wilderness have quieted the voices. There are no words. No analysis, no synthesis. I think in images all the time.

Like yesterday in the rapids. Three-foot standing waves—the longest stretch of big waves I've ever been in. I saw the waves and I felt my fear. But in seeing them, my mind began to work, very quickly and very logically, but without words. The visual problem translated directly into a physical solution. "Keep the paddle in the water for a brace. Angle into the waves. Adjust alignment. Try to keep from shipping water. Keep the bow up. Brace." My eyes saw and I responded without ever using any of the words.

Being this way, living in the physical realm, negotiating with my eyes, my arms, my torso. Bracing, lifting, carrying, learning. This is such a powerful feeling. A powerful way to live.

Yesterday Jan and I were talking about our jobs, about our lives in the other world. A cold shock hit my stomach as I remembered that in that world I and other women are not seen as being as competent and powerful as we are. In that world, I am known, and often know myself, through a very different set of standards. And often feelings of confidence and competence do not follow from the judgments and values I place on myself. Here I feel powerful. Not in a grandiose way—not inflated or too large, like some of the ways I use to make myself feel powerful in the city. If anything, on this trip I've felt weak by my "normal" standard. Sick, or weak, or just feeling dependent. But I'm just myself here, and that is powerful, more powerful than almost anything I've ever experienced.

64

I'm distracted now. Lots of early morning activity beginning around the fire. Time to pack up.

DAY 14. Endings. Judith

We decided a few days back to end our trip at Moose River Crossing, the first railroad access point, instead of paddling hard to cover the additional 50 miles to Moosonee. "Decided" is, of course, shorthand and euphemistic for quite a lot of difficult discussion. Some of us could hardly imagine not taking the challenge of going as hard as necessary to get to James Bay. Some insisted the really important thing was to spend good time together. Some people wanted both, but worried about headwinds. To keep an eleven-sided discussion from becoming endless (and thus making only one decision possible anyway), we "referred it to committee." They recommended (predictably) that we choose the shorter route. Which we did, and after a little more talk to soothe feelings aroused in all this, there was a general contentment. Certainly the last days on the river could be dreamy and relaxed.

Today we floated in a raft of five canoes again, one or two women staying alert to steer, occasionally rousing the others to help run the riffles. Janine read aloud about wind-riding. Lovely spacey feeling.

A driftwood fire, several of us staying up for reading from *Wanderground*. How many of us talk about country land, partly out of an ominous feeling of wanting to be ready for whatever-might-happen.

Then we looked up. A glow in the night sky, black spruce spires, stars above, fireflies below. The light concentrated, intensified. Northern lights! Julie went off singing a northern lights song to wake the women already in tents.

DAY 15. Judith

Our last night on the river was spent so close to the village of Moose River Crossing we could see the railroad trestle from our mud flat. Storm clouds collected. With the smoothness of a group that has made many camps together, we raced to pitch our tents in a circle, with a huge tarp covering the yard between them, just before a violent thunderstorm and all-night deluge.

Almost all of us had quickly crawled into shelter but it was not a night of roughing it. Out in the covered courtyard we could hear four women rummaging in the food packs, and out of the end-of-trip scraps of cheese, leftover buckwheat groats and some sheets of seaweed they concocted an unorthodox gourmet meal, served up by a cheery room service.

"There you are," Jane wrote later, "so tired you can hardly lift your head from the pillow. And women are out there in the dark having a *great* time, fixing you Japanese nori rolls, and wonderful gooey desserts. I don't know how it happens—it's not always the same people either. Something special just takes over."

Maria Brown, Kopka River, Ontario (Judith Niemi)

A Song of Women Travelling

MARIA BROWN

Maria Brown teaches social work at Augsburg College in Minneapolis. She lives near the St. Croix River, likes sharing the outdoors with her two children, and for several years has been guiding wilderness trips for women.

A Song of Women Travelling — Words and music by Maria Brown

Sing a so-ng of rush-ing wa- ter, rock-y sho-re-line, pine trees reach-ing to the sky a-bove us, sun to lo-ve us, shin-ing on the wa-ter.

I write some of my favorite music when I'm in the wilderness, by taking time to be centered, and listening carefully. This song came from a number of events and scenes on a trip down Ontario's Kopka River with twelve women in 1981. It reflects, for me, the extremes of my wilderness experience, from the excitement of learning how competent and connected to others I can be, to the introspective, introverted parts of me that I share mostly with my journal.

The melody and first verse bubbled out early in the trip as we were paddling across a long lake. I was so excited by it, not to mention afraid I'd lose it, that I prevailed on my canoe partner to paddle alone for some time while I got the basics down on paper. She was understanding, both of the

67

importance of the song to me, and of my long silence while I worked on it. I had never shared a song fragment before, but I got stuck on this one midway through the second verse and asked for help. Ronnie Kolotkin helped me sort out the confusion of ideas into two verses. Then the astonishing treat was Kristin Frish's writing a fourth verse, and tentatively presenting it. So this song is a combined gift from the women of the Kopka.

A Song of Women Travelling

Sing a song of rushing water,
Rocky shoreline,
Pine trees reaching to the sky above us,
Sun to love us
Shining on the water.

Sing a song of women travelling,
Strong together,
Reaching outward to the world around us,
Strength surrounds us,
Shining from the water.

Sing a song of woman travelling,
Strong and separate,
Reaching inward to her depths and rising,
Self-surprising,
Treasure from the water.

Sing a song of women travelling,
Reaching out and
Joining hands together in the sunlight,
In the moonlight,
Dancing on the water.

PART TWO:
The Whitewater of Life

Carol Iwata and Judith Niemi on the Missinaibi River, Ontario (Jane Eastwood)

"My maple paddle had snapped from my hands. In impotent despair I looked around at my companion. Until the present trip she never had been in a canoe, and her only knowledge in its management had been gained by my coaching and by less than two weeks of practice. But plainly the river and the forest were now in her veins, and the craft of the paddle had come by inspiration. The hesitation of the city-born was dispelled, and with skillful stroke, she steered safe through the boiling waters."

—Isobel Knowles, "Two Girls in a Canoe," *Cosmopolitan* magazine, 1905.

THE SKILLS AND KNOWLEDGE of wilderness travel don't always come by "inspiration," and the process of learning them has its dangers and difficulties. Women's writings don't often emphasize the hardships: "No inconveniences are legitimate subjects for sympathy which are endured in pursuit of pleasure," wrote traveller Isabella Bird in 1873. But if being tough—the equivalent of the woods "making men out of boys"—is not a theme in women's writing, growth is. Women often make wilderness trips at times of transition in their lives, when their directions are changing and consciousness shifting. These selections are mostly by women taking their first canoe trips, or purposefully doing trips longer or more difficult or dangerous than they had done before. It's about the wilderness skills and the life skills they set out to learn, and the other lessons that they learned along the way.

Yip, yip sur la Rivière

JOAN BARIL

Joan Baril teaches English and Women's Studies at Confederation College in Thunder Bay, Ontario, and writes regularly for The Northern Women's Journal, *the Thunder Bay feminist newspaper. (This article first appeared in* The Northern Women's Journal, *November, 1982.)*

Like most of the other women on her 1982 trip, Joan had little canoeing experience at the time. Since then she's canoed more on her home river, the Kaministiquia, has paddled in the Everglades, and has done a fair bit of white-water.

Two hours out on the South Kawishiwi River in a party of four canoes and ten women I realize that my fears about this five-day canoe trip are groundless. I lean back into the stroke, happy to see the July sun glint off water and paddle drops. The shore of the wide and incredibly beautiful river slides by in cliffs, spruce and swamp. The women are laughing and talking, meeting each other for the first time.

Another tour by Woodswomen, women-owned wilderness outfitters, was gliding off into the Boundary Waters Canoe Area of northern Minnesota.

At the first portage, I make my little speech. "I cannot carry the canoes or heavy packs, only the paddles and lighter stuff. I'm apologizing now for the whole trip."

I scan the women's faces. All are smiling acceptance without a hint of the disgruntled expression so familiar to back sufferers when they have to beg off heavy work. Our guide had been informed of my disability a month previous when I first signed up. Now she smiled. "Don't apologize. We've had lots of bad backs on our trips and people with other disabilities too."

An hour later, over the portage and on our way, my second worry melted away. There was not a "bush jock" in the group, and certainly our two guides, Judith and Kristin, didn't qualify. (Bush Jock: one who insists on paddling thirty miles a day, who trots over the portages and refuses to lie down at night until all muscles are exercised into knots of pain; has a raucous guilt-producing call ending on a rising note, "All right! All right! Let's go! Let's go!")

Woodswomen, I realize, deliberately designs their trips as a relaxed focusing into the wilderness with time to learn camping skills and to zen in on the details – a flower, a bird call, a sunset. This is an over-40 trip, eight women from various parts of the U.S., plus two guides. I am the only Canadian. Decisions are made collectively and amiably, sometimes slowly. "Everybody should do their fair share of cooking and dishes," says Judith. "We don't keep a list, but I don't want anyone to do more than her share." Someone in the group giggles: "That's surely a speech designed for women. I bet when you take a group of men camping you don't have to remind them not to overdo on dishes."

Evening campfire in a world dimming into lavender dark. Women's conversations. A topic moves out, is encircled by our experience, enlarges into a thought-field. We learn and listen and add, we brood and study, we joke and toss the conversation back and forth across the fire like hoop dancers. We can feel our human force field emerging in the black bush and gold light. We do not try to score points, nor hammer home a point of view. There is no thrust and parry talk, no desire to impress or to solve all problems. We are women after all.

We discuss American politics, the "fundies" (rabid anti-women religious fundamentalists), the fifties, children, marriage – surprisingly only one of us is married – divorce, the single life, being 40 or older, living alone and living with someone, the lives of women, and of course the lives of men.

Peg Cruikshank of San Francisco has a definition: "Whatever can be measured, weighed, compared, rated, counted, quantified in any way – that has importance to the masculine world."

The next evening as Mary is fishing, two men in a canoe glide past. "How many fish have you caught? How much do they weigh? How far did you paddle today?" Those of us within earshot fall on the ground in laughter.

I learn something new and deep about myself that sends me spiraling down a well of self-knowledge. I realize I resist learning new things which require manual skill. On a sunset canoe tour of the lake with Peg, I'm happy to learn from her about the San Francisco life style, her teaching experiences, and a book she is editing. I'm fascinated. But the next day, I don't join the group around Marianne who are learning to filet fish. Mmmm . . . Nor do I take out my compass and get involved in the mapping of the course as some women do. Mmmm . . . I grit my teeth and ask

Mary to teach me how to cast. Somewhere in my heart, I realize, is a little black hard pebble marked "Impossible. You can't do it." I fling the rod out according to her directions and the line sings through the blue air in a perfect arc. "To hell with fishing – I'm casting." I am elated and just cast again and again.

Two days later I'm standing on the shore studying a long flashy set of rapids using my new whitewater skills. I'm checking for deep water, for standing waves, for the dangerous rock-concealing pillows. Next, I'm in the bow, twisting through the course, in a tremendous high. After one particularly exciting run, we carried the canoe back over the portage and ran it again, just for the pleasure of it.

So I learn to cast, to run whitewater, to map read, to make a fire with a flint; but the little pebble is still there. I ponder on its origin as we sweep along. There were many times in my life when I tried to learn something but was balked. Lost and enlightening memories ripple in.

For instance, my first driving lesson. It was in Ottawa and my husband, who was my driving teacher, directed me without any prior instruction into Confederation Circle at rush hour. Round and round the War Memorial I went in a complete panic – my first time at the wheel. When I finally got out I was so shaken I decided driving was too difficult for me. My husband agreed, no doubt secretly pleased that his plan to retain control of the car (and me) had worked so well and that he hadn't killed himself carrying it out. He convinced me that he himself had learned to drive instinctively without lessons, but that I was the sort of person who never could learn.

On another occasion a boyfriend, whom I had asked to teach me chess, so confused me with fast talk and jargon that I could not understand him. He refused to clarify, but simply repeated the incomprehensible sentence louder. When I still didn't understand, he shrugged and suggested perhaps I never would catch on. I believed him too.

It was a rewarding sweep down the South Kawishiwi River. Catching on at last, forty-six years old and realizing I'd been conned into incompetence. Negative conditioning doesn't end with childhood after all. I sang bits of voyageur songs I once knew: *"Yip! Yip! Sur la rivière . . . o, fils du roi, tu es méchant. . . ."* ["Yip! Yip! On the river . . . oh, king's son, you are wicked. . . ."]

We saw no moose – though we had seen signs on the shore – or any other large animal, but there were birds, mama ducks and loon families. One day Karin yodelled a beautiful loon imitation and a loon answered back. A conversation developed with the loon sounding each time a little more puzzled.

Occasionally, we saw another canoe. Like Quetico, the Boundary Waters area is reserved for canoeists, and no motor boats are allowed. But the solitude seemed so fixed we were soon skinny dipping or paddling along topless.

The evening circle again. No roughing it in the bush for us as far as food is concerned: we eat curry, felafels, fresh fish and fresh fruits and vegetables – nothing canned or freeze dried. The tents go up and the mosquitoes come out filling the clearing with their horrible hum. I burn a bit of "pic" in my tent to clear them out. The American women have never seen mosquito coils. I offer pieces around but they are suspicious, probably rightly, that sleeping in the fumes is unhealthy. But my tent mate Gayla is thankful I've brought it. "Light it up," she says. "There are millions of things I hate about this trip and all of them are mosquitoes."

On our fifth day, we leave the Boundary Waters area. At the last carrying place, I am dumbfounded to see a large man strolling down the trail toward me, a lit cigar in his mouth. The hum of motor boats is heard and the final mile is lined with summer cottages.

At the landing, some unload, others go for the cars or set up lunch. We all look a bit glum. I'm suddenly struck by "post camping syndrome" – the sudden and overwhelming desire for a hot bath. And I realize I have a long drive ahead of me and I have to return to work tomorrow. "Joan, what are you thinking?" asks Marianne. "I'm thinking I have to stop on the way home and buy pantyhose for work tomorrow," I reply truthfully. Everybody laughs.

At the campground, we eat a farewell meal which includes fresh watermelon and champagne. "You can gold plate these, and make them into earrings, like they do in New York boutiques. These are original souvenirs," says Judith as she hands out momentos – saran wrapped moose berries. I receive the first one "as a symbol of international good will." "Turds across the border," we laugh.

All the things we ten women talked about still float like pollen through my mind. *"Oui, longtemps que je t'aime. Jamais que je t'oublierai."* ["Yes, I've loved you a long time. I shall never forget you."]

40, and at Sea

TWYLA WRIGHT

Twyla Wright of Arkansas is a free-lance writer of non-fiction, short stories, and curricula. For eighteen years she has also been a sex educator, leading workshops in schools, churches, and homes for the mentally retarded. Her two children are grown and on their own.

She took this first kayak trip in 1977, and since then has returned to the Sea of Cortez many times as a partner with her husband, leading groups of students. "I find my confidence and playfulness on the sea increasing," she says. "Between these wilderness trips I find myself a bit homesick, longing for the sea to lift me, to carry me along with it."

I always thought boats were for afternoons on a lake or for fishing. Or for men who had abandoned sensible life and sailed away to tropical isles. As for me, I'd take a four-wheeled vehicle, or my own two feet, please. These modes had served me well as a college student exploring the Grand Canyon, a teacher in rural Arkansas, a comfortable housewife and mother of two, and as a motor home camper.

Then I entered my fortieth year. My familiar preconceptions and self image and my husband's goals all shifted, hanging precariously on their sides. Transition was at hand, and I could feel the quake under my feet. It culminated one evening when my husband said, "Come with me on the sea. You'll have your own kayak, and be a real partner on this wilderness course. Eight students have signed up for it. I'll handle the outer wilderness skills, and you can explore the inner dimensions."

"There are sharks out there! Besides, I don't know the first thing about those little Eskimo boats."

He explained that he could be trusted to teach us, since he had just received fine training, and was well prepared. I toyed with the tantalizing prospect of doing some interesting group interaction work with the students. But in tiny boats? On the huge, bottomless sea?

At last I timidly opted for the shaky side of life. Go with the flow! There was no other way to free Dennis to follow his new outdoor education vision, while growing with him instead of away. At least I didn't have to be the camp cook and nurse. I swallowed my fear and kept it controlled as we prepared for the trip to the western coast of Mexico.

On a snowy day in January, 1977, the new kayaks were lifted onto the trailer racks. We boarded the van for Mexico, all novices in kayaking, except Dennis. He hoped the students would earn greater self-esteem by encountering physical and emotional extremes which would push them to accomplish more than they thought they could. Perhaps it would work for me too. Heaven, help me!

January 6

This morning I stood on the deserted beach and took a long look at the restless Sea of Cortez. A brisk wind whipped the water into small chops, while dark clouds hung overhead. Will it eat me alive, or cradle me gently in its hold?

I lined my loaded kayak alongside the others, pointed toward the unknown. Dennis showed us once again the strokes that would be necessary on the sea, and gave us last minute instructions. I stretched my spray skirt over the cockpit lip, put my gloves on, pulled down my sailor hat, and took up my double-bladed paddle.

I felt the boat slip out with the surf, and within a few yards realized that I could not steer it into the wind. Frantically I paddled in great sweep strokes on my left, but barely managed to keep my bow pointed in the right direction, let alone get anywhere. Panic set in. Dennis glided effortlessly beside me, trying to tell me what to do. I was horrified and incensed at everything, including him. I yelled, "I'm going back. This is too hard. I can't do it!"

But there was no turning back. I had to keep paddling in absolute impotence. I had no power in my arms and shoulders. The sky grew even darker and heavier with clouds, while wind blew salt spray in my face. I leaned forward with each stroke, twisting and pushing with my feet on their foot rests. I was a fool to come in the first place! Everyone was ahead of me, and my arm was like wet spaghetti. Three waves had washed over me, and I was getting cold.

I struggled on. Dennis tried to raft up with me by placing his paddle across our decks. I didn't want to. He asked if he might tow me. I yelled, "No!" I was exhausted and angry and in despair, but I would not bow to defeat. I would not be towed like a child! I asked him to please go on, and let me be.

At last Dennis signaled us to the shore, and I turned the boat, running with the wind at my back. After pulling my kayak up on the beach, I climbed a tall sand dune to be alone. I cried at my helplessness, my age, my inability. Never have I felt so old. I wanted to run away from everyone, especially those young college students! I walked along the estuary, away from the open sea, letting the anger seep out through my feet. I wonder what the future holds for Dennis and me? Can I go on these sea adventures with him, or must I sit alone at home?

Finally, I gathered an armload of driftwood, ironwood, jojoba twigs, and walked back to camp. A fire had already been laid. Sitting down with Christy, I took out my pocket knife and helped her peel potatoes. The wind was terrible and cold. We changed into our wool clothes, and sat huddled around the three tiny fires, eagerly eating pinto beans, fried potatoes, and bannock.

As everyone wandered off to bed, I stayed by the dying coals, feeling like a hypocrite, planning to lead sessions on inner growth, when I'm evidently such a child myself. Dennis sat down and put his arm around me, and told me how proud he was of me. I asked him to go on to bed. He left, frustrated that I wouldn't let him help me.

January 9

A slice of pink on the horizon changing into crimson. A cool breeze blowing softly over the water. Overcast sky with gulls flying low. Lovely! Except that it means that we must start on the sea again after sitting out the storm for the last two days.

But today my boat handled easily! I stayed at the front of the group, dipping my paddle evenly on both sides. As the morning went on the wind rose, and blew my stern hard on port side, and my bow kept heading out to sea. I had to paddle only on my left again. I wish I had a rudder, or something.

The wind dropped, and the sea suddenly grew still and glassy, silvery blue, with the sun shimmering. And a full circle rainbow around the sun! I felt relaxed as I paddled. No fright. No frantic movement. Suddenly dolphins surfaced at our left, arching in the water, some springing completely out of the sea. It was stunning! What companions – wild, graceful creatures. Maybe this isn't so bad.

January 13

The fire was going for our breakfast at 7 A.M. I had been lying in bed writing in my journal, reviewing the last few days and our flawless crossing of the strait named "Little Hell."

This large island is a marvelous wildlife sanctuary with high desert mountains forming its spine. No one is allowed to live on the island, except for two tiny Marine outposts to guard it. We heard a wildcat scream last night, and each evening we hear coyotes and find their tracks around our tents.

We put out to sea through a small surf at 9 A.M. The water was beautifully clear. Far beneath me I could see lots of sea hares, orange sponges, sea fans and star fish. But, most excitingly, we spotted a whole herd of keyhole sand dollars under us, dark purple echinoderms leaving sand trails behind them.

We paddled hard until noon, when Darick, the day's leader, led us into a rocky beach for lunch. We decided to camp there and spend a lazy afternoon, so I put on my swim suit and took a bath and shampooed my hair in the sea. Washed my clothes and hung them out on the low bushes near our tent. I put more zinc oxide on my freckled face, and looked into my mirror. A puffy, red-faced old lady with white circles around her eyes looked back at me.

Two Seri Indian fishermen slowly circled our cove, one standing fearlessly in the high bow of their motor launch. In a flash he swung, harpooning a huge sting ray. As he hauled it up over his head, its flat sides flapped like giant wings. Dennis and I paddled out and I peered into their launch, where huge rays lay, their stinging tails cut off. The Seris will eat them. They laughed at our boats and said they were too little – shark bait!

January 16

This morning is dark gray and overcast with a slight breeze. But the wind will rise as mid-morning arrives. I've learned that much, and I dread the force of the wind on my boat. I imagine it will be a hard day. No one is wanting to go. A coyote tore the cockpit cover off my boat last night, and ripped open three chocolate milk containers.

It was foggy and dismal as we took off. The swells were two feet high, and the wind made for slow paddling. Large flocks of pelicans flew off the southern point as we came near. Around the tip of the island the swells suddenly turned into roller coaster waves. Up on the crest and down in the trough, we lost sight of one another from time to time. Students screamed in surprise. At first it was exhilarating and fun, but as cross swells drew us into them we began to wallow. Over and over huge swells drove down on us. We had to keep at safe distances from each other. It became increasingly difficult to paddle, but I ruddered with my paddle each time a swell hit me. I could hear the ominous spew of breaking waves directly behind me.

I was afraid, yet it did not clutch me; I felt no sense of panic. Tired to the bone, I just kept paddling. The shore seemed to be a mile away and I was making little progress. I watched those up ahead beach in the surf, some sideways and rolling. I wasn't sure how to pick the biggest wave to ride in on, but one found me. It surfed me in, fast. I paddled hard to stay with it. Just before my bow hit the sand, my kayak turned at a slight angle, and the wave broke, drenching me.

Tonight I helped make corn cakes out of cornmeal and boiling water, fried in hot oil. And I kept feeding two fires with piles of tiny sticks. We are sea bums, serving ourselves out of a common pot on a driftwood table, and washing our bowls in the wet sand.

Around the evening fire, I led another discussion, this time about the ways we each manage conflict. Some of us avoid the camp conflict, some confront it, others whisper about it. I tend to mull over it, then confront.

January 18

We're eager to explore a tiny island some three miles off. The sea is un-believably calm, like undulating satin. Dennis stressed that we must not only keep our bows aimed at a point on the island, but our sterns pointed at a landmark behind us, so we won't be carried out by the current without realizing it.

Half-way across I became conscious of the vast cobalt-blue depth be-neath me. I thought of sharks then, remembering the many carcasses left along the shore by the Mexican fishermen, and felt fear break out in sweat on my palms. Just at that moment my paddle hit something hard. My arms froze in mid-air. It couldn't be a rock. Shark? I didn't dare look down. I just sat paralyzed, my heart pounding wildly. Dennis approached and saw a large sea turtle dive beneath me.

I shook all the way to the tiny island. It rose like a giant thumb from the sea, covered with tall cactus. I paddled up close to the sheer bluff, and slipped through a hidden gateway in the rocks, entering a magical place. A bird perched high on a slender rock pinnacle and watched me enter a shal-low pool, an underwater rock garden. Towering white guano-coated rocks brought a touch of Antarctica to the desert scene. A sense of the sacred, the holy sanctuary, flooded over me. I was grateful to my tiny boat for giving me the freedom to enter such a secluded spot. Others followed me, but no one spoke, except in a hush.

As we passed out of the garden, dozens of pelicans stared at me, eye to eye, then laboriously took off in flight.

Tonight I sum up my experience in a haiku:

> Sacred spire of rock
> lifts a feathered guardian
> o'er jade sea gardens.

January 22

The last day of my solo! O Great Sun, how I worship you this morning for bringing me warmth as you climb the sky. Last night's freezing wind tormented me and robbed me of my sleep.

I am filthy. I can't stand the smell of my shirt. My hands are grimy. When I get out of these mountains, I am going to take a bath in the sea, and eat and eat and eat. I wonder how the students have done during the last three days with no one to be with, talk to, and nothing to eat. I have just about drunk my gallon of water. I am sure I have lost weight.

Not until this morning have I been able to reflect on my experience, instead of fighting flies or improving my wind break under the Elephant tree. I have become aware of how finite I am, yet how related I am to the birds, cactus, pebbles, and even the sea. The sea. A great symbol of life. It takes me where it will. Sometimes I can control my pathway on it, sometimes I can't. There are tremendous struggles to survive on it, yet there are also calm days when all its treasures are laid bare in its depths. I must relax, experiment more, lean into the waves. I must face my struggle on the sea again until finally I find joy in riding it.

January 24

Dennis was up at 6 A.M., and called for everyone to get packed without eating breakfast. Today is our last day on the sea—Marathon Day. The first person back to the beach, where we left our van nineteen days ago, will be declared the winner. I haven't got a chance against ex-Marine Doug, or powerful Jack!

I pulled a muscle in my shoulder as I pushed off. The water was rippling smooth, but I felt frustrated at being so far behind, for everyone quickly left me. I watched the flashing blades and tiny boats ahead of me vanish into specks as the sun broke on the horizon. And suddenly I relaxed, paddling smoothly, evenly. I found myself singing a haunting old Judy Collins song, "Farewell to Tarwathe."

Without warning, a large fin split the water at my side. I sucked in my breath. What irony to be eaten by Jaws on my last day at sea! I sat immobile, watching, and a dozen other fins broke the surface, circling me. With immense relief I saw their backs arch, and heard them snort. Dolphin. A dolphin escort! Could my song have called them up? I paddled with them, singing, playing. A moment of joy.

Hours later, I spotted the kayaks on the beach, and felt a twinge of shame again. I was the pig's tail—the old lady of the sea. But as my aching shoulders and paddle blades thrust me onto the beach, a great cheer went up from the students. And I laughed with pride in spite of myself. I had done what I set out to do!

The Bush

KATHRENE PINKERTON

Kathrene Gedney, of conventional upbringing, married footloose news-
paperman Robert Pinkerton in Milwaukee in 1911. They "settled down," but
within a year his health collapsed from what would now be called acute stress
or "burn out;" his doctor ordered him to quit his numerous jobs as press agent/
writer/editor and return to an outdoor life. Kathrene and Robert headed for
northern Ontario, to build a cabin, live off the land, and earn cash through
free-lance writing.

He had considerable backwoods experience; she had none. "You'll get the
hang of the North," he assured her. "That country was made for a feller who
flies into things like you do." They located a cabin site within a day's travel of
the railroad near Atikokan, Ontario. Before settling into cabin building and
true to their belief that life is to be enjoyed and experienced to the fullest, they
travelled around by canoe for several weeks to explore their new surroundings.

In this excerpt from Wilderness Wife *(New York: Grossett and Dunlap,*
1939), Kathrene Pinkerton gives an account of her initiation into canoe camp-
ing in 1912.

For weeks we saw no canoes except those made of birch bark. The sun
was our time clock in a country where it rose before five and did not sink
until nearly eight. We wakened to the twitterings and early stirrings of
birds in trees beside our tent. I took my morning dip while the first shafts
of sunlight gilded the wind ripples of the water.

We were in the canoe by seven and did not stop until late afternoon
shadows stretched far from shore. Supper was eaten and camp tasks finished before the last red glow lighted the pine trees in copper tones. We
watched them as we lay before the tent, tired, comfortable and terribly
content.

I had become the "map eater." Robert grumbled to hide his pride. "If I'd

Ojibwe women sewing a birch bark canoe, Mille Lacs, Minnesota, 1940 known you were going to be a paddling fool, we could have gone to Hudson Bay."

Ease in the Ojibwa stroke, or awareness of it, had burst upon me suddenly. I did not realize that I was paddling and was thinking only how joyous the tiny sparkling wavelets made the lake look. Robert broke into my absorption. "You've been setting a pace that keeps me humping."

I had fallen at last into the steady motion which eats up miles, and I enjoyed it. There is a beat in it, a rhythmic appeal much like that of dancing, a forward sway of the whole body and a quick snap backward. Travel was not a succession of weary paddle strokes. It was fun.

The discovery opened up the waterways of the North. We dared long, wind-swept traverses and swift rivers. I faced my first rapids with some terror as we studied the hundred yards of whitewater ahead.

"We'll have to shoot for that big rock in the center," Robert said. "Then turn sharp to the right."

"Yes," I agreed weakly while I wondered what would happen if we did not turn.

Once in the grip of that tearing water, I knew no power on earth could keep us from striking the boulder at which we rushed. I closed my eyes and waited. Robert did nothing. I could tell by the feel of the canoe that he did not take a stroke. That fact shocked me into looking. The deflected current had already carried us safely past the rock. After that I was kept so busy grabbing water with my paddle, pulling the bow this way and that at his command, I could not take time to be frightened. Before we were through the rapids the excitement of the wild dash had caught me and I demanded that we return at once and run them again. But Robert refused to pay for our Northwoods "shoot the chutes" by tracking the canoe upstream or carrying it back on the portage.

My enthusiasm for swift water made him rather canny as we consulted on our routes and he began to offer alternatives for rivers which promised thrills. The possibility of an Indian village was his scheme one evening to get my mind off a stream marked with rapids.

I could never resist the appeal of the little settlements in which Indians gathered for summer visiting after lonely winters on the trap lines. We had called at several of these groups of birch bark wigwams set behind big sand beaches. The sites were always well chosen, sunny, and commanding a long view of the lake.

The villages were happy, friendly places. The children laughed and shouted and played games. The men, finished with their early morning hunt, lounged on the beach or worked on birch bark canoes, mending old ones or building new. Near the wigwams and racks of drying meat and fish, the women were gathered. Every village had a sewing circle with much laughing, gossiping and making of moccasins.

Robert's Ojibwa always won us a welcome. He was not fluent. After each halting effort the whole village would hold a conference to make sure they had caught his meaning. His songs went over best, especially with the women. A lumberjack ballad began with a line in English, "I went into the wigwam to pass the time of day." From there on it was Ojibwa and did not sound like the sort of thing to be sung to strangers. The sewing circles ate it up.

My clothes fascinated the Indians. Groups gathered around me. I thought it was admiration until the chief of a small band, apparently a wit, convulsed his villagers by pointing at me and repeating, *"Kaw-win ish-quay! Kaw-win ish-quay!"*

"Not a woman! Not a woman!" Robert interpreted. "He means your riding breeches."

The village roared and shrieked its mirth. That became the summer's joke. And durable. Years later I would turn a bend in a portage and hear a giggle, *"Kaw-win ish-quay! Kaw-win ish-quay!"*

Moose became very much a part of our camping days. We played a game. The first to see a moose took the scores. An antlered head counted three, a cow two, and a calf one. By running across the portage first, I collected the heads in the next lake, but Robert often matched me by seeing a fine set of antlers in the lake we had just left when he returned for the canoe. The straight count of moose for the summer was one hundred and fourteen.

When I had learned to paddle in the bow and in the stern and to handle the canoe alone while kneeling amidship in the Ojibwa manner, we began to make shore explorations. Food was our excuse: ruffed grouse, berries and later, a small deer, which we converted into jerky. That supplied the commissary. Then we broke down and admitted that we started off on a day's tramp for the sheer joy of covering country, discovering an uncharted lake or wandering along game trails in the deep soft moss of muskegs. I never learned to skim over windfalls, but I got very adept at crawling under.

Camp cooking edged over until it fell entirely in my province. Never having been a cook was a help. I had no technique or kitchen fetishes to be shocked by primitive methods. I expected poultry to arrive intact, with insides and feathers. I had not been spoiled by the nicely groomed fowl that market men deliver.

All the flutter of adaptation was saved me. I began with the simplest methods and I sometimes wondered if an oven could be controlled as easily as I moved the reflecting baker around the fire. And the thought of a rolling pin and a board as pie making utensils lacked the appeal of an empty bottle and the bottom of a canoe.

Mostly I cooked by ear. It was a strange medley of lumber camp dishes modified by formulas from a cooking booklet, my impressions of how food ought to taste, and by the limitations of the grub sack. The products were often sporting events, and adventure for me, but much more so for Robert. Some still lay buried on the shores of distant northern lakes.

Nomadic camping reduced life to essentials and gave us the freedom of simplicity. An insect-proof tent, a campfire, cooking kettles, plates, cups and cutlery were all we needed. A windfall, flat clean rocks or brown needle matting, were tables, chairs, or couches; camping life should have touch with earth. Every night we had a fresh swept world to live in.

We evolved a camp making system. Each had his tasks. At night these were completed, and the meal ready, a half hour after the canoe touched shore. Unless it were raining, the tent always went up last because under its waterproofed floor cloth was built the balsam bed.

The weeks wrought changes in my attitude toward physical conditions. Wet feet were no longer a discomfort. Journeying in the rain was not unusual and I made the important discovery that hardship, so called, exists almost entirely in the imagination. But the most astonishing change of all was what that life did for my body. Physical exertion always had appalled me and unused muscles had rebelled at any task. But when they were toned and hardened I discovered pleasure in their use. A new sureness came to my walk. I could see farther, could distinguish projecting points, shorelines and distant hills in what had been only a green confusion. My hearing was more keen. I was sentient to the world around me.

I said all this to Robert one evening as we lay before the campfire watching darkness engulf the lake. Soon it would be black velvet and the night was far too lovely to miss in any early bed hour.

"It's a shame," he said. "Just when you've got to be a damned good woodswoman, we have to quit."

I had known the end was approaching. It was time we built the cabin. But the travel idea had shown me Ontario in summer and no one could paddle through those lakes, each beautiful and each different, some dotted with islands, all sparkling in the sunshine, and not feel the enchantment of the land.

It was no longer the empty, desolate country I had watched flash past the car windows. It was wilderness, but a wilderness of beauty and of adventure, of swift rivers rushing to the north, of camps where no one had ever camped before, of deep soft game trails leading into the forest, and of intimate friendly contacts with the forest's people.

Intensity: Journal of an Arctic Expedition

LAURIE GULLION

Laurie Gullion of Northfield, Massachusetts, is an outdoor educator and photojournalist. Since 1982 she has led whitewater canoe trips in the Canadian North as assistant director of Arctic Barrens Expeditions.

This journal, however, was written before her days as a trip leader, on her first Arctic canoe trip in 1980 on the Elk, Thelon, Dubawnt and Kazan Rivers in the Northwest Territories. She calls this journey a turning point in her life; she left her job as a newspaper reporter, explored a true wilderness for the first time, and came to understand its call.

BUGS

"The struggling black flies drowned in my chicken and rice dinner. I debated whether to pick them painstakingly from the bowl, but the layer of blackness obscured the meal completely.

"The flies demonstrated, without a doubt, that they were the victors in this battle. I ate the exotic garnish, my raging appetite muted by the unwanted extra protein. I was more tired than I have ever been. When I decided to join this 1200-mile canoeing expedition into Canada's untravelled Barrenlands, I hadn't realized the toughest challenge would be mental stress rather than physical endurance."

I wrote these words shortly after the end of my first trip to the Barrens. I vowed that I would never go again. It was a beautiful land and an exciting adventure, but the hardships were challenges to be met only once.

Given the opportunity to return to the North two years later, why did I accept so quickly, so joyfully, and with such yearning? An acquaintance asked the same question with painful bluntness: "I read your words about eating those black flies, and it sounded horrible. It sounded like you hated it! I can't understand why you went back."

"Well," I stalled, shifting uncomfortably, "I did hate it on some days. But there are scattered images of my travels in the Barrens – pictures and sounds and smells – which shadow me every day. I learned so much and lived so wildly and achieved things beyond my greatest expectations. Beyond the bugs. But the bugs are much easier to describe."

The essential element in living in the wilderness is understanding the danger. Staking one's life and limbs on one's own judgment is a challenge and a commitment that few people ever accept. We are rarely forced into a decision which involves clear cut and immediate risks. We spend most of our lives avoiding those situations. But in meeting the North's challenges, one is not "fighting nature and winning," either. That approach is the height of egoism.

Perhaps the reason I hated the bugs so much was because I couldn't win that battle. In my egotistical self-assurance I never thought I would be undone by an airborne enemy, thousands of which weigh less than an ounce. I was confronted forcefully with my limitations. And not only did the bugs show me that truth – sit in a wind-battered tent for four days, cold and wet, and one quickly realizes who is the victor. Satisfaction with the experience, though, is derived from accepting one's limitations while meeting nature's challenges. In the process, adversity becomes enlightening and enriching.

⋆   ⋆   ⋆

June 29

An ecstatic feeling when the planes depart. Commitment. Wet feet already. Rennie Lake is so shallow that we unloaded gear from the planes 50 feet from shore.

The first campsite is a beautiful esker (sand ridges left over from glacial times). A solitary walk behind our tent reveals a caribou graveyard; bleached skeletons loom in the subdued light. I find a perfect set of antlers. Fresh wolf tracks on the beach.

June 30

My first long walk. The permafrost has created an entrapping terrain. A sandy well-drained slope changes abruptly to jello-like ground. A vibrant environment beneath the immediate desolation. The life is minute; it requires a look from many levels. Caribou bones everywhere. I found *anook-*

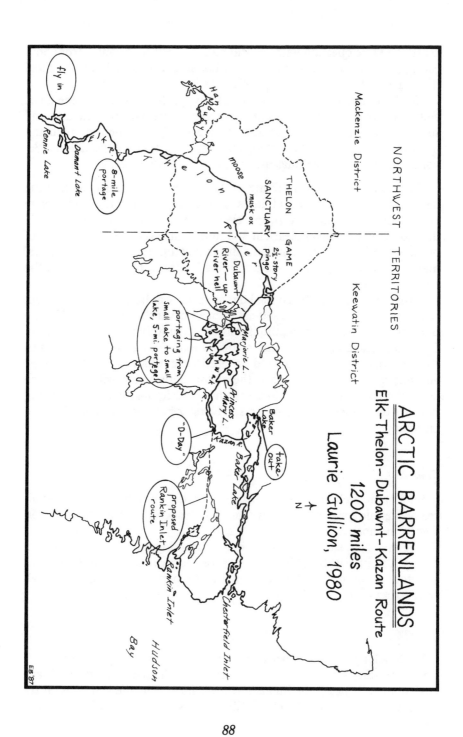

ARCTIC BARRENLANDS

Elk–Thelon–Dubawnt–Kazan Route

1200 miles
Laurie Gullion, 1980

NORTHWEST   TERRITORIES

Mackenzie District

Keewatin District

fly in

Rennie Lake

Damant Lake

8-mile portage

Elk R.

Hanbury River

Thelon River

moose

musk ox

THELON GAME SANCTUARY

2½-story pingo

Dubawnt River—up-river hell

portaging from small lake to small lake, 5-mi. portage!

Marjorie L.

Kunwak R.

Princess Mary L.

Kazan R.

"D-Day"

Baker Lake

Baker Lake

take-out

proposed Rankin Inlet route

Rankin Inlet

Hudson Bay

Chesterfield Inlet

N

E.B. '87

88

shooks (stone men) piled by the Inuit along the ridge to divert caribou into their ambush. Such contentment to just walk.

By mid-morning the sun dies abruptly. Rain begins and waves build. The wind hits 35 mph but dies after supper. Our first night paddle, across Rennie Lake—20 miles. The trip leader sets a fast pace. These damn loaded boats sit so low in the water.

July 1

Rain. Slept until noon. The wind is raising white caps, but such a minor detail! We start paddling at 2 P.M., against head winds and swells. Much bailing and cursing. Squalls finally force us to stop on an esker at the head of Damant Lake.

Bathing parties. Crazy to some who can't stand the numbing water, but the feeling is superb. Washed off the last dirt of civilization, and now I'm ready for the layers of genuine Arctic crud.

Munching in the tent before sleep—food to warm the toes, conversation to warm the heart.

A rare experience—the women are definitely the most interesting group, the men lacking in character. A change for me, since I've often found female company insipid. Twelve women and nine men, not the usual ratio found in the outdoors. There have to be more opportunities like this one, where women can be comfortable with their bodies, comfortable with each other, comfortable facing a formidable physical and mental challenge.

Thanks to Selina, our canoe has been named *Aqanat Umiak*. In the language of the Inuit, it means "women's skin boat." We are the lone female boat on the river. A good challenge.

July 2

Rain all night. Gale winds.

Trout for lunch—exquisite. Selina, who has lived in Point Barrow, Alaska, for three years, introduced us to a native delicacy, fish eyes. I felt queasy, but the eye tasted like a mildly fish-flavored gumball. Chewy.

Wind died to a passable speed, and we began paddling just before midnight. Gorgeous sunset to accompany the pain of head winds. The first 25 miles felt good. The last 10 were like death. Never felt the ground before I fell asleep. Cold, cold, cold.

July 3

Bug city. A black fly hatch. Millions of the blasted buggers hitting the tent so hard it sounds like rain. I can't phase out the noise yet.

The Elk is a shallow, rocky river that requires much scrambling in and out of the boat to get over the shoals hidden just inches below the surface. No plastic boats to slip smoothly over the rocks—800 pounds encased in aluminum just doesn't slide. But I like the challenge.

July 4

Celebrated Independence Day with 10 gallons of popcorn. I'm getting nervous about the portages, so I decided to lighten my food stash early.

There is a clubhouse syndrome among some of the people who have travelled with the trip leader on other rivers in the Barrens. They appear unwilling to share their knowledge with the newcomers, yet they find ways of reminding us that they have Been Before. I find these divisions distasteful. There is an increasing separation between the experienced folks and the masses. Their remoteness from the remaining group limits their experience and ours. I wonder if they realize that.

A great solidarity among the rest of us who cluster around the fire at day's end to talk, to tell stories, or to be silent when the loons sing. Nancy had an atrocious day in the bow of her canoe, visibly shaken by close encounters with boulders. The popcorn party worked hard, yet seemingly casual, to bolster sagging spirits.

July 5

Slipping through nice rapids on the Elk today. We are truly in the Barrens—the trees have receded entirely. Sandy beaches along the river, the sand so pure the banks look like snow in the bright light.

I can feel the effects already of the bust building program built into this trip. Thirty-eight inches and it's all in my back. I can feel my muscles, every last one of them.

So many black fly bites that my face feels like the Pillsbury Doughboy's. Nancy's wrist is inflamed, perhaps tendonitis. It's splinted to immobilize it, and she can't paddle for a few days. There now is a hospital boat. Misery for Nance to do nothing.

July 6

Rotated partners *again* because of problems in other boats. Now I'm with Dawn, a model from San Diego, whose mother gave her this trip as a present. She hustles.

I'm so angry at the shifting of partners, not at Dawn. I seem to be the Good Samaritan who can be counted on to fill in the gap when people don't get along. I'm increasingly upset with the reluctance to split apart other strong pairs who could help resolve the problems with canoe combinations. Meanwhile, I have to keep adjusting to yet another new partner, and it makes building a partnership so difficult. Just as we establish good communications and an awareness of how the other operates, time out again. Another change.

July 7

Musical canoes again. I failed in my appeal this morning. Now I'm canoeing with the trip's least impressive male. We broached twice today because he paddles with his eyes closed and his head down. I think he's frozen with fear, actually. The river demands quick reactions, and he is rigid in the boat. I have an uneasy feeling he may be afraid of the water or a poor swimmer. But what is he doing here? I have got to talk to him before we start tomorrow. A miserable day. I knew this venture would be a challenge, but I never suspected it would be one of this kind.

An amazing contrast between people is becoming more apparent. A more serious conservative group and then the loose ones, the liberals from California and Massachusetts. A major part of the trip is the challenge of living with 21 new people for six long weeks. The best part is the humor in the face of adversity—the bugs, the raw rain, the long paddling days. The hilarity generated by the delegates from the East and West is wonderful.

July 8

Another gorgeous day except for an 8-mile portage around Granite Falls at the confluence of the Elk and Thelon Rivers. A mile of rapids preceded the falls. We lined the canoes the entire distance—anything to avoid or shorten a portage.

Dawn and I hustled the 25 miles of river after the portage. It looks as if she and I will be together for the summer. I am relieved the switching is finally over. We are still the only female boat on the river. We will talk our way across the Arctic and enjoy companionable silences. Dawn's strength is like the Incredible Hulk's, only in her brain as well. She is a grumbler on the surface, always growling about something, but it's just her way of dealing with tension, of letting off steam.

The pressure is on. Two hundred miles down, and 1000 miles to go. The route is incredibly difficult; I'm able to translate the mileage into real terms now that I'm familiar with the terrain and understand what it means to paddle loaded boats against the wind. We have to paddle at least 40 miles a day on the Thelon to provide safety days in case of bad weather.

That means early wakeups and long paddles. Low water is also a problem this year.

The Thelon is a smooth bowl carved by the ice with a fast current and few obstructions. The land is continually amazing—miles of unpopulated beaches with a serene beauty. Ancient rocks that remind me of my miniscule presence in the passage of time. Already I have a yearning to return.

July 9

72 goddamn miles. 12 hours of canoeing since a 7 A.M. start. We established a trip record under perfect conditions— sunny, hot, virtually no wind.

I remember absolutely nothing about the scenery. I am numb. Functioning on automatic pilot long enough to get the tent up.

July 10

55 miles today. Seven of them across ungodly Eyeberry Lake. Rolling swells, a tailwind, paddling like we're sure to die.

My anger with the trip leader propelled me across the heaving lake. After resolving the disagreement on shore, I ruined the resolution by crying. Tears of frustration and release of tension. I astounded myself with the quickness of the tears because I just don't cry in front of people, and I didn't want to with a person who dictates unexplained "rules."

So many situations here are hard to comprehend initially— especially the fickle weather. I want to understand the reasons *why* decisions are made, and "commanding" with little or no explanation invites mutiny. I want to learn as much as I can to develop my own good judgment. What a battle to do so!

The grueling pace has proved to be a greater challenge to my mental state than to my physical condition. And it was my physical strength that concerned me the most in preparing for this trip. I wonder if I would have preferred the Caribbean for my $2000.

July 12

Headache. An incredibly tense 14-hour day. Six hours to line the boats down a half-mile stretch above the confluence of the Thelon and Hanbury rivers. Glad I am with Dawn—she is so good in understanding the river currents.

Wet, wet, wet. Cold, cold, cold.

July 13

40 miles in 9 long hours. The Thelon is magnificent. The canyons are filled with millions of swallows and an occasional raven. Hills in the distance are bathed in pastel colors. I saw a whistling swan, a beautiful white bird which emits a raucous honk, quite unlike its name. Canada geese joined us for the night. I discovered an abandoned wolf den in an esker.

July 14

60 miles in 11 hours. Began at 6:45 A.M. A hot monotonous day of canoeing. An exercise in mind control.

But we're seeing wildlife now. 12 musk oxen. We followed the first one this morning up over a ridge. It's like playing Red Light – stopping and pretending to be a rock when the big beasts look. A graceful animal with long flowing brown hair dancing in the sunlight.

Another tawny colored wolf and a whistling swan. The Thelon is beautiful. The bugs and ferocious weather must be nature's way of protecting this land from human ravishment.

July 15

30 more miles of monotonous canoeing. The only relief is the experiences on the land. A trek to a two and a half story pingo [a hill pushed up by frost], perhaps the largest in the interior of the North. Two moose. Sandstone canyons with rough-legged hawks and peregrine falcons and bear scat everywhere. Fear of the grizz follows me into sleep.

July 16

I slept late – until 10 A.M. My body needed the luxury. I hated the mental debate which preceded my decision last night to visit the pingo. The canoeing fatigue is seriously interfering with my desire to explore the country. I question the wisdom of ripping off so many miles that it becomes a major effort to walk or take pictures. This expedition is obviously The Impossible Trip. Next time, I will have the knowledge to examine the route more carefully. I would rather have more time on shore to enjoy the land.

18 days in. The time is flying, but we are approaching the 550-mile mark – amazing hustle. But the worst is coming. In about three days we face a trip *up* the Dubawnt River. I've thought about this upstream business, yet I feel as naive as I was about the 1200-mile target. I guess inno-

cence is bliss, although I know I'm not going to feel too blissful after hauling boats upstream.

July 17

50 miles of windy, cold river. I'm rapidly exhausting my supply of Gothic romance fantasies and house-building ideas.

A wolf on the beach today. The canyons of the Thelon recede, the terrain becomes less hilly, and the land is finally treeless. The true tundra. I carry constant images of the wildlife and the awareness that few people live within a thousand miles. Humans become unimportant creatures next to the natural grace of form and movement found in Arctic life.

The wind has dropped. A silence pervades the cooling sunlight.

July 18

55 miles. It's getting colder at night, and I can also feel a change during the day. As I watch some flowers turning to seed I realize that we will witness three seasons within a few weeks.

We are in the Keewatin District, the land of rising North winds. The wind is a changeable force whose howling can establish a day's mood. Never have I cursed anything so much.

The climb up the Dubawnt begins tomorrow.

July 19

20 miles of hell on the Dubawnt. Six miles of lining upriver, jumping in and out of the boats, walking them up drops, lining around points where the current slams into the boats.

Not an ounce of enjoyment. Rubbery legs from wading in cold water and along rocky, sliding banks. We stopped at a beautiful ledge which heralds a canyon up above and camped with the knowledge that we face a long portage in the morning.

A perfect moment: Eric threw me a hard cherry candy as I reached shore. I stood in water to my thighs, carefully unwrapped the precious morsel and slowly consumed it before stepping on to shore.

Dawn and I communicate well. The ability to talk and relieve any building hostilities eliminates major problems encountered by some of the other boats.

July 20

20 miles of lining up the Dubawnt. Plod, plod, plod. Blisters on the balls of my feet. Rope burns on my hands. I walked that shore, head down, rope over my shoulder, and inspected every rock. Beautiful striated rocks of orange and red, broken off in layers.

Two more caribou and an Arctic hare. A peregrine falcon was stalking the hare; we ruined his chase and his meal.

July 21

Current milder, so we paddled upriver and then portaged up a mammoth hill for the last half mile to Marjorie Lake. The food packs were consolidated, and a 100-pound pack shortened my neck by several inches.

Winded in at Marjorie. We're camped on a point where gale winds threaten to lift us into the marsh. I love the sound of the wind.

As supper ends, the wind is beginning to die. I hope there is no night paddle.

July 22

Still winded in. Temperatures are getting colder.

Almost two months have passed since "legitimate" working days. The rigors of this trip have only confirmed my wisdom in quitting my job. My body and brain demanded relief from a 40-plus-hour week. Perhaps the challenge of a new, completely different occupation would change that feeling, but I'm not convinced. Seasonal employment is an appealing concept, if I could handle the economic insecurity. As I grow older, my life becomes more unsettled. Television and fairy tales lied.

July 23

Ten hours of portaging from small lake to small lake. It might have been manageable, but I've developed tendonitis in my heel from walking the uneven shores. So I hobbled.

July 24

Winded in on an unnamed lake, recuperating enough to survive a 5-mile portage.

I began reading Liv Ullman's *Changing* and found the book potent enough to have to go for a walk. She made me think about many changes in my own life—pinnacles and depressions which haven't received enough thought. Ullman remarked that no one owns anyone: together, we have each other, nature, and time.

July 26

Never before have I hurt so badly. A 30-mile walk on crippled feet. I shall never forget this.

Being on the disabled list is miserable in this environment. The Doc says I have the nicest example of Achilles tendonitis, and the cure is to stay off my feet as much as possible or use them in restful activities. Then he just grins.

I'm on the cook crew tonight. Portage for 12 hours, cook for 2 hours. Disgusted, tired, numb, dead.

Nancy blew up my air mattress!! I yelled "I love you" across the tundra, and applause rang from other tents.

July 27

Winded in. Helped Jim celebrate his birthday with cheesecake, apricots, watermelon candy and lemon drops. Mary modelled a 75-cent negligee from the Goodwill store, purchased to honor Jim's birthday. The lace went well with her bulging muscles, bruises and hiking boots.

Chased more fall colors with my camera. The air is crisp, the sun shares no warmth. The bearberry, bilberry, and caribou moss are becoming crunchy underfoot.

July 29

Left camp yesterday after the trip leader renewed his commitment to the original Rankin Inlet route. But sentiment is increasingly high for the shorter Baker Lake route down the Kazan River, a more favorable choice in face of advancing severe weather and low water.

I really question the push for The Impossible Route. The routine which we must embrace to get there is much like what I left behind in the States. A tense, energy-consuming enterprise, which leaves little time for reflection, sharing and experiencing the natural environment around us.

Paddled 20 miles across the lake, an icy-cold traverse over untroubled waters. A smoky sky with a peach moon suspended in it. I became transfixed with paddling in the stream of moonlight.

Unnerved by the rumble of approaching rapids on the Kunwak River.

Visibility was poor, and we searched for a campsite along the rocky shore, dodging shadowy forms concealing suspected ledges.

July 30

Still winded in. Cold, rain. Weather is our greatest foe – changeable, unpredictable. But I am praying to the Demon for more windy weather. Stalling our progress will make Baker Lake a more likely route, possibly the only route. Strangely, I feel no guilt about not reaching Rankin Inlet. By the cutoff point above Kazan Falls, we will have travelled 950 miles. We're 31 days in now. With time constraints, and low water suggesting the prospect of puddle jumping, the Rankin route is very unappealing.

My competitive drive is so vastly different from a racehorse ethic embraced by some. I have pushed myself physically beyond what I thought were my limitations. The intensity of the trip with its weather problems is an experience I've survived with relative mental grace. I don't need to cling to our original plan; I don't mind "giving in" to the alternative, if it means we might have a more enjoyable, less pressured ending.

July 31

A 4:30 A.M. start under a cold sun. The Kunwak drops 45 feet in the first mile – a nice series of rapids to wake you up fast. The water is so brutally cold that I can't imagine lining or jumping in if broached. Ice is beginning to form along the shore.

By lunchtime, swells fill Princess Mary Lake and force us ashore on a huge island. The first bath in two weeks.

Such lovely women on this trip. We are an odd bunch – a collection of differing personalities who would probably never take the opportunity to discover each other at home. For the first time since the crew team, I've met athletic women in a situation with a substantial physical challenge. And the major partners in the deal are not male. It is wonderful to share two months with women whose adolescent "tomboy" years have definitely shaped their selves.

The kinship spirit among us is significant for me too. I need to make time to uncover such interesting women who can add their unique perspective to my life. Too often I have let the pressures of a job or a relationship with a man usurp my time.

August 1

Mega-paddle beginning at 5 A.M. Gusty winds. By 10 A.M. it felt like the afternoon. The Kunwak finished with a roar—*fast* current. We covered 15 miles in 45 minutes, unbelievable, frightening speed.

Orange moon after a sherbet sunset. The moon is mesmerizing through the tent screen.

August 3

D-Day. Decision day about the route for the final stretch of the journey. This morning I walked to the boats and discovered that my canoe was missing. "But I thought I'd parked it right here." Four of the more dissatisfied trip members left in the middle of the night without addressing the group. They did speak with the trip leader before they took two canoes and food and headed to Baker Lake. But a little too late for me to have much respect for them. Why didn't they voice their displeasure with the trip's pace and character earlier?

But their departure has erased the underlying tension of the past few days. No more small group discussions which never lead to total group communication, a divisive and inaccurate way to find out what's going on. There is much unity now among the remaining group.

We camped at the mouth of the drainage that leads to Rankin Inlet and walked the route to check the terrain. Bad news about the water level. Islands in the lakes have become stretches of land blocking passage. The forecast is at least three or four days of portaging *through* the lakes to get to the new river system.

So, for a more enjoyable end, Baker Lake became our choice. The trip will end in three days, weather permitting. With my foot still aching, that route is definitely more enticing. I'd rather paddle than walk.

With 13 days' food left, it was a free-for-all for dinner tonight.

August 4

I walked across the tundra by myself this morning to visit an Inuit grave on a hillside. Enjoyable solitude.

The intensity never ends. To avoid excessive portaging, we lined the canoes through the rapids right to the lip of Kazan Falls. So frustrating, as my heel hindered the mountain goat moves required to line around the ledges. But Dawn carried the show, almost single-handedly dropping the canoe over the small waterfalls and ledges without incident.

Paddling the canyon below the falls was the most incredible canoeing rush I have ever encountered. Tricky, where the water struck the canyon walls and rolled back in whirlpools. A narrow tongue of runnable water twisted down the middle. My knees were trembling as we scouted from above.

Dawn and I nailed it perfectly. We hit the haystacks at the bottom with precision and never got a drop of water in the boat. A wild half-mile ride and a major personal victory.

We camped overlooking the canyon, down the street from two angry peregrine falcons. When we discovered their nest we moved the tent farther away; I felt guilty crowding their neighborhood.

August 5

We finished the Kazan River after a long, long day of paddling. The intensity definitely never ends.

August 6

A 5 A.M. start to find our way across Baker Lake. Eric, Nancy, and I sabotaged the boats last night by changing all the names. Our "women's boat" became Vaguely Vogue a.k.a. The Blister Sisters. Contrary to its name, Vaguely Vogue has proven it has a surplus of style.

We hauled our tired bodies 50 miles across the lake under sunny glare and mild headwinds. One last unbearable, undesirable portage with the settlement in sight. The sand by the Thelon River's mouth had shifted and created unbroken sand bars between the islands. Trudge, trudge, trudge. It was agonizing to watch the hillside of civilization grow no closer for hours.

It felt bizarre to face new people for the first time in almost six weeks. Our isolated armada had become so routine, so natural.

We have accommodations in the school. Soft chairs and toilets. I immediately travel to the restroom and undress before the mirror. My muscles are sharply outlined in my back and arms. I'd felt the changes all summer, but now I could see them. My body looks as healthy as I feel.

The Noatak: Getting Back

CARYL WEAVER

Caryl Weaver of Seattle is, in this period of her life, a family intervention counselor and a teacher of vocational skills courses for adults. She has also been a Quaker peace activist, a Lesbian rights activist, and a founding member of a women's support group called "The Wrinkled Radicals." In 1983, for her 49th birthday, she joined seven other women she didn't know for a canoe trip in Arctic Alaska. The Noatak River flows through the Brooks Range; the women flew into Pingo Lake, near the headwaters, and ended at the Inuit village of Noatak, 370 miles downstream. Along the river there is one ranger's tent, a hunter's cabin open to all travellers, some rapids, endless tundra.

Caryl Weaver's story of why she made the trip and its effect on her is from her reminiscences first published in Woodswomen News, *Spring 1984, and from an interview with Judith Niemi in March 1987.*

I had always dreamed of going on a wilderness trip, off into the wilds where my skills, endurance and common sense would be tested. (Remember how you used to hear that word "fortitude?") I grew to know that I would go someday, and that when I did it would be with women.

I have lived mostly as a city person, except for six glorious summers at a girls' camp in Wisconsin. That's where I was really happy. Camp taught me that tall trees, my "talking trees," healed me. Since then much of my life has been spent raising four children in urban settings, mostly as a single parent, working hard just doing day-to-day survival. As my three older children grew up and moved out on their own, I began to have time again to learn about me.

In 1981 I went to New York, slept on the floor of a friend's house, and wandered all over the city alone. Then I went to Washington and was arrested doing civil disobedience at the Pentagon. I went to jail, where I had to face my claustrophobia and my terror that I'd go "crazy." In 1982 I filled a backpack, flew to Europe with my lover, slept on trains, and walked and walked for eight weeks. I learned a lot, including a new sense of my limits of endurance. Then at a feminist conference in Seattle, I heard about the Noatak trip. I knew that was it. I had no idea how I'd do it, where I'd get the money, but I went up and said, "Hi, I'm Caryl Weaver and I'm coming."

I don't call it impulsive. If there's one thing I've learned, it's that the part of me that I can trust absolutely is my gut reaction. That's the part I denied for so many years—but it's a healthy part, the part that takes care of me. I never had any doubts. I had lots of fears, mixed with excitement, but it was the right thing for me to do.

I wanted to learn my limits. To know I could do it—not just physically

Caryl Weaver, Noatak River, Alaska (Judith Niemi)

survive, but really *be* there for it. I wanted an intense physical challenge (I had been working for a year to get in shape). I wanted real wilderness, no having a phone or train available a few miles away. I wanted the eight of us to bond, to get so close with each other that we would always be connected. I wanted nothing superficial – every thing and every interaction to be *real*. I wanted adventure! I'd played it safe for so many years.

It was the most intense confrontation with myself I've yet had. I got a whole new level of knowledge and understanding of myself. I got to know and understand each of the women. It didn't always work out the way I wanted – we never did bond as an entire group – but I came to appreciate the uniqueness and strength of each woman.

It was a wonderful feminist experience. There were no rules laid out. We agreed to let our bodies, the river and the weather guide us about when to rest and when to be on the water. (We still managed to be on the water when the Arctic winds were strongest.) We agreed to disturb the environment as little as possible, to bury and scatter all signs of a fire, to let no soap in the river. We tried to accommodate different individual needs.

I learned to chart where we were by compass sightings and map reading. There were wonderful plentiful blueberries, ever-present willows that always let us start a fire even when wet. And there was the intensity of feeling so alive that all my senses were fine-tuned not to miss anything: the sound of silt hitting the hull, the quiet presence of animals everywhere, the incredible silence.

I got everything I expected in the Arctic and more: it was cold and overcast and rainy 19 out of 22 days. My back got stiff and ached, my fingers split from helping to haul gear and boats up and down the banks whenever we stopped for any length of time. The awesome feeling of laying into the paddling when the headwinds were fierce. The terror at being "frozen" on the side of a shale mountain, unable to move up or down, until finally with a guide's gentle help I could take a breath and continue. The scare when the flooded river wiped out the eddies and I wasn't sure if or where I could stop. The pure ecstasy of going through some rapids and almost losing it, but putting it all together and coming out just fine! That moment when after 370 miles of paddling and floating this river, I saw the village of Noatak and felt relief and sadness, knowing it's all over – I did it!

It was very, very hard for me when I came back. I wondered, what's wrong with me? I was working at the Quaker meeting house, it couldn't have been a more gentle transition back into the world. But I went into a deep depression, an existential crisis. Nothing seemed real anymore. The only thing real was back up there in the Arctic. I was dismayed at the insanity of my daily life, going to work, the smog, the pollution we've brought to the earth.

I wanted a more sane way of living, and I didn't know how to do it in the middle of a big city. I thought of living up in the Arctic, but I knew I wouldn't choose that. I did need to find some way to make my life more real. Which was ironic. Among my contemporaries, I think I've had a pretty real life – my relationships, the way I choose to earn my money. But I wanted more. I wanted the intensity again. I remembered that incredible awareness, when you're going down the river knowing the rapids are coming up. Or taking the boats up at night, knowing the waters could rise. It wasn't the basic survival questions I missed – I wanted that feeling of being so alive, so aware, instead of getting into routines and taking things for granted.

For a couple of months after I got back, I was walking around saying, "What's the purpose?" Nothing mattered. I didn't want to live, and I thought I might just will myself to quit. But one friend was there for me, consistently. And I have an incredibly powerful life force inside of me, as I'd learned years before. I don't think we've got too many options in life – we're either going to go ahead and grow or we're going to curl up and essentially die. So I had to get it together.

Remembering the Arctic today, four years later, I see things I'd gotten out of touch with. The depth of the sky. None of my photographs showed that incredible sky. I paddled for a while into that wind, remembering what it felt like. The whole thing comes back, those little wildflowers that were so perfect. The big purple droppings from the grizzlies, and how impressed I was by them. I thought a lot about my fears when I first went, especially my fears of wild animals. I guess I had been so brainwashed by wild animal pornography – the idea that they would come out raging and attacking just because we were there. I learned how sensitive they were. We were too big a group – even though we were quiet – and disturbed the animals. My understanding of wilderness is so different than before I went.

The Arctic gave me incredible joy. You know, I've done it, I don't have to do that kind of trip again. Physically, it was very tough for me. But I'd like to go back. I saw the goddess in the Arctic. I remember exactly where I was on the river and the feeling that came over me that this is women's land. That everything is OK. And that feeling has never left me.

I don't share my Arctic trip with my clients, but it still is the basis for how I operate with folks, with women. The women I work with have not been "successful." They don't need *one* more person to make promises, or teach them nifty skills. They need to see the strength in themselves. What I learned in the Arctic, the confidence I found that we could do it, has affected what I'm doing with the rest of my life.

A Day at a Time: Winisk River Journal

SUE BUCKLEY

Sue Buckley lives in Iowa City, Iowa. She made this trip in 1980 with editor Barb Wieser, whom she asked to write the introduction.

HOW WE GOT THERE, by Barb

In 1969 and another era of my life, my first experience in wilderness canoeing was a week with my husband in the Boundary Waters of northern Minnesota. I did not have a great time—scared of bears, undernourished on a diet of instant mashed potatoes, frustrated and angry at my husband's berating me, "Paddle harder!" Still, I left with the beginnings of a love of the Northwoods and a vivid memory of our outfitter, Janet Hanson, saying, "Only a few people have canoed from here all the way up to Hudson Bay and no women have done it, as far as I know."

Ten years and a couple of identities later, I was talking with my friend Sue Buckley about doing a long canoe trip "somewhere up North" and remembered Janet's words. By then the lives of Buckley and me and all our friends were usually involved in doing things "no women had ever done," so we wrote to Ontario for information on routes to Hudson Bay.

They sent us a trip report from six high school boys who paddled 600 miles to Hudson Bay, starting at Armstrong, Ontario, wandering northward through a series of lakes and rivers (and 42 portages) to the settlement of Webequie, and then down the 280-mile Winisk River through Polar Bear Provincial Park. That wasn't quite getting to start in the Boundary Waters—but the fact that few people ever travel down the Winisk and that it is the site of polar bear denning grounds made our decision. No roads crossed the area; the scattered Indian settlements were accessible in summer only by canoe and float plane.

We spent the winter figuring out things like how to get home from

Winisk, the settlement at the end of the river (a complicated journey by supply plane, train, and helpful friends with cars) and how to mail ourselves two food packages to be picked up at settlements along the way. We had little equipment; we borrowed a battered aluminum canoe from a nearby Quaker school.

We didn't try to recruit others to go with us. We really didn't know anyone with the skills or desire, and we wanted the trip to be just the two of us. We know now how unsafe it is to travel big rivers with only one canoe, but at the time, we really were ignorant. We didn't know about ferrying, eddy turns, back paddling—all those whitewater techniques that keep one in the canoe. We also didn't know much about the Canadian wilderness, although a 1200-mile backpacking trip the previous summer had taught me a lot about extended time in the wilderness.

When I read my journals and remember Winisk, I'm appalled by our lack of knowledge, but I'm glad of the determination that took us there in spite of our ignorance. It was an experience that changed my life.

The following excerpts are from Sue Buckley's journal of our 43-day Winisk trip in 1980. It tells of what we learned, two novices not knowing what to expect.

★   ★   ★

Riding up in the car, a friend reads a Hudson Bay journal of six Minnesota women who went to York Factory by canoe. One line catches my ear—"we are getting too old not to be doing what we want to do." There's something about having set this trip up and doing it that keeps me sane, a sense of self and power in the world. Sometimes I know this principle in other parts of my life: it has to do with wanting a sense of control, other times a sense of honor.

Day 1

At a very used campsite now, trying to write by flashlight, wishing it was daylight and that I had lots of time.

Lots of flashes—the waves today brought to mind Girl Scout camp and Reenie. How we canoed together, how utterly crazy we were. We had to be the best, strongest, fastest, most daring. And I remember talking to the ocean, being friends and connected to her—but always from a position of great respect. I recall an old tie with the water and start a new one, asking if I may live with her for the next six weeks.

105

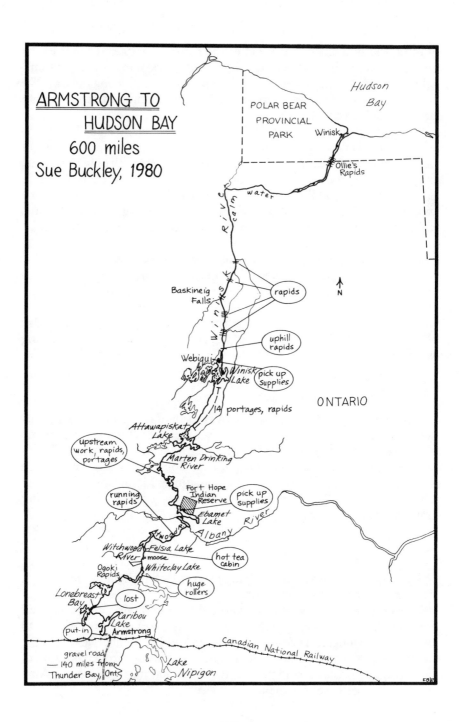

ARMSTRONG TO
HUDSON BAY
600 miles
Sue Buckley, 1980

Hudson Bay

POLAR BEAR
PROVINCIAL
PARK

Winisk

Ollie's Rapids

calm water

River

Winisk

Baskineig Falls

rapids

uphill rapids

N

Webigui

Winisk Lake

pick up supplies

ONTARIO

14 portages, rapids

Attawapiskat Lake

upstream work, rapids, portages

Marten Drinking River

running rapids

Fort Hope Indian Reserve

pick up supplies

Ebamet Lake

Albany River

twoo

Witchwood Felsia Lake River   moose

hot tea cabin

Whiteclay Lake

Ogoki Rapids

huge rollers

Lonebreast Bay

lost

Caribou Lake

Armstrong

put-in

Canadian National Railway

gravel road
— 140 miles from
Thunder Bay, Ont.

Lake Nipigon

106

Day 2

It has been a good day. Three portages on the Caribou River around three sets of rapids which were almost runnable but not quite. Then we did run a fourth one and hit the main rock. We learned a good lesson from that – both of us should go check out the rapids. I think Barb and I will go back and forth on whether or not to run a rapid. It's almost like Barb teases me, or herself, saying we should try them. I think part of her knows it's not safe, especially this early in the trip, and then there's the part that knows and wants the thrill, that feels bad to have a challenge unmet.

Us – just us. It's very hard to understand that this really could be my world for the next 40 days. An incredible solitude – some birds, humming of insects, a sun that moves . . . little else. In a lot of ways my mind feels like one big jumble, not knowing what to think about first, a hysteria from all the space it will be afforded.

The sunset is huge, throwing a red column across the lake. Already I don't understand how I'll be able to go back.

Day 3

What a day – very exhausted, yet can tell my muscles will get used to it. Got lost rather badly trying to find the opening for Lonebreast Bay. It was frustrating paddling the extra miles, but we now know we can find our way back with map and compass. I can't imagine how we are going to do the complicated stretch leading into the Winisk River – but we learn so much every day, so I hope our skill level will be higher by then.

The water and the woods up here seem inviting, friendly. Losing a lot of fear about meeting "bad" people. For one thing we are alone, truly alone. I'm not even hoping no one will appear – I know they won't. It's hard to believe that we can be somewhere so beautiful, in such peace.

Day 4

It is sort of silly to write that we canoed ten miles today – we seem to be going twice the map distance because of wind, looking for entrances, getting lost, and not finding portages. But today, as every day, was full of lessons. Couldn't find a portage so we tried lining the canoe down a river connecting two lakes – did most of it in knee to hip deep water, some rapids. Very good feeling of really being *in* the environment. But we discovered our equipment wasn't tied in. We are so careful, and then make such a stupid mistake; it's a kindness that we didn't go over.

Barb and I have very different rhythms. I want to go on and paddle more, even when I am tired, where Barb listens more to her body and says it's time for a break. I am into setting goals and keeping on schedule, probably at too high a cost. But there is the other side of me that wants more time to write in this journal, write to Sue, fish, read. Our sense of risk is much different, too. I am more comfortable with the big lakes and waves; Barb with the rapids. It will be interesting to see how that shifts.

Day 5

We had another big discussion today about rapids – when it is sensible to run them, when it is groundless fear blocking us. I considered Ogoki Rapids for a bit, but they were pretty much out of the question – too big, too long, too early in the trip. Not to mention how scared I was of them.

Barb and I also locked horns over planning the coming day. She thinks I am obsessed with completing daily mileage goals, and I think she spaces out on them. But a lot of that is sporting conversation, and when it comes down to it, what we each think is good judgment is very similar.

Thinking about this trip beforehand, I never thought I would see it as being so much fun. It is very hard work – but so beautiful, enjoyable, where I want to be. Maybe if it rains for ten days, the bugs get bad, we swamp a lot, get lost even more, I'd change my mind, but I don't know. Beginning to wonder how I could ever not keep coming back.

Day 6

Canoed at least 30 miles today, maybe more. The wind on Whiteclay Lake made huge rollers. We had to zig zag in and out, using the shore for protection. Everything I learned at scout camp fifteen years ago assisted me today.

Camped at the beginning of the portage into Witchwood Lake. This feels like the most remote spot we have been in yet. There are moose and bear tracks all over the beach. A very strong sense that few people ever come this way.

Day 7

I'm writing at the fire with the full moon staring back at us. The feeling of remoteness is growing.

Every day there are new challenges. Today I thought maybe we filled our quota at the first portage – a half mile, plus two beaver dams we climbed, pushed, and dragged our way over. But apparently the event of the day was to be the second portage—one mile through a moose run. Big ruts, muddy, lots of mosquitoes. But the reward was soon. Going around a bend, my response is "holy shit" and Barb's is "jesus christ." Twenty feet in front of us a bull moose is rising from the water where he had been totally submerged except for the crest of his head. Graceful, as if in slow motion; total elegance in this huge, bulky body.

Day 9

Raining hard these past two days. Today on Felsia Lake, with the weather turning from rotten to more rotten, we managed to miss the outlet leading to Hurst Lake and started to canoe in a big circle around the lake. Stopping to consult the map, we realized how gone our bodies were from the wet and cold. I kept asking myself if I was delirious. We had seen a fly-in fishing cabin about one bay back, so we went over to it with the idea of asking where the hell we were, but of course hoping that it was empty. It was; and complete with a wood stove, chopped wood, a gas burner with a kettle of water and tea ready to go, and a map on the wall which showed us exactly where we were. We spent a couple of wonderful recovery hours there, and then continued to a small beach some miles away to camp.

Every day a challenge is being thrown at us, but never too much. Every day we push against some other limit. I feel like my mother, who died so many years ago, is truly the guardian of this trip. It would be her way to have it rain and us get lost only to accidentally find the wonderful haven that we did. I'm feeling her presence, appreciating Barb's acknowledgment of her. As we took off from the cabin's dock, Barb yelled, "Thanks, Ollie."

Day 10

This day had an odd ending with our total inability to decide whether to continue or to stop. Our discussion of where to camp was mindless, although the truth coming from it is that I do need to check the maps and have a better sense of our schedule and daily mileage goals. Barb, of course, just assumes we will get to the end on time. Washing our hair and underwear and having a snack seemed to restore some clarity to our thinking and conversation. It is probably true that if we are too tired to figure out whether we can go on—we are too tired to go on.

Day 11

Camped on a breezy rock ledge of the Albany River, nearing the settlement of Fort Hope. This feels like the completion of step one in our journey to Hudson Bay. A motor boat has already passed us, I hear another drawing close. We will lose our seclusion for a couple of days. I'm trying to make that be all right with myself.

Ran some rapids today on the Atwood River—quite the experience being in the bow in a series of standing waves, getting very wet, taking in a fair amount of water. I am starting to get a taste of the thrill of rapids, sensing the fun and challenge. I can feel my fear lessening. We will probably make better judgments on whether or not to run them, and already I'm getting a glimpse of why it is hard to say no.

Day 12

Nowhere, really. Huge wind this morning, but we decided to cross the channel, paddling with everything we had. Then we followed the shore a ways until it seemed utterly absurd; the wind and waves were strong and large, and progress was oh so slow. So here we are on some rocky beach, hoping that with sunset the water will calm.

I felt a lot of responsibility this morning in choosing whether we should cross. Many voices in my head: caution; meeting a challenge; not wanting to underestimate us; not wanting to say yes when Barb probably felt no. They were big fucking waves. But with luck there was a lull in the wind after breakfast, so we made a decision that I think was right even after doing it.

The day has been a lazy one—napping, munching, writing, telling a lot of stories. I asked Barb if she thought we would try and make this day up. Clearly by her response she thinks I'm obsessed with time goals. Well, sometimes I think I am but I'm trying to change that, to relax more. I wonder if Barb will give me that room.

Day 13

This day has been, by far, the hardest—both physically and mentally. Started before sunrise with battling a hefty northwest wind, heading towards Fort Hope, our first supply pickup point. Discovered that the government had moved the settlement to the opposite shore of huge Ebamet Lake. I thought of Girl Scouts, and how I have canoed across stretches like that and said we should go. The water was sort of calm, though I did see very threatening clouds behind us.

I have not been that scared for a long time, even knowing I am good at those times, fighting real hard to get through an almost impossible situation. We worked so hard and were very lucky. We were so close to going over in the huge waves that blew up in the middle of the lake, and I don't think we could have made it to shore by swimming. I'm encouraged that we had the endurance when we needed it, but if possible, I don't want to be in that situation again on this trip. Terror, there was truly an element of terror in it.

We spent a couple of hours in Fort Hope picking up our supplies and re-packing the food bags, and then took off again in the blowing wind, des-perately looking for a place to camp. We finally found a tiny beach not far from the settlement. We needed to stop badly – I don't remember being this far gone.

This trip is intensifying day by day. I still believe nothing impossible will be thrown our way, but I also feel strongly that none of it will be easy. Tomorrow we need no wind. Rain would be okay; cold, too. But no wind. Day 13, and we are lucky to be alive.

Day 15

Today we got back lost momentum. Got up an hour before sunrise to fi-nally beat the winds of Ebamet Lake after being stalled out again yester-day. Two portages, the second very long and the path hard to find. Had to drag Winnie the canoe upstream, so here we are with the nightly ritual of drying out socks and boots. Funny how one day of motion has me thinking that of course we will get to Webequie. Yesterday, I felt certain we would not.

Day 16

A long day, wading, pushing, and dragging old Winnie upstream. Wet all day. But a good day too – sunny, nice breeze that kept the bugs down, and we worked hard, canoed the day's length. No conflict about whether we should be going any further, we went as far as we could. But I couldn't take many of these days in a row, it would be utter exhaustion.

Tonight there is such a feeling of remoteness to where we are, it seems we could almost hear wolves, if we deserved it. Underneath that I feel we haven't yet "earned" hearing them, and certainly not seeing them. What I *can* hear is the incredible forest hum of mosquitoes – the sound that lets you know there are millions, everywhere.

Day 17

Three portages, including a horrible one of one and a half miles. I threw the canoe down a lot today, frustrated with getting stuck in mud over my boots and with walking the wrong way on the barely discernible trail. Temper, I could feel it cooking. Yet, with all our aches and pains, it has been a good day, feeling so here.

Talked with Barb tonight about the type of knowledge and skill we are developing, a being-out-here sense. Looking at weeds for the flow of the river, following the flights of birds and the shafts of sunlight to sense openings in the shorelines, intuiting the weather and realizing the power and impact of even her most subtle shifts. Slowly knowing this could be home.

Day 18

What a day. Got caught in the middle of a set of rapids we thought were the "extraordinarily difficult" ones described in our guide. The water was too deep to line back, but we were too scared to go ahead. Scouted the woods, shoreline, a lot of discussion. Finally we shot the rapids and did all right, it poured rain, and then we discovered the real rapids ahead with a terrible portage—hard to find and to follow. We arrive at our campsite in total darkness and collapse. A day at a time. It's the only way I can make it.

Day 19

Another long day. Seems all we have time for is to paddle, make camp, eat, try to write in our journals, and then crash. My idea of lounging around, reading, writing thoughtful letters, is quite gone. And Barb and I had another one of our typical squabbles over stopping or not. We both get so tired by the day's end that our ability to communicate is way down. We need to be more careful about kidding each other so late in the day, and we need to support each other's desires more—mine to complete goals and plan for tomorrow, Barb's to be into what's happening now.

Day 21

Probably if I wait until later, maybe after dinner, I would be in a better mood, but I need to write about the continuing conflict between Barb and myself over stopping for the day or going on. Originally when we talked about this trip, we even spoke about taking days off. Then at Ogoki Falls we spoke of some half days. Well, we have had twenty days, almost all long and filled with hard work, with no days off, and that is what I have gotten used to, perhaps addicted to. I wonder if this is another example of my liking routine so much that I don't care to switch. I think we are both probably half right. Barb thinks it would be good for us—and fun—to relax some; I think we shouldn't get so locked into trying to find campsites at the sacrifice of our daily mileage goals. I think I come from the old school of if you don't work hard you get punished, and if you do, things will turn out in a fair, just, and usually agreeable manner. I go overboard, I know, fearing we won't get to Winisk on time.

Day 23

A difficult portage today after an easy day yesterday. Overshot the entrance and had to line back up. Part of the mile long portage was burned out and it was difficult finding the trail and picking our way through a boulder field and burned logs. But, tonight, even with the exhaustion, a hurt ankle, I feel so *here* in a good way and feeling more and more confident that we'll make it to the end. Today is the halfway point.

Day 25

Nearing the settlement of Webequie these past two days. I'm beginning to think the Winisk River might not be that bad. Anyway, we have gotten this far, hard as it has been. Barb tells me we have only eight portages left in the whole trip—that's good news. Tomorrow we'll go into the settlement, pick up our supplies, and then head out on the Winisk River for the rest of the trip, all the way to Hudson Bay.

Feeling pretty good about going into Webequie, don't anticipate any hassles. A couple of times today I would hear a motorboat and have all these negative feelings that we are going to be bothered. Then an Indian family passes by and waves, and I remember that all the fear and paranoia comes from my city experience.

Day 26

We have arrived at the doorstep of the Winisk River—and what an entrance. We are camped at a huge set of rapids, not runnable, that span this very wide river. The rapids give much warning—they are loud! But before that are the Winisk River's immediate headwaters, like a door mat into a great hall: shallow, wide, fast, and full of rocks. We entered the shallows with a very strong head wind, blinding sun, and seemingly many different currents, but with one main channel to follow. And then the impossible was happening: we seemed to be going uphill in the rapids. Probably the

113

wind was most responsible, with the aid of the sun, but both Barb and I admitted afterwards to being totally freaked out – I think not only because of the sensation of going uphill, but of this being our first taste of 280 miles of what has become to us the legendary Winisk.

It feels right to make some offering to the river, something. I ask Mom to take care of us, put us through the paces as she will, but to take care and help us complete this journey. I don't want to wipe out on the Winisk, but in some ways just getting here and starting on the river has been the goal. Finishing seems convenient.

Day 27

The Winisk River – today we discovered her. I've felt everything from terrified to bold, and now I am quite grateful to be at our campsite in one piece, dry and exhausted.

The first rapids threw me – big standing waves. It wasn't in the guide, not even on the detailed maps. I couldn't believe what was probably to come with the rapids that *are* listed. Barb wanted to talk; I wanted to be quiet to calm myself down. How we need opposites. Felt her pushing, which was pushing me to the edge. Finally got enough said so Barb knew I needed not to talk.

From then on, every turn seemed to have rapids. Between the wind, low water, abundance of rocks, and a wide river, where to go was anybody's guess.

Finally we reached the rapids rated "difficult," where you have to cross a strong current above a waterfall to get to the portage. Good fate was with us; somehow we made it in time. Then more currents crisscrossing, wind, a shallow rapids where we got caught on a ledge. Finally, a campsite. Relief, satisfaction, hunger, exhaustion.

Emotionally between Barb and me, this was the hardest day. We got pretty frustrated with each other, probably from all the pressure we were both feeling. But we didn't do so bad, considering what we were dealing with.

It's hard to imagine starting the trip from Webequie, as some people do. I think we have been fortunate to have three weeks of a preparation of sorts. It doesn't make the Winisk any easier, we still must battle and flow with her, earn our days; but we can be *here* while doing it.

We left home too long ago, too many experiences ago, to wonder why we are out here. Supposedly the Winisk River will get easier as we go. I don't think I'll believe that until my feet are walking around the settlement of Winisk on Hudson Bay. And at that point I can't imagine sharing the jumble of emotion with anyone not here – it has gone so far beyond words.

Day 28

Today was so much better than yesterday. Everything seemed a bit out of control yesterday—us and the river. But today we ran plenty of rapids and did fine. In one of the early rapids we did have a tight moment at the One Big Rock. I thought for sure we were going to get creamed. Canoeing is so much a matter of inches, of moments.

I am curious, but I can't get myself to read further ahead in our guide to the descriptions of the remaining rapids. So far I feel safe in studying one day at a time and glancing ahead to the following. I feel we can always muck through, struggle with whatever each day brings, but to see the whole picture—that would be too much. I don't think I want to know it.

The land is starting to change. All of a sudden it seems that the trees are getting leaner, shorter, the clusters are getting thinner. It makes the idea of tundra more real. It feels more like wolf country, more space, a place they could roam and stretch. I still hope.

Day 29

Early today we got caught on a ledge. We still have no idea of where to go over ledges, where we see lots of whitewater or where we see none. At noon we went over another ledge—a big drop, huge waves, most water we've taken in yet.

Later as we sat at Baskineg Falls, we started to grasp the dangers of going over a ledge in the middle of the river with rapids and falls right below and no chance of a self-rescue. Realizing that the biggest danger of this trip is paddling such a huge river with only one canoe. A capsize anywhere, especially in the middle, would be a disaster.

So we were taken care of again today—hard work, but we did what we set out to do. I asked Mom for a cooler day, no capsizes, let storms wait until camp, general well being. She's doing what she can, and it seems like a lot.

Day 30

If I didn't think it was so important to stay humble and quiet about our accomplishment, I would like to celebrate this night, Saturday night *alive* on the Winisk River. Today we finished the designated portages and rapids, except one at the end. That's not to say there won't be surprise swifts, the fearful ledges—the Winisk River has too much character to have no surprises left—but in my heart I know we have gotten through what was threatening, the real danger of this trip. I'll miss the big whitewater; yet, I know I can't take the concentration, the total state of readiness it demands for many days in a row.

Day 32

The river, for now, has smoothed out. The new challenge is the weather — rain, cold, wind. We did well canoeing into the wind all day, our endurance has really grown in a month. But now I'm pretty bushed, wanting space and quiet. Not being by myself is finally getting to me. I'm trying to do little things to help it — going to the tent early, mending my pants way off from Barb, being quiet and spacing out.

Perhaps it is the influence of movie images of the North, but I really get into the exuberance/vigor of paddling when it is cool and windy. I feel more bold than powerful, more right out there with the elements than challenging or conquering. It makes me feel strong and alive.

Day 33

Barb is fishing, but not with much luck. The fish really add to the meals, but I feel that with less work I should eat less, not eat out of boredom. I try to sit on my desire to eat like a horse, Barb talks about it all the time. I don't know why verbal focus on food gets to me, especially since we share a lot of humor around it. It feels very gluttonous to speak as if we are starving, when I think, "Yeah, the truth is that we are overly stuffed white Americans." But another truth is that I have lost some weight and Barb has lost a huge amount. We clearly need as much as we are eating or more.

How I wish there was nothing but the weather, water, paddling. I know this whole camping experience is a gift, rich, but there are moments that the routine, chores, meals — especially in the morning — frustrate me so. All I want to do is get out there in the sun, rain, wind, whatever, and paddle. Mystical, that is the word that comes to mind; this is all beginning to feel very mystical, very intense. Now, perhaps for the first time, the idea of being here alone is becoming mine, to be alone with the weather, woods, water. It's faint, a glimmer, but it's coming through that I will someday have that.

Day 36

The cold wind continues to blow as it has for the last four days. Becoming more okay, familiar to me that I am tired because of the wind and the cold, not the paddling. Barb just asked me if I wished the trip was over. No, I just wish for a windless day.

Before me many old spruce trees pulsing at their base with the wind, raising the forest floor as if the moss breathes.

Day 37

Finally, a day of sun, calm winds, warmth. Able to paddle without our shirts for a while, now at a spacious camp next to a fast flowing creek, lots of beach, we can wash our hair. This day is needed.

Tonight, the night of the full moon, has been the night that we've said we might hear the wolves. Well, I don't think we will see or hear them this trip; perhaps on the 4th, 5th, or 8th trip, but this is too soon. We have earned much, but we don't deserve the wolves, not yet.

Day 40

The joke is on us. So complacent, so lulled into a drowsy, dreamy state by the calm Winisk River of the last nine days. Then today, she once again showed us that she can't be predicted, taken for granted, that we will earn Winisk. She has not lost her force, she is not tame; she had only chosen calmness for a while.

Suddenly, a canyon, and we had four miles of almost continuous rapids with huge standing waves. I have never seen waves that big from a canoe. Barb says they hit her in the bow with incredible force, like being under a waterfall. I don't know how we got through; twice we went broadside in big waves. We fill up, very tippy, but get to shore to empty out. We wonder, we laugh at how this is not on the map, not in the guide. It is the hardest, the biggest yet. I suggest it is my mother's humor, that the rapids are only real to us. We name them Ollie's Rapids.

The gulls are growing in number. We are getting close, yes – the tundra, the ocean.

Day 42

Hot, muggy day. Going into the settlement of Winisk tomorrow, the end of the trip. Both of us are in a semi-drugged state from this weather of the tropics.

Went for a long walk yesterday, felt strongly how this land, a land with space, a place to roam and range, is where wolves could be. And that bird, that wonderful bird that has followed us from the beginning of the trip to here. Who calls with a sweet whistle to wake us up, who welcomes us to a campsite, who's with us when we watch the sun lie down. That bird, whom we have never seen but is always there as we paddle; that bird, I think, is not a real bird at all. We've started to call it the Ollie Bird, to wait for its call. The sounds have made me smile, brought me comfort, made me feel at home. Barb asked whether she should tell me if she finally identifies it. I realized it would make no difference; that reality and mine can be held together in my mind.

Day 43

It is evening here at the settlement of Winisk. I tried to make this day be like the others, but it's not, a lot of the trip has ended here. We're inside now — it is very hard to be inside. Windows don't open, too quiet, too still.

We did this journey through our skill, our ability to deal with things as they came up. But I know it was the Winisk River and other waters, good fortune, my mother, who allowed this journey to happen. I could never assume we would get here. For me that would be arrogant, and I needed to be humble, respectful, and think of a day at a time and perhaps the days would add up and we would get to Fort Hope, then Webequie, then Winisk.

This is a sad and hard time, the trip's end. But I know that I can choose to begin again, a new focus. And I know, too, I will not do that until this trip has had her due, her rest, her mourning for the end.

Going Alone

BARB WIESER

In 1985, I did a ten-day solo canoe trip on the Steel River loop in the rugged country near Lake Superior in northern Ontario. My life was changing that year. I'd quit working at the women's press I'd been a part of for eleven years, ended a relationship, and was moving to California from my Iowa home of the last sixteen years. Most of that summer I had spent canoeing in Canada, but I wanted to go back one last time— and this time alone—before driving to California.

For years, I had been travelling in the northern wilderness, mostly with the same three friends. We weren't a particularly noisy group, but some of the times I had enjoyed the most were after everyone had gone to bed. I'd take the canoe out into the bright northern night, and just float there, watching the shooting stars and the reflection of the moon on the lake. I would think about travelling alone. To have that kind of solitude and quiet *all* the time. To travel at my own pace—spend as much time as I wanted looking at wildflowers, floating with the current, watching a soaring bird. To be in the wilderness in a way I only get glimpses of when I am with my friends.

I had done a five-day solo trip on the Flambeau River in Wisconsin two years earlier. I went late in the fall, it rained the entire time, and I had a *very* big canoe to paddle solo. But I had a wonderful time and knew I wanted to go again and this time to northern Canada. I thought about the reasons not to go into that kind of wilderness alone. I had answers to my more obvious doubts. What if I get lost? (I have the skills to prevent that.) What if I twist my ankle? (I haven't had that happen yet, and I'll be extra careful.) Do I need to worry about being a woman alone? (That should be less of a worry than in the city.) What I didn't know was what I would find when I no longer had other humans to remind me of my self. What would happen in my mind in a wilderness alone?

I really wanted this trip to be a trip *alone*. So I picked a time and route accordingly—late September and the Steel River. Though the route has gotten some publicity for its spectacular scenery, I knew the legendary awful portage at the beginning of the trip would keep a lot of people out.

I debated for a long time whether or not to do that portage. It was reputed to be straight up over a mountain, and I did not have a lightweight canoe. The alternative was to fly in, but I was pretty broke, needing what money I had for my move. The plane flight won out—it would be hard and dangerous to make it over that portage alone. And the pilot turned out to be a woman. Liz has been flying in the North for 25 years and was full of great stories and sound advice on how to be spotted by a bush plane. I wasn't too happy about carrying the bottle of fuel oil that she insisted I take to create smoke signals, but her compass with the mirror came in handy when I lost mine.

The plane dropped me off close to sunset on a quiet lake. The drone of the engine faded away, leaving me in silence. No human sounds, no people anywhere for a long distance. Just me, with no way out. I looked around for a place to camp and paddled over to the nearest rocky point and got busy with all those tasks I knew so well—setting up the tent and tarp, collecting wood and getting a fire going, cooking dinner. I tried to ignore the butterflies in my stomach, but I couldn't eat a bite of my dinner. How am I going to stand this quiet for ten days? Why did I think this trip was so damn important to do?

I was a lot more scared than I had been on the Flambeau. Scared and not wanting to be there alone, not wanting to be moving to California, wanting back the security of my little home on the Iowa River. Somehow in all my thinking about this trip, I hadn't really anticipated what this would be like. I had lived alone in the country for ten years, but this was different. The quiet was absolute, the aloneness unbroken.

But in the next few days my nerves calmed as I settled into the routine of a canoe trip, and the joy that I always feel in the North began to take over. I forgot my fears and just got into being there—the beauty of the granite cliffs lining the river, the sunlight on the rippling water, the late blooming wildflowers, the lichen and moss-covered meadows. With no one else's rhythm to keep, I slowed down a lot, napping after a portage, paddling as slow as I wanted or not at all, eating when I felt like it.

I saw a lot more wildlife than on my other trips. One day as I came around a narrow bend in the river, three moose slipped into the water near me and swam across the lake, unaware of my presence, or uncaring.

More than anything, I loved the quiet. I like singing and do it a lot while driving, or working in the yard, or paddling. But not on the Steel. My voice faltered after the first few notes. The sound seemed out of place in the silence of that land.

I spent a lot of time trying to figure out what was happening to me out there alone, what it all *meant.* I didn't feel content to just leave it that I'm doing a canoe trip alone and having a fine time. I needed the trip to have some special significance.

But I never could find it. I told myself that later it would come to me, that I wouldn't be able to understand what was happening while I was living it. But when I think back on the Steel now, what I remember is simply a beautiful land and some of the most peaceful times I've ever known.

And I want to go back—maybe not for so long and maybe just to stay in one spot without the constant unknowns of where to camp and what the rapids are like. But to go back again and again to experience that aloneness. Whatever I'm searching for, I know that's where I'll find it.

Mucky Waters: A Hudson Bay Journal
JUDITH NIEMI

When we made this trip in 1978, I'd been canoeing for 18 years, and had started guiding women's trips, but I hadn't yet given myself the kind of big trip I'd been dreaming of—someplace Up North, more remote than my home waters of northern Minnesota, someplace I'd have to learn new skills. I just knew I needed to do it.

Of the six friends who went, only two had much canoeing experience, and even we weren't very knowledgeable about whitewater. But most of us were deeply involved in various exuberant and ambitious feminist projects spring- ing up in the mid '70's, and the idea of paddling to Hudson Bay caught our im- agination. It seemed to us a bold and joyous gesture, the sort of thing women weren't supposed to do.

We spent a month travelling 380 miles along an old fur trade route, the "Middle Track," which appealed to us partly because even in Minnesota we hadn't been able to find anyone who had been there. We also liked that it would bring us to York Factory, a Hudson's Bay Company post established in 1693, open now as an historic site; from there we returned by charter plane and rail- road. We appeared to be the only travelers on that route that summer. Even our supportive and loyal friends, the ones who spelled out "Welcome Home, Amazons" on our refrigerator, sometimes called it "a crazy trip." But our health was better there, we felt stronger, clearer with each other than before or after. We often used "Hudson Bay" as a shorthand way to say a saner way of living. And we often talked of the almost tangible sense of safety we felt there, of being at home.

This story, a version of which first appeared in The Lesbian Path, *edited by Margaret Cruikshank, 1980 (San Francisco: Grey Fox Press), is from the jour- nal I kept on the trip and in the following weeks. Revisiting it makes me nostal- gic, amused sometimes, and very grateful that we made this trip.*

Day 1. Cross Lake

First campsite, a pink and violet granite shelf, thrushes singing their questions across the channel, four of us writing in our journals. This afternoon when we were finally on the water I felt suddenly calm, at home. "Prayerful" too, I thought, a word I haven't used for twenty years. A recognition that what we're doing seems big, an act of faith. As we paddled off Connie said, "Think how many women in Minneapolis are thinking about us today."

For me this trip is fulfilling a fantasy. For years I've wanted to make a long canoe trip and didn't do anything about it. Then on a ski weekend a group of us started talking about our dreams, taking ourselves seriously, I guess. I said out loud that I wanted to canoe to Hudson Bay, and Jean instantly said, "I'll go with you, Judith." We're both too old not to start doing what we want.

In recruiting other women we decided not to look for expertise and muscle but for women we wanted to share the experience with. At our first we're-really-going-to-do-this meeting last December Jean said, "Well, I want to go with feminists – not someone who'll sit around the campfire and say, 'Gee whiz, isn't it great to be just us women?'"

"What would an opening campfire line be, Jean?"

"Oh, maybe, 'This is what the matriarchy was like, I just know it!'"

The six of us have spent a lot of time discussing our greatest fears, and what our personal low thresholds are (bugs, cold wet feet, rain, people who crab about rain). We had a group chart done by Moonrabbit, who told us there are so many fixed signs among us that there's no doubt we'll hang in there – we might have to try to remember to have fun. She suggests that Kristin and I, with the most fire in our charts, not paddle together in the rapids. We say that we are going to live "tribally," and we figure that we'll find out what we mean by that in doing it.

Day 5. Cross Lake – Muck

After a late afternoon dinner, we come to the shallow bay where Réal Bérard's annotated map, our main source of information, tells us we may have to wade and drag the canoes for several miles. Connie splashes over to a big rock to scout and shrieks, seeing only waving green reeds in all directions. We find a narrow channel marked by a birch pole and start a long evening of wading knee deep in fine muck. Dead jackfish float belly up, and sometimes ooze out cold under our bare toes. This is not Nature we are contending with, but Manitoba Hydro; the new dam has lowered the lake level about ten feet, angering the Crees who live here and rely on the fishing, which is badly disrupted. The patriarchy as usual messing

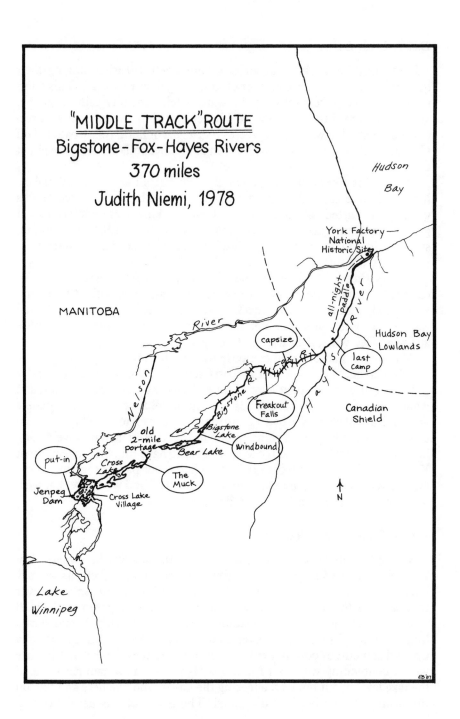

"MIDDLE TRACK" ROUTE
Bigstone - Fox - Hayes Rivers
370 miles
Judith Niemi, 1978

Hudson
Bay

York Factory —
National
Historic Site

MANITOBA

Nelson River

Hudson Bay
Lowlands

capsize

Fox R.

all-night Paddle

Hayes River

last
camp

Freakout
Falls

Bigstone

Canadian
Shield

old
2-mile
portage

Bigstone
Lake

Windbound

put-in

Bear Lake

Cross
Lake

The
Muck

N

Jenpeg
Dam

Cross Lake
Village

Lake
Winnipeg

EB '87

things up because it thinks it needs more of what it thinks is power.

At sunset we make camp on the mud flats, which Connie refers to as "the aspen glade" when she declares a stop. We unload only our sleeping bags, one tent, the Svea stove and a packet of soup. We let the mud dry on our legs and scrape it off with Swiss army knives before being allowed in the tent.

Scene in a bog: incredible scarlet sunset over the boreal forest. Mosquitoes rise in clouds from the drained lake bed. Three canoes lie stranded far out in the muck. Through the swamp grasses two tiny heads appear, Kristin and Connie, squatting sociably. "Considering the options, this isn't a bad campsite." "No, actually it's quite nice." Jean and I overhearing this get pretty hysterical.

In the morning Jean is up early hiking on the mud flats, and comes back to report several more miles of this. We agree to stick with our present canoe-dragging partners however long it takes us to get through this. Lorry and I become Muck Sisters. Lorry and I were also together a couple days ago to see something floating in the shallows that looked like a bloated moose haunch, until we got closer. "Look at the *feet,*" she whispered, tense. "It has *toes!*" Well, it might have been a bear, like I said. Or a human.

Until the muck, I couldn't let myself totally believe this trip would work, that others really shared my dreams. Some hold-out, untrusting part of me secretly thought someone was going to say, "This is too hard. Let's go back and just take the train to Churchill." But my friends were trucking on, kvetching, smiling, inventing madrigals—"Mucky wa-a-a-a-aters." Faith cautiously settled down on me. Besides, I knew no one would ever consider going *back* through that muck.

Day 7. The Long Portage

We had been thinking the casual and vague directions our map gives for finding the portage trail were pretty funny: "In a jackpine cluster by a large rock." Arriving at the end of this dried-up bay after hours of mud-slogging, we spent all the late afternoon and evening checking out innumerable jackpine clusters and rocks. Nothing.

That was a little scary and frustrating for a while, but I really loved the search. After all the mud, to be in the sweet-smelling pines, hiking alone across the hummocks in the intense late light of the North, free, unlimited space all around me. I was also so exhausted that when I saw my very own Muck Sister across the beaver stream, I couldn't recall her name or her face.

In the morning we collect our wits and information, organize search parties— we'll check the other stream, following the hunter's trail—you guys go back inland and hike due east. We had the fun of finding the trail a couple different ways.

The portage is two miles through a peat bog; when the walking gets especially nasty, we name it the Richard M. Nixon Memorial Bog. The trail is worn deep in the sphagnum moss, a path used by the Cree people since York Factory was established in 1693, and probably long before that. It's a day's work to get everything across. On my last trip carrying a canoe I find my second wind and feel elated, euphoric. We're all very tired when we're done; I suppose that at 27 to 41 we don't have the resilience of kids. But we're all better than we used to be – tougher, beautiful leathery tanned faces. We're going to make it.

The portaging is slow, because only four of us can carry heavy loads. In March Connie broke her ankle, and it's not strong yet. Two weeks before we left, Aurora put her back out again, could hardly walk. Crises. Each of them decided to risk the trip, the rest of us decided we were willing to carry extra.

It fits the way we want to travel. We chose not to take the Hayes River, easier, more travelled, where the European explorers pushed into the interior in big York boats. Ours is an older Indian route on the Bigstone and Fox, suitable only for small canoes. The British did this heroic military-style stuff, travelling at top speed to get somewhere else. The Crees lived here, women, men, children, aged people; when they went to York Factory to trade, probably the whole family often went along.

Even before they were injured Connie and Aurora took on all the food packing, and now they have appointed themselves head cooks. Sugar-free, vegetarian food, not an additive around. One day Connie got hilarious spying out the inventory in Aurora's Handy Bag of Necessities: agar agar, chia seed, black bean powder, hijiki, ligaplex. Mu tea, Aurora assured us at the beginning of this portage (less than tactful timing), would give us a zip that would last all day, not like *coffee*.

Day 10. Bear Lake

A fine day of riding huge rollers in a tailwind ends as we paddle around bouldery islands looking for any tiny clearing to camp in. We land in waves and spray in a tangle of spruce and Labrador tea. We've been up since early (for once), and it's now last light, maybe ten or eleven, but after clearing out space for one tent, we fix *two* gourmet dinners – Asian rice and noodles-with-something. We put wild roses in a Sierra cup for a centerpiece, and eat by candlelight. For dinner music Lorry plays Morley songs on her flute, and I try to sing along, "Flora, beauteous and fair, alas hath slain mee."

Canoe conversation the other day: how for once we haven't had to think about being political, how great it is to feel no opposition, to take ourselves for granted and live unselfconsciously. Back in the city this trip seemed like a physical risk, and like getting out of line. But once out here, I relax, trust myself, feel like my real self. I'm a physically very cautious person, and I guess I value risk-taking not for thrills, but as a necessary survival skill, one I actually need much more in the other world than here.

Clouds. I think what I may remember most about this land is the clouds, great fields of them. They are very low, and the horizon so wide we can see miles of them as they build up in the West every afternoon. We time our lunch by the daily storm. The first words of Sylvia Plath that I ever read, before I knew she was famous: "It took two days of driving North to find a cloud so big the polite skies over Boston couldn't possibly accommodate it."

Day 12. Windbound on Bigstone Lake

A Gale from the North, cold wind, huge waves. We have no choice but to rest, with 130 miles behind us, and over 250 miles to go before we meet a plane only 14 days from now.

It takes four of us a while to get the fire going without using up any of our white gas. We feast on millet and barley and decide to enjoy the layover, sorting and drying things. Jean and I take a canoe out in the storm to pick up a couple of fish for chowder, wearing life jackets and paddling like crazy to stay in one place. Most of the day I spend at the fire, baking bannocks and writing.

Last night the six of us stood around the fire in the damp and drizzle and talked painfully about what we're wanting and not getting from each other, about feeling angry or resentful or insecure. Nothing got resolved, but I trust our willingness to keep working on it. We're also in conflict about time. We worry about reaching York Factory on the 26th, and we differ on how important it seems to do that, how confident we feel, how we can get going earlier. The problem, I think, is that we're still partly on white man's time, needing to meet a plane, a train, to get back to jobs in the South on the day we said. Otherwise, I'd be just fine with wherever we are.

Near this camp, Jean hears women's voices singing in the rapids. I've often heard voices in the wilderness, speaking quietly. She recalls legends of the sirens, of Rhine maidens. In the morning a bear politely visits our camp and goes on her way.

Day 17. Bigstone River. Rapids

We're feeling a lot more confident, running more of the rapids than we thought we would. The river gets bigger. Today started with an exciting bit of lining canoes through little waterfalls, an elaborate ferry system. ("Good," breathed Connie, "a group activity.") Very pleased with ourselves. Then we really stalled out at the next rapids—not runnable, not lineable, and no portage in sight. Not much energy in us. I got pissy and irritable. Finally we detected ancient blazes on the trees ("The James Fenimore Cooper Trail"), and playing scout totally restored my good humor.

At the next rapids we took for the first time what seemed like a reasonable and deliberate risk, first Kristin and I, then Kristin and Connie taking loaded canoes through by three different routes, none of them quite the planned one. In the middle of this we stopped to wait out a downpour. Huddled in our rainsuits, we recall Farley Mowat writing that the Eskimos' real dwellings are their clothes; we patiently listened to rain on the roof. Problems here are so solvable.

Day 18. Stopped again. Bigstone River

Aurora is sick—not just the familiar "camper's crud," but fever, hallucinations. Lorry is dosing her with belladonna from the homeopathic first aid kit. By afternoon she's still weak, but able to be up and join a group conference about whether we should try to push on with her as "passenger," about what we think this illness is, about our group dynamics generally.

This has been building for days. Now all six of us spend the afternoon sitting in the sun in a difficult talk that ends in a lot more clarity and good feeling. Some new excitement—I feel a burst of energy.

Can we possibly make it to York Factory on the 26th, even with this additional day's delay? We don't know, but are willing to give it a hell of a try. I'm more eager, agreeing with Jean that I don't want to see us not meet our plane because of our own inertia. It will be OK to give up fishing time, photography time. Are we being too task-oriented, forgetting to have fun? I think we've been mistakenly calling paddling our "work" and stopping in camp "fun"—that is not the distinction I feel. Maybe we're finally starting to unlearn some city thinking.

Day 21. Fox River. Rapids

A good thing our talk brought us new energy because the trip is getting rougher. Two days ago Lorry and I went into a rapids feeling unconfident, stuck on a ledge, and I had to go for a swim to get us off. Angry at the others for not waiting. At the big burn we decided that carrying through the pick-up-sticks tangle of charred logs was impossibly difficult, and we roped, ran, and hassled our way through a rapids we would never have tried a few days ago.

The map-maker clearly travelled through in August at lower water levels. The Fox is getting very big, the water level is very high. The power of it is awesome.

Today we came to what the map calls the most difficult part of the Fox. It starts with our picking our way down through a maze of channels, getting stuck once on a rock island with waterfalls all around us. Up ahead the river drops right out of sight. We drag, rope, and portage our canoes, then edge cautiously down the left bank right under the alders until even this makes us too nervous. Connie then finds a sort of portage. This one, unmarked on the map, is about half a mile around very heavy rapids, and ends below *five* thirty-foot waterfalls across the wide river. "Freak Out Falls." I mean, they weren't even *mentioned* on the map—what's coming next?

Actually, I'm relieved. As the river gets bigger, I've been feeling a lot of anxiety. Now that there's such an objective cause for fear and others share it, I relax, and take on only my one-sixth of the responsibility. We ferry across the strong current, and I get back my rapids nerve and judgment leading down the inside of the bend.

And now we're only 300 feet above sea level; in the last few days we've dropped 400 feet, sliding right off the Canadian Shield into the Hudson Bay lowlands. Last night we passed through a layer of beautiful red igneous rock, where four otters swam around us, snorting and laughing at us, and ran the rapids with us. Tonight we're below the rock, surrounded by high clay banks. Somewhere in that long brushy portage today we saw a beautiful mushroom in the middle of the faint trail, and after all our tromping back and forth it was still there, everyone having carefully stepped around it.

Day 22. Fox River. Capsize

Kristin and Lorry capsized today. This was just what I'd been afraid of since last winter—someone would capsize, and I wouldn't be able to help them. (And of course whatever happened would be all my fault for thinking up this trip in the first place.)

Four of us had pulled ashore to scout a bad place. Kristin and Lorry cut to the other side of an island, and when we saw them reappear, way downstream, out of the canoe, it was like a bad dream, paralyzing. Then we snapped out of it, and although we'd just decided this chute was too iffy to run, we ran it anyway, trying to catch up with them.

The whole thing worked out well, and everybody got in on the rescue. Lorry stuffing daypacks back into the canoe as they floated down the rapids, she and Kris gallantly aiding each other. Aurora and I caught up, and with one hanging on each side of our canoe, ferried furiously toward shore, managing to crash land on some rocks just above the next big rapids. Connie and Jean arrived and threw us ropes to get us ashore on their island.

The last scene was pretty comic. Four of us and a canoe lodged on two tiny rocks, wild rapids around us. Rain of course. By then we were all perfectly safe, but it seemed complicated and I felt absurdly cautious. We were flinging ropes around in this Marx Sisters routine, using the canoe as a ferry to the island. Does anybody remember how to tie a sheepshank? Connie watched her new paddle, dunked in the capsize, go spinning off downriver where Kris and Lorry didn't go and called after it cheerily, "Bye, sweetheart, and happy birthday!"

Then we had the job of collecting the other canoe, dealing with wet gear and leftover feelings. Some of us insisted on making the portage, walking off our anger, fear, relief. But of course it was not a smart time to push on, so we had to carry some of the packs partway back, to a campsite.

The day was sobering, but in a pinch what we found was that we were all there for each other, willing to take risks, competent.

Day 24. Fox River. Home Free

One last day of rapids, and Kristin and I wanted a chance to paddle together, although Moonrabbit had warned us that with all our Aries stuff we could egg each other on, escalate the excitement. We're all being very cautious. Kris, subdued, tells us to keep our lifejackets on even eating lunch. And still we get a chance at a rapids bigger than we'd have any right to choose to run.

Scouting ahead, the two of us underestimate the speed of the smooth current, and find ourselves stuck on a tiny island. We yell to the others that the rapids ahead is out of the question. Then we find that it is not possible to paddle back upstream. Unless we wait for fall to lower the water level, our only choice is to run it. We wait for a potential rescue canoe to be lined to the bottom and then push off. I'm afraid, but even more excited and pleased. Washing out below the last big ledge, in a canoe half full of water, I'm intensely joyful, every cell alive. I realize I believed we'd make it, but I felt so much a part of this river, these woods, that whatever happened, it really didn't matter. If I can just remember this moment clearly, I think, I may never be afraid again.

Day 26. Hayes River and York Factory

When we came out of the last rapids of the Fox we had 120 miles to go and a plane that might be waiting for us in a day and a half. By evening there were only 90 miles left. At the last campsite on a gravel bar we cooked up most of the remaining food and planned our strategy: four hours paddling, a rest stop, another four hours, all day and night until we get there. We estimate 16 to 20 hours.

Some of us suspect this is nuts, "linear," crazy white man stuff. (The pilot, for sure, is not going to come for us without radioing York Factory to know we're there.) Others of us say it *is* sort of crazy, but it's fun, witchy. The plane doesn't have much to do with it anymore. We said the 26th, and we want to see if we can do it.

Just before dark on the 25th we stop for dinner, and finally get around to making a trip flag, partly for our friends back home. Magic marker women's symbols, letters torn from canoe-repair tape: "We Are Everywhere." Then we paddle off into the dark. There's a band of beautiful yellow light ahead on the northern horizon, but otherwise it's heavily overcast, and we can't see a thing. We navigate only by the silhouettes of the largest islands.

Sometime in the middle of the night Aurora is too exhausted to go on. I keep falling asleep, but can half hear Connie facilitating a discussion that gets us all what we want. Aurora and Lorry wrap up in sleeping bags and space blankets and bed down in the middle canoe; those of us who insist we'll keep going tie our canoes up on either side and set off again. We make a very sluggish raft, and are paddling into a stiff cold headwind, but the fast current still carries us on. We start singing. Connie makes up a lullaby. I hardly look at Kristin next to me in the stern of the other canoe, or say a word, except as we push off the sandbars, but we're comforted knowing neither of us will ever quit.

Just before dawn Kristin tells us we need to stop NOW to get warm. We stumble out onto a dark beach, and as the sun rises, realize how nearly hypothermic we are, what a task we've just finished. We're coming into the tidewater. We put on every stitch of warm clothing we have. Aurora cooks us miso soup.

Paddling the last few miles into York Factory, I'm very sleepy, very high. Intense sun and blue sky, cold wind, socks on my hands for mittens. Jean and I are paddling the flag ship, the orange flag is snapping around my head and still Jean has to keep waking me up to steer. I tell myself I may be missing the climax of the trip and then realize the whole idea of a climax is nonsense and anyway, in my spacey, sleepy state I'm soaking up impressions with my whole body.

131

Aurora, Cross Lake, Manitoba (Judith Niemi)

Permafrost-tipped trees are sliding past, mirages lie ahead where the river opens up to the sea, and I feel—how?—prayerful? Foggily I remember having felt that sometime before, and then I remember it was on our first day, at Cross Lake. Now we've done this, and I don't really want to go back.

We finally seem to be there. Gunshots. What do they mean? The Indians were shooting at a polar bear out on the island, we learn later. Doug, the caretaker of the historic site, is warm and welcoming, shows us where we can stay, and then he and his daughter tactfully leave us alone, to return much later with eggs, dry crispy crackers, fresh plums.

We drag our gear up above the tideline and one by one fall asleep on the grass, wherever we happened to collapse. One by one we wake in a few minutes or a few hours and quietly start unpacking, walking around the old fort, looking out toward the sea. Jean takes out the kite we've been carrying all this way, and without a word goes out to fly it in celebration.

PART THREE:
Urban Wilds

Ann Wilder, Bobbie Smith; St. Paul, Minnesota (Judith Niemi)

"The concrete bridge is a most delightful, a most spacious haven. Cuddled beneath the arch, there was a space of ground at least as big as a hall bedroom. Thickets of sumac grew all about, and though the doctors' Fords and the bakers' carts and the touring cars of New Jersey rattled above our heads, nobody ever looked down to see us three raggle taggle gypsies squatting about a blackened tin pot and feeding the fire with cedar twigs."

—Ruth Murray Underhill, "A Near-Home Canoeing Weekend," *Outing* magazine, 1921

"CANOEING ALWAYS MEANT WILDERNESS to me," Barb said. "For ten years I lived where the Iowa River flowed right through my backyard, and I only got out canoeing on it twice. I wish it had occurred to me that any place water is going somewhere could be interesting canoeing." Non-wilderness canoeing—paddling around Manhattan Island or on local ponds—is often accessible to people who could only rarely travel to our few remaining wilderness areas. It's a way to get into out-of-the-way places, travel a long mental distance in a short time. It can offer new perspective on our surroundings, reminders of when the Hudson, the Connecticut, and the Mississippi were the major highways. Often there's a curious and delighted audience when canoes appear where people think they're not supposed to be. That sense of audience, and interactions with the city world, are part of the experiences in this section.

Clarissa and Seraphine on the Canal
RUTH MURRAY UNDERHILL

We have no biographical information about Ruth Underhill or about the author of the following piece, Anna Kalland, or about their companions, beyond what's evident from their articles. They were uppity women, all of them, with whom we'd have loved to share trips. They were well endowed with one of the main qualities needed for canoeing in "civilized" areas, a sense of humor. Both articles appeared in Outing, *a popular outdoor activities magazine. In the early twenties, canoe trips were common enough, yet still news enough, that canoeing articles appeared in every issue.*

(Excerpted from "A Near-Home Canoeing Weekend," *Outing*, February 1921)

"This camp," said Seraphine that evening, "is a poacher's lair." (*Outing*, 1921)

137

The route is an old canal.

"And could we really see it all in a weekend from New York?"

"If ye're any good at paddling. But ladies *isn't.*"

That settled it. That was enough to make a Friday to Monday on the Morris and Essex Canal into an adventure. Seraphine and I are always looking for adventures but sometimes we do not find polishing our shoes in the morning and taking the subway down to the office quite as thrilling as the optimists of the New York cult would have us believe. So we have decided to have weekends sometimes costing as much as a dollar and a half apiece.

The canal seemed to fill the bill. It was ancient and abandoned according to the boss; it wound its way through half the backyards of New Jersey from Lake Hopatcong to Newark Bay. With carfare enough to take us somewhere near its middle, a canoe, a can or two and an extra day off, we might have a weekend close to the heart of Nature – or, well, fairly close, for Nature is very respectably clad in that region and her heartbeats are muffled by her tailor-made costume.

"Clarissa, my dear," said Seraphine, spilling a little more bacon grease on her last year's khaki skirt, to make the spots symmetrical, "it will be a lesson to us. You see, up to now, all our camping trips have been taken under the wing of virile young American manhood and our duties have been to squat around the campfire while men yelled to us to bring things. But the time has come for women to have some adventures alone."

I hauled out the Rocky Mountain camping outfit.

"How about our Child?" I ventured.

Seraphine and I have adopted a child, like all spinsters who, after stormy careers, attain the solution. We think we are going to be awfully good for his mental development. His name is Alfonso: he can speak quite a little English, and recites, "Aye, tear her tattered ensign down" just like the teacher. We lend Alfonso our smocks to wear and listen with startling eyes to his stories of Italian ghosts in a Harlem tenement.

We had wise plans for training him to be a carpenter, but the other day Alfonso brought us ten carefully written pages and stated that he had decided to become an author. Then we realized too late what we had done.

"We owe the Child something," said Seraphine solemnly. "If you have a flannel shirt for him, let him come."

I sent my canoe to a place called Mountain View. From the station we saw nothing but an expanse of melancholy flat. We plodded quite up to it and slung our packs on the grass and then, up a little embankment, we found the canal, fifteen feet wide and six deep, gray green, like the wrong side of a grape leaf, with a neat little tow path on either side.

They built it ninety years ago, the boss told me, and now one of the railroads keeps it up for purposes of its own. That means sending a lumbering barge along it once a month to repair the mouldering locks, and see that the moles don't tunnel the banks away. Except for the barge and a canoe or two, it lies in peaceful emptiness all the year round, with the weeds growing long under the water. Other people go to the canal in summer when every bungalow is full and the mosquito swarms just as badly as we have always been told it swarms.

But I do not like mosquitoes and, to be really honest, I do not like bungalows. So I am an Octobrist. I was about to explain that that is nothing revolutionary, but, on second thought, it is. It means I go canoeing when other people do not go: when the air is cool and the mist floats off the water in great streamers after sunrise; when the flaming maple and woodbine and sumac stand over the opaque green water like the pictures in the colored fairy books.

"Can we get a permit to be taken through the locks?" This I asked of the boss, leisurely mending an oaken bridge beside the blacksmith shop.

The canal is no fun at all without a permit, for it runs over high country, downhill, and its course is riddled with locks, most difficult to negotiate with a laden canoe.

"Well," said he, "the feller went down the canal somewhere – or maybe up. You might catch him tomorrow."

"Is there an office where I can telephone?"

"No. Ye can't telephone."

"Couldn't you give me a permit?"

"Me?"

Now, the fact was that the boss was empowered to give me a permit. But it was a fearsome power which he had never dared to exercise. No one likes to exercise it: getting a permit is a sort of mysterious task in which the applicant is hurled from pillar to post, continually seeking elusive personages in unknown villages and lucky if he attains the important yellow ticket before the end of his trip.

I could not get a permit from the boss, and that day Seraphine and Alfonso and I sweated and used blandishments and otherwise exerted ourselves to get the canoe over the locks between us and the Big Town. At the Big Town the very big boss would be found, and he would put the document into our hands and smooth the way before us.

It was difficult loading the canoe. But at last the tent, the blankets, and the canned goods were properly stowed amidships around the person of Seraphine, who was to read to us "The Sentimental Journey" while Alfonso and I paddled.

"We might read *The New Republic,*" she suggested tentatively, "or something that would be good for Alfonso."

"Seraphine," I said, "I can be pushed just so far. And if you don't amuse me, I will not push this canoe."

"We might as well have a man along!" wailed Seraphine.

But one doesn't really read. And the paddling was interrupted in any case whenever Alfonso joined in the conversation, for he cannot talk without his hands and they always went flying into the air at the very moment when I needed him most to help push under a bridge.

"Clarissa, it is exactly like Holland!"

It really was, at that moment. The canal ran like a footpath between two rolling fields of cabbages; a black and white cow strolled along the tow path; a long gray barn squatted in the distance; a fleet of dazzling ducks cast off from the grassy banks and sailed across our bows; two tiny boys in overalls leaned on the curving bridge above us.

"I feel, Seraphine, like an old Dutch woman paddling her produce to market."

"Say, lady, are you in the movies?"

Alfonso belongs to the guild of the young. We left the small boys on the curving bridge to him, and he silenced them with a gesture well known and effective.

Then, suddenly, cabbage fields and bridge disappeared, for this is one of the charms of the canal. In a moment, we found ourselves alone in a stretch of autumn woodland where the reflections of white birch trunks danced in the water like black and white harlequins among the yellow leaves.

"We gotta camp here," said Alfonso, who has perfect intuitions, and Seraphine and I bowed to his word. A little promontory with the stones of an old fireplace already placed, a stretch of leaf mould for a bed: no resting place can be better.

"Seraphine," said I, for I am trying to teach her to occupy a woman's sphere, "you make the fire and get the blankets ready and cook supper, and Alfonso and I will walk to the Big Town, which is half as far on foot as by canoe, and get this famous permit."

"Yea, lord," said Seraphine, so we got her some dry birch sticks and left her.

Alfonso and I walked to the Big Town: we found it was ten miles. We found the boss in his parlor with the harmonium and the green velvet rocker. He was very serious about permits: he thought we must come around tomorrow.

"I should have," he said, "to write it all out. It's six lines."

"Six lines! To say we may go through the locks!"

"You have to say that you release the railroad from all responsibility if you get drowned."

The permit matter was still a mystery. But the boss assured us that if we would present ourselves in the flesh tomorrow, at a certain lock, the document should be waiting for us. In the meantime, he wished to know where we were camped, and we answered him meekly. The canal people govern by a sort of benevolent paternalism. They wish to know not only every mole that burrows along the banks, but every camper who sleeps above them. Then the tow boat gang for weeks afterwards discusses the route and the behavior of every canoe party.

A big raindrop splashed at our feet as Alfonso and I started home. We were walking through the lighted streets of a comfortable little town. Umbrellas were to be bought there, and night's lodgings. Be it said to Alfonso's credit that he never mentioned either of them. As for me, I was a camper.

"It's going to be great fun, Alfonso, to walk along the tow path in pitch darkness and not know whether the next step will plunge you on your nose into the canal."

"Yes," replied Alfonso.

I did plunge. Not my nose, but two knees.

"Isn't this ripping?"

"Yes," replied Alfonso.

"Are you wet, old man?"

"Yes."

There was something grim and laconic about Alfonso's yea. "It may be," I considered, "that I've taught him a bit too much Anglo-Saxon self control."

"Would you like to go into this store until the rain stops?"

"Yes," replied Alfonso.

We entered a general store which seemed to have risen out of the night.

"Ye're kinder mussed, ain't ye?" asked the postmaster who kept it.

"I guess," I told him, partly vanquished, "that I'll have to borrow a lantern to get home with."

The postmaster went on sorting mail.

"Can you lend me one?" I clinched the matter.

"No."

"Can you tell me where to get one?"

"No."

"Can you?" I asked a bystander.

"No."

"We're either ostracized," I told Alfonso, "or these natives have no bowels of mercy. I guess I'll try next door."

I got quite thoroughly drenched on my way next door, but it was long enough for me to meditate, "A dramatic appeal's the thing. These people can't believe I'm in trouble when I seem so business-like."

So when a woman opened a kitchen door on my draggled form I gasped, "I've come to ask for help. I can't get home. Can you lend me a lantern?"

"Why, bless your heart, come right in," said the woman. And I haven't decided yet whether it was because she was a woman or because I was dramatic that she was so kindly.

But Alfonso and I reached camp at nine o'clock and sat down in the six by three tent to eat cold bread and raisins with Seraphine before rolling over to sleep.

What variety there is on the canal! The next day was as brilliant as a Maxfield Parrish picture. We paddled through lots of woodland all flaming with color, where drifts of yellow leaves blew over the green water and settled on our heads and shoulders. And suddenly we would find ourselves nosing under a high stone wall, with a red woodbine trailing over it, like a corner of Venice.

I understand that the towns we went through have front yards, neat railway stations and automobile roads. But the canal passes only through back yards. There stand old stone farmhouses built before the Revolution, apple trees hang over the water, and flocks of geese go waddling to and fro. Corn fields stretch away uphill, and elms stand beautiful and solitary on the little knolls.

The permit was forthcoming and we went through four locks that day. I have never seen anything so ancient looking as the locks on the Morris and Essex Canal. The big black doors rise above you as if they belonged to some sort of dungeon.

"They must be oak," I said to Seraphine. "Huge timbers like that won't fit in my mind with any word but oak."

We asked each of the lock tenders who put us through. But we shouted our question down the wind as we plunged through the gates three or four times, before we got the answer.

"White oak. You don't get that kind no more."

I adore going through locks in a canoe. We steal up, so tiny, before the high beetling gates that shut off the canal. We shout, we wave our permit. Then, out on the little wooden platform above the gates, comes a veteran lock tender. He cranks an ancient rusty wheel, and slowly, to a sound of swirling water, the big gates swing open. The lock is just the size to fit a canal boat, but, at the bottom, twitching with the current between its mossy walls of old masonry, we feel most tiny and helpless.

The ancient tender closes the gates behind us and putters over to the far end of the lock where he cranks another rusty wheel. Far down under the water the little flood gates open, and the tide comes rushing in. Hold fast and keep her away from the walls, the back wash will throw us against them! How fast, how steadily we rise! It is like being on some giant chest which takes an enormous, steady breath and raises us indomitably, up and up, until the old moss-grown walls seem sinking at our sides and suddenly the blue sky looks into the slimy cavern and our heads are level with the green grass at the lock side.

"Some ladies is nervous in a canoe," says the lock tender. "Maybe you ain't that kind."

And he refuses to wave us farewell until he has been told where we came from and where we camped last night and whether we was the same parties that come last year.

"Be ye comin' back tomorrow?" asked one, and we affected a lofty indifference and refused to reveal our plans. But in this we did an unkindly thing. For the lock tender had planned to go away and dig potatoes, and had his plans much fluttered by being obliged to stay on the job and attend to the one craft of the month. After that, we carefully explained our plans to everybody so that they might dig potatoes and gossip with the neighbors until the last moment before our passage.

"I don't see why we never have to show the permit," said Seraphine.

In truth, after our labors in procuring that yellow document were once over, it very nearly passed from our minds. By some secret process the lock tenders seemed to have word of our advent: we generally found them nodding over their rusty wheels and ready to scold us for being late.

"I'll be along after ye in a minute," said one.

And we discovered that we had entered a succession of grades and that our ancient friend would have to trundle after us on the tow path for a mile or two, opening and shutting locks.

"This camp," said Seraphine that evening, "is a poacher's lair."

We had passed some delightfully desolate spots during the day, spots where the canal ran on a ridge between two valleys and one looked from the water down on brilliant woodlands obscured in blue mist. But, of course, that wasn't camping time. And now, at half past five, when the chill of evening is creeping on us and we want nothing so much as to "hear the birch logs burning," we seem to hear nothing but the screeching of Lackawanna trains and see nothing but villagers in derby hats hastening along the tow path to supper.

"It's a comfort," Seraphine finished, "that for a woman almost everything is an adventure. For a man, now, it would be nothing but a bore to camp in a New Jersey back yard with people stamping about on the other side of the fence. But for us it's a real deed of daring."

"You think you can handle the rustics, Seraphine?"

"Perfectly. That's one of the privileges of sex. We may not get much praise for the way we carry a canoe, but for persuading an irate farmer it seems to me that no one in the world has a better chance than we."

I have forgotten to mention that Seraphine is beautiful. Really strange that anything can be written about a woman in which that fact is immaterial. Seraphine is one of those fragile appealing blondes. But the fact is that in a khaki skirt and big boots, and with a sunburned nose, no one looks tougher than a fragile, appealing blonde.

"I think it's more better we go in and don't tell the farmer nothin'," said Alfonso.

"Child, you are right."

So we encamped in the poacher's lair, an alder swamp with a most delightful dump heap adjoining, whence we abstracted bushel baskets for kindling and pieces of rusty sheet iron to shield the fire. The farmers tramped beyond the stone wall and did not even see our smoke. We decided, after trying it, that a soft swamp was really no worse to sleep on than dry rocks.

"I think," said Alfonso the next day, "it rains."

Alfonso has lived all his life on the east side of New York, but he has an invincible peasant heritage. He is friendly with the sky. When, in the morning, Seraphine and I hastily pull up the dumb waiter to consult the morning paper about the weather, Alfonso merely squints up the air shaft and remarks blandly after consulting the square foot of sky which hides there. "It don't rain. That's all."

But when Alfonso says it rains, then it rains.

It rained. Slow drops at first, making circles in the leaden water, a vague blueness that tinged the bright foliage, and a whiteness in the sky.

"What lots of fun!" said Seraphine, putting on two extra coats and a pair of gloves.

"It rains all day," said Alfonso gloomily from the bow.

We paddled silently through a deserted country: dripping vines along the bank, slimy black roads with skidding automobiles, muddy tow path from which rustics stared at us in amazement.

"How awfully dry it is under that concrete bridge," murmured Seraphine in an impersonal tone.

Alfonso had relapsed into intense gloom. He never turned but merely remarked hopelessly, "It rains all day."

"I feel," I said, "that it would be quite entrancing to encamp under that concrete bridge and cook pork and cabbage. Pork and cabbage take all day anyway. It will give us a great deal of exertion."

A concrete bridge is a most delightful, a most spacious haven. Cuddled beneath the arch, there was a space of ground at least as big as a hall bedroom. Thickets of sumac grew all about and shaded us from the road and canal, and though the doctors' Fords and the bakers' carts and the touring cars of New Jersey rattled above our heads, nobody ever looked down to see three raggle taggle gypsies squatting about a blackened tin pot and feeding the fire with cedar twigs.

"Why not a night under a bridge, Clarissa?"

"It does seem better than the wild wet woods—if, indeed, there are any wild wet woods, for yonder seems to me to be a Lackawanna freight yard."

"It rains all night," said Alfonso.

An evening under a concrete bridge: what a delightful and spacious haven! Of course it was chilly when the fire died down, and one got drenched searching in the adjoining woodland for cedar twigs. Alfonso recited twice, "Aye, tear her tattered ensign down!" He got very warm with the gestures, but Seraphine and I seemed to know no verse but those about Celtic Twilight, which plunged us into deeper gloom.

"It can't be worse than the trenches," said Seraphine.

"It rains all night," said Alfonso.

There was a moment of solemn silence.

"Why," exclaimed Seraphine, "the weekend is over anyway. We shouldn't be really quitting if we—if we—took a Lackawanna train tonight."

A wild, brilliant light blazed in the eyes of Alfonso; he began energetically to fold up the tent.

"Aye, tear her tattered ensign down," he recommended. "It's more better we go home and cook macaroni."

But it was a glorious weekend.

It Can't Be Done

ANNA KALLAND

"Yes, we had gone up the river – in the good canoe *Ward Fifty*" *(Outing, 1923)*

"Two lone women up the Hudson River in a canoe! Sleeping on the banks where the railroads run – cooking your own grub for the tramps to eat! Gosh! You don't know when you are well off. The steamers will swamp you – it's awfully rough, anyway – and the barge crews! Why in the name of common sense don't you ship your canoe out to a lake somewhere and sleep at a hotel – if paddle you must!"

"Wouldn't see a sister of mine do it – that's all!"

When a man says that, further remarks are not in order. We made none, nor did we mention such small matters as a .38-caliber, mother-of-pearl handled and a beauty; a black jack and a nightstick lent by a friendly cop; a hypodermic syringe to be filled with plain water, but called vitriol (this last idea, however, was given us as being too Borgian).

(Excerpted from *Outing*, March 1923)

The smell of woodsmoke was still in our hair and fingers since our early breakfast on the Palisades, where we had stirred our gruel with a stick and broiled our bacon before the sun had lifted the mists from the waters, swearing by the tides, the winds, the sun, stars, and moon, that our next weekend should be three hundred miles long.

One fine morning in early September we headed out on the Hudson River in the good canoe *Ward Fifty,* hope of adventure paddling bow, hope of adventure paddling stern, a goodly supply of potatoes, bacon, Aunt Jemima, and Mocha and Java to feed it, oilskins and a tarpaulin to keep it dry. And the sharp-edged, newly sandpapered and varnished paddles reached out for more, always more of the muddy, oily river; a soft pat, a firm swish—and eighteen feet of Old Town slipped by all the old weekend landmarks.

As we sat in front of our own campfire, we scarcely offered a thought to patients, notes from night nurses saying that someone had "ceased to breathe," telephone bells, ambulance clangings, and ether vapors—all—all of them were buried in the sub-cellar of our consciousness.

We unrolled early the next morning and made haste to get started before the wind came up. We discovered a huge sign immediately below the canoe, which we had hauled up over the rocks to a place of safe keeping. It read, "Private Property. Keep Off." A watchman came by while we were turning our flapjacks.

"Can't you read?" he queried with a surly grin. Then he looked around, to the right and left and all about us. But there were no more.

"Why, yes—but that is ours—that sign. Don't you see?"

"The devil take ye," he growled and moved away.

"Score number one. He deserves a cup of coffee, but that would have been an anticlimax."

As we pushed out from the little cove, he had returned from his round and, leaning on the private property sign, he watched and, no doubt, wondered us out of sight.

The mists were hanging low over Tappan Zee, that wonderful cruising place for ghosts and goblins. As it closed in about us and our paddles plied silently in an oily sea, we expected any moment to sight the "storm-ship" that comes and goes, "flying swiftly before a wind which no one can feel," or the boat of Rambout Van Dam rowing forever and ever on these haunted waters, or the headless horseman riding toward Teller's Point along the Old Post Road.

But we reached Teller's Point all alone, mists and visions alike gone before a wind that had its own way with Haverstraw Bay. So this was Haver-

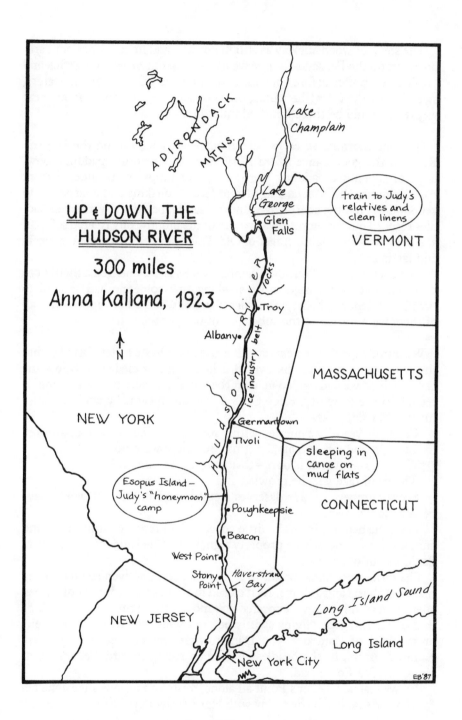

UP & DOWN THE
HUDSON RIVER

300 miles

Anna Kalland, 1923

↑
N

Lake
Champlain

Lake
George
Glen
Falls

train to Judy's
relatives and
clean linens

VERMONT

Troy

Albany

ice industry belt

MASSACHUSETTS

NEW YORK

Germantown

Tivoli

sleeping in
canoe on
mud flats

Esopus Island —
Judy's "honeymoon"
camp

Poughkeepsie

Beacon

CONNECTICUT

West Point

Stony
Point

Haverstraw
Bay

Long Island Sound

NEW JERSEY

Long Island

New York City

EB '87

straw Bay! We had heard many descriptions of it from other paddlers, but the reality outdid them all. It sluiced as much of itself as possible over our bow and sides, and all afternoon it was a game of hitting square, now tacking, now going straight before, taking advantage of lulls, always with a growing attachment to our ship that rode like a log, running away from the following sea, each try out egging us on to press her closer and closer.

With the wind there was a blistering sun, which tormented our faces and arms and backs as all that afternoon we paddled and paddled toward the Highlands. At Stony Point we had to give up. There was no passing thereof 'til the wind had died down.

So we beached *Ward Fifty* in a cove below the point and got ready for chow. The place seemed too near the railroad tracks for night camp, and, when the wind had died down, we pulled out, heading north, sparing as to speed and comments. We felt hurt all over, crosswise and lengthwise, each muscle fussing to find a position it had not tried and found wanting.

About an hour later we found ourselves half asleep, making camp on a small sandy beach on the west shore. No sooner had we rolled up than the trains began to thunder by, right over our heads. But we were too tired to move and dozed off fitfully, trying to find a spot on our anatomies that didn't call for help. Finally, when the milk cans began rattling overhead, we again took refuge on the river, which flowed like a silent protest between rumbling shores.

It must have been about five or six o'clock in the morning when the watchman of Iona Island saw a blue waif of a smoke trail skyward from an outpost of the island. There was a gruel pot trying to come to a boil. Gruel? Yes. That seemed to be the dish tacitly agreed upon as most becoming to our status of mind and flesh.

The watchman probably began worrying about his ammunition, for we saw him coming toward us in rapid strides, the white tail of his little dog bobbing up and down among the gray stones, like the tail of a rabbit. We made friends with the dog and attended to our gruel and oranges in an absorbed manner that precluded interruption. He allowed us to finish our breakfast and carefully watched our intentions as we slowly paddled upstream into the heart of the Highlands.

With one day of arduous labors behind us, every neuron on the jump from the night under the railroad track, our faces so blistered from the sun that it even hurt us to laugh, we felt totally out of place in these grand surroundings. But as we slowly forged ahead, we gradually forgot our various hurts, and the paddles again fell in of themselves as paddles should.

Late in the afternoon we saw the promontory of Beacon run into the side still waters that were beginning to take on shadows and evening tints.

Storm King, Old Crow's Nest, West Point, and Cold Springs had been duly marked off on our map, which was already aspiring to the oily appearance of a hospital deck of cards. We also marked off Pollopel's Island, once the dwelling place of a ghost, now inhabited by an ogre of an arsenal, creeping down to the water's edge. Looking at the architecture, we felt the ghost had shown its good taste in departing, and mentioned this in our marginal notes.

We made camp at Beacon in our most finished style. There was even a neat trench dug around the tent, which consisted of a tarpaulin tied to the canoe on one side, and belayed to stakes driven into the ground on the other. With the main house built, one of us got into shore togs (a skirt and sweater worn over the bathing suit) and went foraging, while the other built the kitchen and procured wood and water.

The night was clear, and we rolled up in front of the fire, outside of the tent, listening to the soft lapping of the waves on the beach, agreeing with Henry Hudson that "it is a good land to fall in with, and a pleasant land to see." We finally slept 'til the tide had come and gone and was coming again.

It looked like a promising day, but a wind came up, a wind which gathered into a storm as the day wore on. We marked our chart "Stormy Day at Beacon" and lay down on the rocks to enjoy it. The gray-green waves, topped with white, were racing toward us, breaking against the tall grasses, but where they struck the sun-built road across the waters, they played in all the colors of the shore. There was a little bit of yellow from the goldenrod, a little bit of red from the thornapple, a touch of violet and purple from the asters, silver from the willow trees – it was like an oriental mosaique on a background of delicate green.

That night we crept under our good ship, for it looked like rain, and before long, huge drops were tambourining on our roof, trickling, we hoped, into the waiting trench. Some did; others were of an inquisitive nature and wandered into wind-blown places, looking for knees and backs to slide downhill. But the ropes held and after we had wrapped our oilskins about the firewood, we returned once more to the tent, to be lulled away by the tides, the wind, and the dripping rains.

The next morning was clear and calm. We broke camp and stocked up with firewood and water. We hoped to make at least twenty miles that day, bringing us to about seventy miles from New York. We hailed the cantilever bridge at Poughkeepsie in the late afternoon and registered ourselves and *Ward Fifty* at the Yacht Club. The commodore treated us to much good advice, and a glowing description of a beautiful island a little farther upstream, an island where none but campers were allowed.

We swept under the bridge on a strong tide and pushed on, passing bend after bend. The sun had gone down on our search for the island, but the moonlight lay white over the wide reaches; the air was so filled with light that we seemed to be drinking it in with each breath. Our brains were visited by strange visions of islands created out of clouds and promontories and trees, rising in grotesque forms out of the all-pervading, illusory light.

The commodore had told us it was about five miles beyond Poughkeepsie, but we counted it nearer ten when our canoe finally took the sands of Esopus Island. It was all as he had said – and more. Near the landing place were three huge logs placed on end, with fresh balsam boughs, all turned down and ready. If we had found slippers and a dressing gown tossed across it, we should have been no more amazed. There was also a grate placed over bricks, which were still warm.

"Campers," we said, almost with one breath.

It was the handshake of experts in a life of give and take, connoting membership in a club as exclusive as it is delightful, although members but seldom meet.

After dinner we stretched out in front of the burning logs. Before us was a picture exquisitely framed and hung. We curled up in the corner thereof, where the signature of the artist should have been, and watched it, 'til the white light was gone and the stars were alone.

"This is where I am going to spend my honeymoon," said Judy.

"So," I inflected, somewhat incredulous, but as it was said in front of her mirror in the bright light of the following morning, there was no doubt that she meant it.

And yet, like the prophet among the junipers, we could not dwell forever among the balsams and, having left things as we found them, we set out in quest of a new port.

The green thing beneath us moved rhythmically and smoothly all day long. The sun was gradually changing our skins from a bourgeois lobster to a dull coppery red, which would have been quite artistic had it not been for the huge flakes of skin which persisted in coming off and dropping into everything. Yet we felt that we were arriving. Our appetites were all that we ever asked of our patients – and more: we supplemented our visits to grocery stores by calls at farm kitchens, leaving the money on the door sill and helping ourselves when the owners were away.

We paddled for a long time, the sun shining, the waters glistening, the miles slipping away. We passed Cruger's Island, where, according to Indian tradition, no one ever died; we paddled through North Bay where Fulton played with his "folly," and toward evening reached Tivoli of frivolous name and an excellent grocery store. It was twilight when we left Tivoli, and what we should have done was to look for a camping place then and there. But we didn't. We felt like moving on, and move on we did, 'til the shores seemed like long, undulating black masses, we ourselves a black mite moving between them.

The east shore was unfriendly for camping purposes and, near Germantown, we crossed to the west side of the river. We paddled on, waiting for the moon to light the way. Instead of the moon came black clouds, borne on a strong north wind, and all was not so well with us. We hugged the shore to keep out of the wind, looking for a possible camping place. But every desirable spot seemed occupied by workmen's shacks; what seemed an inviting sand beach proved to be a white cliff overhanging the river.

We crawled on and on, against the wind. It was a strange and sinister thing, this moving along on dark waters under a stormy, threatening sky. At times we seemed to be standing still; at others we shot forward or downhill with headlong speed; now the waters were choppy; again we struck a snag that set us worrying about the boat. Remembering our night under the railroad track, we were determined not to make asses of ourselves this time.

On toward midnight, having doubled back on our tracks, we tied up to an old float, and fell asleep in the bottom of the canoe, too tired to take bearings, too sleepy to care. We had paddled over forty miles that day, part of the time against a strong wind and tide. When I unfolded myself in the morning, Judy greeted me from the raft, where she had squatted in that attitude of a meditating oriental:

"See that shack—and that one?"

I looked, and seeing, beheld them both, close to our canoe. They were covered with black tarpaper and invisible at night. Tousled heads were now and then displayed at the open flaps, to be hastily withdrawn. The waters had receded, and we were beached on a mudflat reaching yards and yards away from the river.

But the Providence which is partial to women, children, and asses seemed to be with us, and so we took heart and began pushing our canoe through the mud, taking a photograph of our moorings as we went. We waded in mud to our knees, guiding her tenderly away from stones and wire and broken glass. She was a most particular, persnickety sort of a canoe; wouldn't even let us inside 'til all that mud had been washed off. Then we headed for the river, where a strong north wind made upstream progress impossible. We tacked across and camped out near North Germantown for the day and night.

It had not rained since the second night at Beacon; it was ideal summer weather, summer heat and mosquitoes gone with the dog days. The next day we passed through the ice industry belt. There were huge icehouses where the harvest had been stacked away during the winter season. Out they came, from the dark, damp places, crystalline blocks, travelling down the incline in pairs, acting like two good pals coming home of a Saturday night, melting into the waiting barge.

In the afternoon the towers and spires of Albany rose out of the river. We did not land, but made speed to reach a landing place before dark.

As it looked like rain, we tied our canoe to the piles under a pier and slept in the bottom of it. As if by some mysterious communication, we both awoke just in time to see the *Trojan* bear down upon us in the small hours of the morning, paddles going at full speed. A few more minutes, and we would have been smashed against the piles by the breakers. We got out from under in due time, and without a scratch. We proceeded leisurely upstream, and this time we didn't even blush at our asininity. We were beginning to think that our lives were charmed.

We should soon reach Troy and the first lock, where we had been told that no canoe was ever taken through by itself. Accordingly, we kept close to the fairway and were on the lookout for a possible tow. We finally marked a large barge, with her load waterline barely showing, as worthy of our attention: she was easy to board, she looked hospitable. We hailed the captain, who proved to be a French Canadian. No man ever walked a ship's plank more proud of his ship than he. To be sure, she was only a barge, but we had our weakness for our own *Ward Fifty* and understood.

Shortly before noon the whole float was locked through and we anchored near the west shore.

As this particular float was going no further that day, we shook hands and lifted ourselves and our belongings over the edge. We stopped at North Troy for provisions and paddled on our way, wondering how we might get through the next three locks, for the river seemed empty of craft going our way.

We arrived at the second lock at supper time. The lock superintendent was interviewed. No, of course not. A canoe could not be locked through alone! Perhaps there would be a float in the morning—perhaps not. No, there were no good camping places above—nor below for that matter.

This was encouraging. I slid down the pole leading from the locker wall to the little strip of shore below and reported the setback. We should have as much privacy on that beach as zoo animals—not even a chance for our September Morn bath; but we decided to stay, as there really was nothing else to do. It was, moreover, a lovely evening, and no unpleasant official on top of the wall could take it away.

No boats and no floats had been locked through up 'til nine o'clock the next morning. We became tired of waiting for boats to come and for men to change their minds and, having paddled our canoe over to the other side of the lock, we carried it to the top of the hill. The hill was steep and long and, as we appeared on the brow of it, a group of workmen came rushing to a man to take it away from us, babbling about "What a shame not to let a couple of poor women through!"

We did not feel exactly that way about ourselves, but it evidently pleased them to make Don Quixotes out of themselves, and we did not restrain them. Our keeper of locks had not expected this: when we had our canoe and trappings safely on the upper level, he sauntered over, with a half disdainful, half admiring air about his perfumed person that was as comical as his whole make-up. But he was very young and we forgave him.

The next lock was only a short distance away—after that was still another—and yet another. We had hoped to reach Lake George that evening, and there was no time to waste. The next warden of locks was not so young and, therefore, not so important. We told him what had transpired at his next door neighbor's. He seemed greatly amused and unconcernedly told us to paddle into his empty lock.

It was a strange sensation to see the heavy mitre gates close on our little craft; it seemed like a huge trench, with our little duckboard sticking to one side like a crab. The operator set the switches in the controller box, the valves of the feed culverts at the sides and bottom opened, and the whole trench was like a boiling cauldron. Just for a moment we had the sensation that someone was picking up coils of intestine inside of us and dropping them again. But, as we crawled up the wall crabwise and the waters had subsided, we let go of our horseshoe position and sat up like the braves we were.

The next lock was passed as easily and we now had a long stretch of slack water 'til we should reach the last. The scenery was changing. Woods and fields were closing in around us: there were cowbells and crowing cocks and meddlesome ducks. Chimneys, ice houses, and brickyards were gone; instead, there were silos and farmhouses where we could get eggs and milk that was still warm and tomatoes right off the porch railing.

We passed through the last lock again alone, having evidently broken an unwritten law in three out of five cases.

Having decided to take the train at Glens Falls to Lake George and then proceed on foot to make a midnight visit on Judy's relatives, we left *Ward Fifty* and our possessions in a friendly backyard.

We felt quite out of place on the train, among so many dressed-up people. Once away from the railroad, we took our shore clothes off and arrived, after a six-mile hike, at the house of Judy's aunts. It was 12:30 A.M. and there was a reception, where nightgowns and bathing suits were worn. We were told that we looked terrible. We knew that and demanded something to eat. Then there was a lot of business with soap and hot water, to make us feel equal to those large soft beds with hemstitched linen.

"Doesn't that feel good? After sleeping on the ground for so long!"

We did not wish to be impolite, but we were hot and restless the whole night, feeling stuffy in that large, airy room, with windows open and with wind blowing. Less than two weeks it had taken to rub off our painfully acquired civilization, and that vast sea of concrete called New York City seemed but an empty dream. We were ungrateful for almost everything except the automobile lift given us back to Glen Falls the next afternoon.

The last week it was a question of making good time, and yet we took no towing 'til the last Sunday. So all the week we paddled, our muscles getting harder and harder. And the passing show continued all up and down the mighty artery of the Empire State, supplying the wants of thousands, touching, it seemed, the remotest ends of the earth.

There was an unforgettable night when we had rolled up in the shadows of the Ontioras, talking softly in the light of a low moon of the legends of the Cloud Mountains. We had tied up to a float near a railroad junction, sleeping in the canoe as always, when we were uncertain of the locality. As we talked on and on, we became aware of a face grinning at us from the pier-head. Followed rapid consultations and call to arms, during which the iodine was upset over the tarpaulin. After that, silence, suspension and, finally, subdued laughter. For from that black pier-head floated a sweet, mellow voice:

Vide 'o mare quant' e bello!
Spira tantu sentimento . . .

We were being serenaded! Naples and Sorrento and the blue sea! Venice and the lagoons! Who says that romance is dead?

E tu dice: "I' parto, addio."

It was fresh and altogether lovely, almost golden—that voice. We listened 'til the last notes had died away and nothing was heard save the lapping of the waves against the boat. We waited for him to continue, this fellow who signaled trains by night, and whom men called a "Wop." But he slowly moved away, and we put away our weapons.

On the last Sunday morning we caught up with a large float above Haverstraw Bay and engaged passage, on account of a high wind and lack of time.

It was a family barge. There was piano music in the cabin and singing of hymns. Geraniums in tin cans dripped red in the little curtained windows. The barge was going under her own steam and had a prosperous air about her, as witnessed by white, clean dresses on the children, shirts and collars on the men, and a tantalizing odor from the galley. The youngsters, we were told, lived on the barge all summer, and went ashore in winter to attend school.

The barge moved on, carrying us nearer the end of the trip that "could not be done." We had been seeing the world in real truth; the moving human life all up and down the wide river, new discoveries at every bend; the poignant beauty of the blending of earth and sky and water, and we had been in the midst of it all, tasting the infinite delight of things as they are.

In the early evening we reluctantly pulled away from our float at Yonkers and slowly paddled across the river to home waters, leaving the barge on her way to Erie Basin and the river to its winds and tides.

Backyards of the Connecticut

CATHERINE REID

Catherine Reid, now of Deer Isle, Maine, spent many years involved in radical anti-nuclear and anti-military politics. "I grew up in an ecological background," she writes, "trained to be a birdwatcher by my grandmother and to be energy conserving by my environmentally aware parents. It took me a while to make the feminist connections. As I did, I wrote a great deal about feminism and non-violence and taught a course one semester on Eco-Feminism at Goddard College. A goal of mine is to live as consistently as possible with my sense both of the environment and of the responsibility we all share for consumption of natural resources. I no longer have to live quite so simply, however; I now have electricity, hot water, a telephone . . . and a sea kayak."

For several years she and Norma Kawecki offered workshops for women in canoeing, bicycling, rock climbing and backpacking. During this time they decided to paddle the entire length of their home river, the Connecticut.

May 24, 1978

What a relief to leave all the preparations, all our projects right where they stand—moving out of the cabin, readying for the Seabrook Action, organizing our summer workshops. It was a good winter, living in the little cabin without running water and electricity, proving that we could take care of ourselves and figuring out ways to earn a livelihood doing wilderness trips. But it's so easy to get burned out, it's important to do things for our own sanity. So now we are off on this trip for just the two of us.

We plan to paddle the whole Connecticut River from its headwaters in wild country up near the Canadian border to where it flows into busy Long Island Sound. Norma and I both grew up in western Massachusetts and it is the major river there, a life force pulsing down through New England. We know it isn't going to be an exotic trip, paddling a river so close

157

to home, but it feels like a primal thing to do, an adventure, and it feels real secretive to be down low on the river.

At the last minute our friend Annie decided to join us for half the trip and Leigh and Kathy agreed to transport us, staying on an extra day to shuttle us from lake to lake.

To really "do" the whole Connecticut River we felt we should canoe the length of each of the Connecticut Lakes, located up in northern New Hampshire. We paddled across Third Lake and then took off into the woods on foot, trying to locate the headwaters of the river. The going was slow—we were barefoot, the underbrush was thick, and there were frequent large patches of snow. Norma found a swamp that we decided was Fourth Lake (they seem to be numbered in reverse), and we turned back. Somewhere near there was the Canada-New Hampshire border.

Paddling back across Third Lake, we were aware of two loons drifting along the lake edge, silently watching us. Suddenly, Norma's body seemed to shout as she whispered wow! wow! this huge fish! It was a loon swimming under the canoe, the mottled black and yellow back looking like scales on a streamlined form.

We decided to stay at Moose Falls Campground and passed a young bull moose feeding by the roadside on the way to the campground. We didn't find the warden, but we pitched our tents anyway, ate a quick supper of cheese and crackers and trail mix, and headed down to Second Lake.

What a ride! The lake and the sky were the same sunset colors of pink and orange. We surprised a great blue heron, several ducks and a beaver. As it darkened the courtship activities of the loons became ever more inspired. Their crazy laughter rose in giddy swells. One would suddenly burst up and run across the water's surface with a great flailing and splashing. After he settled, they would resume calling, only to have an hysteric take off again.

The next morning, pulling the canoes out of First Lake, an official and steamy-looking man met us: the warden from Moose Falls, who wanted us to explain why we had skipped out without paying. He accepted our answers, and then informed us that the Game Warden, with our license plate number in hand, was also searching for us. What explanation did we have for the barbecued rabbit remains they found in a trash can near our tent site? With a lot of laughing we cleared it up. Winter (my Malamute puppy) had dragged back the remains and I had pegged them into the can. Besides, we emphasized, you want to argue with vegetarians? We paid our fees and parted on good terms.

Even this early in the spring, the water is too low to canoe between lakes, so the next stop was just below Beecher Falls. Then the truck and

Leigh and Kathy were off, and it feels like our trip has really begun. The lakes were beautiful, but doing them was a bit of a formality; the river, in comparison, feels small and wild and protected.

May 27

Yesterday we came about 20 miles. The puppy proved to be the most frustrated and frustrating. She was in and out of the canoe, sometimes falling off the bowplate, sometimes howling to be put on shore. As soon as we discovered that, contrary to popular myth, Malamutes can swim, we let her tire herself out paddling behind the canoe. When she was finally exhausted, she slept in Norma's canoe (Norma's turn to solo), and we rafted up while Norma fly fished.

We're all getting stronger and we each feel it paddling solo. Four would have been an easier number, but Annie's decision was pretty spontaneous. Fortunately, time doesn't matter on this trip. We have no final deadline that we have to keep. We're stopped now for a long noon break. Winter is sleeping off some frustration in the shade, Annie is painting, having just given me a breezy short haircut, and Norma is fishing and eating pickled eggs.

Yesterday we swam and bathed in the river, but I doubt we'll be able to do that much longer. I dread the arrival of Groveton: we've heard many tales about the pollution generated by the mills there, with graphic descriptions about the number of fish floating belly up.

We're seeing a delightful variety of birds as we paddle slowly though the different habitats. Mergansers persist in flying ahead of us, and we put them up again and again. Evenings, it's the thrush songs and the woodcock's aerial dance. Through the night we hear grouse drumming, and an occasional owl or loon. A surprising sight are the big yellow splashes on the muddy riverbanks that turn out to be great meetings of tiger swallowtail butterflies.

June 1

We met Norma's folks today in a perfectly timed noon rendezvous. There they were, friends, people we recognized, waving to us from a bridge. After a picnic and a visit, they helped us portage the Gilman Dam. The dam comes up fast, there are no warning signs for boaters, the river just drops over the top.

We're camped tonight alongside Moore Reservoir, a huge man-made lake where the river once cascaded through Fifteen Mile Falls, dropping 375 feet in those 15 miles. When the dam was built the falls disappeared and now we see stone walls coming out of the woods and going down into the lake – one of the remaining signs that this is all flooded farmland. The loons do seem to like it this way, though – they're calling back and forth this evening.

We woke to a gray and gusty day and paddled about four miles to Comerford Dam. Some of Annie's family – her mother, grandmother, sister, sister-in-law, and nephew – met us there. We quickly took advantage of their station wagon for the next two portages. With emptied canoes, and with Annie's sister paddling with her, we raced down the seven miles to McIndoe Falls Dam. They were letting water out of Comerford and it was a great stretch of whitewater: a powerful current pulled us through the high haystacks.

June 3

We spent much of the afternoon holed up in a steamy hot laundromat in Fairlee, Vermont. It poured hard all morning and we had gotten thoroughly drenched and chilled. We dried all our clothes, though they still didn't look too clean, and headed to a diner for sandwiches and pie. We left Winter on a leash outside, but she wasn't used to having us inaccessible and she complained in her wolf howl until a waitress found her a bone to chew on, much to the amusement of the diners.

The thought of returning to the wet and cold of the rain and the river made the idea of renting a room for the night real attractive. We tortured ourselves with images of clean sheets and soft dry beds. We went so far as to inquire at one tourist home, but the no dogs policy sent us packing. The sky cleared as we headed back for the river, and camping suddenly seemed most appropriate for the likes of us.

When we returned to the canoes, hastily tied up under the Oxford-Fairlee bridge, we found the Blue Hole had drifted under a culvert coming off the bridge. It was full of water and, worse yet, the tent had swollen up like a sponge. We started paddling with lots of pathetic laments and soon found a small point of land to camp on. It turned out to be a sweet little homestead – a small cabin, woodshed, guesthouse and garage, a covered bridge over a stream nearby – all grown over with weeds and grapevines and tall grasses. We spent a happy evening at that camp, making up stories about the people who once lived there.

The next day we rigged up ponchos and lazily sailed most of the miles. Annie was miserably sick and just slept on the bottom of the canoe; she blamed it on an overdose of town goodies – sugar, chocolate, caffeine.

June 6

A day meant for canoeing, but instead we're in transition. This is Annie's last day on the river and she's playing tunes on her dulcimer in a sad and nostalgic way. I have mixed feelings about her leaving. She's fun and easy to be with, but we'll travel faster with just one canoe, and oh, I do love being alone with Norma.

Robin should be here soon to pick us up and take us back to Montpelier to catch up on plans for the Seabrook Action and to deal with correspondence for our summer workshops. The caretaker of this campground recognized me from my trip on the Appalachian Trail and has cheerfully agreed to store our canoe while we're gone.

What a full day, what a change from the river pace. We caught up on news with Robin in the ride in the truck, and then visited people for hours, finally dropping him off and arriving at the familiar cabin about sundown. Everything glows in an intense spring green, and the mosquitoes are horrible.

June 7

All morning we "worked" (far different from paddling). I finished an article about the history of the river for the *Recorder* and Norma answered mail. It looks like most of our Alternatives for Women in the Environment workshops will go this summer. Then we sat through hours of meetings for the Seabrook Action. Norma and I both volunteered to be medical people, and offered the truck as a ambulance.

Plans for the Action escalate: over 150 people attended the meeting. A lot of enthusiasm is being generated for a mass civil disobedience. The plan is for an illegal occupation, for as long as people can stay. Camping out on the power plant's ground won't be too different from what Norma and I are doing already.

June 8

Back to the security of the river. If it hadn't been such a high to see the turnout yesterday, and all that momentum for a big civil disobedience, I would definitely have resented an interruption in the rhythm of this trip. But the trip and the action feel consistent — we're trying to live as self-sufficiently and as in touch with the environment as we can, and part of that way of life is helping to undo the nuclear power plants.

So now it's just the two of us, one puppy, one canoe.

June 10

After so much time researching the hazards of the proposed Seabrook Nuclear Power Plant, we both have a creepy feeling that we're so close to the Vernon Nuclear Power Plant. When we planned this trip, we were hoping to time our arrival here with a demonstration at the power plant, but it looks like that is going to happen later.

Huge carp love the warmer waters slowed down by the dam. When they roil the shallows, they look like the backs and tails of giant serpents. Frequently they thump the sides of the canoe, and Winter anxiously dashes back and forth, rocking the canoe in her efforts to see what they are doing.

We had a ferocious headwind all day. If we hadn't committed ourselves to seeing family in Greenfield and Gill, we would've quit. We portaged the Vernon Dam, watching people fish for carp, "just for the hell of it," said one older man. Then the wind came up. Lots of motorboats were on the water, too, this Sunday, and their wakes, combined with the high wind-whipped haystacks, made for much smacking and the need to be constantly alert.

June 15

Yesterday, Norma called the Holyoke Power Company and they portaged us around the dam. We were pissed when we realized that by being picked up at the marina, as the guidebook encourages, we were missing about five miles of the river, including the stretch by Smith's Ferry where dinosaur tracks have been found.

The next section of river deserves the expression, "too thick to drink, too thin to walk on." It's a technicolor eyesore, the Holyoke section, with dyes and foul smells pouring straight out of culverts into the river.

It's an intriguing and slightly bizarre feeling that we can pass so quietly through these cities. Down low on the water, not only are we protected from the urban sounds and some visual assaults, we're not noticed. The highlight of the day was the canal around Enfield Dam: it was like canoeing through someone's secret garden. It was sunset, so the waters were even more still, the colors more dramatic. All kinds of plants clung to the ledges above us, dangling down in leafy clumps; we were in an insulated world, protected against the close urban sprawl.

We've had some good vantage points for looking at old and new Connecticut. A prejudice of mine shows: I'm surprised there is so much farmland. We were paddling along, shirtless, in the morning, passing miles of tobacco farms and planted fields, when Hartford was suddenly in front of us. The riverbank was crowded, but not with people. We saw scarcely any dwellings, just bridges, highways, industries and refuse. The city had long ago turned its back to the river. We did see some remnants of former boat travel, including a huge flatboat being used as a dock and a big barge sunk in Hartford's port.

In the afternoon we passed Rocky Hill Ferry, the oldest continuously operating ferry in the country. Since 1655 it's been driven by pole, paddle, horse and steam. Currently, a tug pulls it. Cost: 25 cents for a car and a driver, 5 cents each additional passenger.

We headed down to Wilcox Island, through a stinky pink spill from a shore pipe, but the island was just above the Portland Bridge and too loud for our country nerves. So we continued paddling to sunset and found a perfect sandy beach. Lots of fireflies light up the campsite and Winter dances among them.

June 16–17

A sadness settles over us: our last days of canoeing. We could continue for weeks at this steady, comfortable pace. We're lunching now below the Haddam Atomic Plant. (Is it safe to breathe? to eat?)

We stopped in Haddam at the Goodspeed Opera House, beached our tiny canoe next to a huge ferry, and bought a few beers. A tremendous Texaco freighter headed upstream; we began to feel like we were on the wrong river.

The tide and wind changed, both coming against us. The beer didn't stick by Norma as we maneuvered in the rough chop. When we encountered another ferry and I (in the stern) refused to head for shore as she demanded, she blasted me with panicked insults. Surprise! It was fun riding the waves. I was off the hook and she cried in relief.

Gillette Castle looked tempting, perched high above the river, so we stopped for a tour. William Gillette, the actor who gave Sherlock Holmes his stereotyped image, had the drippy-stone fortress built in 1919. The caretaker informed us that we couldn't camp at Selden Neck, where we were headed, and somehow got permission for us to stay at Gillette State Park. (Little did he know how invisible we are on the river, and what kinds of campsites we had previously found for ourselves.)

From there we called home to arrange the pickup. The people whose phone we used were impressed and interested: "What? All by yourselves? No men?"

The last night on the river felt scrambled and disorganized. Norma was up and down in the night, following noises. Winter kept racing by the tent, her tags jangling. Finally I got up with a flashlight and saw that she'd treed some furry critter. Eventually, exhaustion got us all and we slept.

We embarked late in the morning, wanting to coordinate our meeting with my brother. I'm sure the treed raccoon was glad to see us go. Quickly, the river life was being left behind us. The sky filled in gray and the air was damp on a south wind. We caught the tide as it was turning, and rode out with it towards the sea. We saw increasing numbers of swans, egrets and cormorants and, unfortunately, ever more boats on the water.

Rounding Saybrook Point put us on the ocean, counting down the miles, hustling in and around the marinas and dock pilings and coves, angling into the steep wakes from cabin cruisers. We tried not to think about the trip being done, we just headed for the lighthouse. Doug appeared in the big green truck as we pulled out the canoe. He greeted us as though we'd really accomplished something. It helped; we both went on automatic as we emptied the canoe into the truck. It was over.

Not a Vacation: Mississippi River Notes

MARSHA BERRY

In the fall of 1978 Marsha Berry and Janet Dalgleish, two Minnesota school teachers restless with their lives, canoed the entire Mississippi River. They started at the northern Minnesota headwaters in August, took their time on the river, and arrived in November at the Gulf of Mexico. Actually, Marsha says, they gave a year of their lives to the trip—four months of preparation, four months on the river, and another four months of sharing their trip through slide programs in schools and old people's homes, and trying to re-adapt to city living. She now looks back on the trip as "a starting point, a place where I learned how important journeys are in my life," and a start toward new career directions. In the winter of 1987 Marsha talked with Barbara Wieser about her experiences on the Mississippi.

When I decided to do the Mississippi trip, I had been a teacher of the hearing impaired in Minneapolis for six years. My roommate, Janet Dalgleish, had been teaching for three years. We both had taught long enough to be bored, but we weren't sure if we wanted administrative positions or to move on to something else. I considered teaching overseas; Janet began looking at clown school. I knew I needed to shake myself up in some way, to do something really different.

Then, in the spring of 1978, Janet and I went to a slide show two guys did about their trip down the whole length of the Mississippi River. When we walked out, we looked at each other and said, "Let's do it!" I knew this was it exactly: there would be time to think, to be outside, and to be free from the daily responsibilities of a job.

I had been fascinated by the Mississippi since I was a child in Washington, D.C., hearing the phrase "west of the Mississippi" on T.V. What *was* west of the Mississippi, I wondered. When I moved to the Twin Cities, I spent time walking along the river, thinking about it, but I hadn't done much travelling on it at all.

In fact, neither Janet nor I had done any long trips. We both had done a lot of canoeing as kids. I had done some backpacking, and had a goal of someday hiking the Appalachian Trail, but I thought that was something I could do when I was fifty or sixty. The Mississippi trip seemed like the right thing for me to do now.

We worried about leaving the security of our teaching jobs, worried about what kind of jobs we could come back to. I knew I could stay with teaching, make money, and live comfortably, but I was more afraid of being bored, of getting really fried at my work. I knew I would never be effective that way. Over the long haul, avoiding that burn-out was more important to me than worrying about job security. However, we both did take summer school jobs before we left on the trip, even though we would have preferred spending all summer getting ready. Fear of needing extra money drove us to that.

When we told our families about the trip, both of our mothers were absolutely horrified. "Something is going to happen." Our fathers worried about our leaving those cush teaching jobs. But both sets of parents changed their tune and were really impressed once the trip got going and they realized we were going to get publicity out of it.

Friends had varying reactions. Everyone was supportive, but some were more hesitant than others. Some people that Janet was teaching with got so excited about the trip that they flew to New Orleans and spent Thanksgiving weekend with us. These weren't people that we knew particularly well, but they treated us the whole weekend. They were just ecstatic about somehow participating. That was the feeling that I got from a lot of people—that we fulfilled people's dreams and if they could participate in any way with us, they would.

Preparing for the trip was like a second job. It ended up taking about four months. We would go to school and teach, then meet at the apartment to work on the trip. I might be on the phone all afternoon, while Janet would be out scrounging up equipment and sponsors. Grumman Canoe ended up sponsoring us and we did a lot of promotion for them—slide shows, TV, all that stuff.

We spent a lot of time talking to folks from the Army Corps of Engineers because the Mississippi River south of the Twin Cities is in their jurisdiction. We asked about the locks and dams and about the maps so we would know what to look for. North of the Twin Cities the Mississippi River is in the Minnesota Department of Natural Resources jurisdiction, so we also talked with them.

One of the neat things that came from researching the river was that we got hooked up with people from the Freshwater Biological Institute in Navarre, Minnesota, which is doing a lot of the freshwater quality research. They had been doing some tests on the Mississippi, but what they needed from us was a totally unscientific viewpoint. They wanted us to say, "Oh, we're going to camp here tonight," grab a bottle of water from the river, not looking for anything, and perform four simple swimming pool-type tests. We tested for nitrates, phosphates, dissolved oxygen, and the pH of the water. We would send them postcards with the exact mileage of where we had taken the water—there are mile markers all down the river. When we came back, Janet wrote an article on what the river was like from our point of view and the Institute wrote the scientific part. That data has been used quite a bit.

We also talked to canoeists who had paddled the entire river. There was a big thing about doing the trip as fast as possible, but that just wasn't our objective. We planned to spend four months. We had some general time goals in mind—otherwise we would have still been in Lake Itasca in December—but we never thought of it as any kind of race against time.

We started the trip August 1st and finished in Louisiana on December 1st. We decided to leave in August because in the spring the water is high, and the river is dangerous. The entire trip was 2,552 miles. Instead of trying to average a certain number of miles per day, we looked at the river in sections: Lake Itasca to the Twin Cities, the Twin Cities to St. Louis, St. Louis to New Orleans, and then New Orleans to the end. We knew we had to be in each city at a certain time, and that helped us decide how much travelling we wanted to do every day.

The river changed so much. Above the Twin Cities, it's a small, recreational river. It began as a pretty stream bordered by asters and Joe Pye weed. Deer, beaver and bluebirds were with us the first days—one afternoon a bear swam across just ahead of us. Occasionally there were rapids and riffles; sometimes we had to portage around power company or paper mill dams.

Once we hit the Twin Cities, we had to take into account the opening and closing of the locks and dams. The first time we went through a lock we were so scared, we thought we were going to be dead for sure. Janet started putting on her shoes and socks, and I dug out a fresh t-shirt. You know how your mother says to wear clean underwear, just in case. . . . But once we actually were inside those cement walls, it was no trouble at all. Then word spread down through the system that we were coming, and all the people were friendly and helpful.

South of the Twin Cities, you can't paddle along the edge of the river because the Army Corps of Engineers has built wing dams to channel the river. These wing dams go out perpendicular to the current; sand gets caught behind them and the water channels out into the middle. The horror stories of the river are about boats getting caught on the wing dams, so we paddled out into the center of the river and listened for the barges. Sometimes we had to get off the water to avoid barge traffic. Those tows could move 36 barges—six long and six across—and when they came up the river and turned, it was whitewater city. Mostly they were real easy to spot—they are very noisy—and we had to be well off the water before they reached us. The barge captains got to know us after a while, and they'd toot, and all the guys would come out on deck and wave. We got to know which companies the different colored barges belonged to. We wanted to put the canoe on one and ride, just to see what it was like, but we never got to.

Paddling through the big cities created other problems. There wasn't just traffic going up and down the river, but also across the river, and people weren't watching out for a canoe. St. Louis was the worst—it had a lot of commercial traffic. After thinking about it for a long time, we decided not to paddle through St. Louis because there the river is cemented in like a large canal. If we had to get out, there would be no place to go. So we took out at Portage des Sioux, and put in again at the Arch. We paddled only about four hours south of St. Louis, camped on a wooded island, and the next morning, we saw a red fox. That quickly we got out of the city and back into what felt like a wilderness area.

The entire trip was an odd combination of wilderness and civilization. We never really thought of it as a wilderness trip, but along the whole length of the river, there were places where we would find beaver and see deer. And then we would come to a big city. Trying to move in and out of both worlds sometimes confused us.

South of St. Louis there are no more locks and dams and the river becomes much bigger and more commercial and is contained by levees and revetments. The levees are sand and dirt walls ten, twelve feet or even higher. The revetments are made out of street-size concrete blocks that are piled up on the levees creating huge walls. We would camp out on the sandbars and be alone—people don't use the river for recreation down there.

As the Mississippi River got larger and more and more rivers poured into it, we expected it to become increasingly polluted, but that wasn't the case. In some places the river seemed polluted and in others it felt clean. Above the Twin Cities where the river is very clear you can imagine that it is clean, but you know small towns are dumping into it. Where the river was muddy, it didn't necessarily feel dirty to me—big cities are almost cleaner than small towns because they've worked at cleaning up their sewage. We never drank the river water but we saw people doing it, all the way down in Louisiana.

We only saw one really bad landfill spilling into the river. I was so up for Hannibal because of reading Mark Twain, but as we came around the bend at Hannibal there was this dump—washing machines, tires, old cars—going right down into the river. It was awful.

When we talked to people in the small towns about the polluted condition of the river, they pretty much seemed to accept it. Older people would tell us stories of swimming in the river as kids, about the fish they used to catch. There was one hopeful sign that the river is being cleaned up. A naturalist told us that there had been a hatch of mayflies in Iowa, the first in 25 years. Mayflies don't hatch unless there is pristine water.

We took Mark Twain's *Life on the Mississippi* with us, and would read parts of it as we travelled. Because we were right on the river and travelled slowly, we could often tell exactly where Twain was referring to and could get a sense of the history of the river. We could see why the communities of Native Americans would build way up on the bluffs—of course, where else would you build your burial mounds but up on the bluffs with those wonderful views.

We liked to see how the river has changed through time. South of the Twin Cities are huge rock bluffs on the outside bends, carved out in glacial times. In New Madrid, Missouri, the river once ended and dropped 200 feet into the ocean. Driving down the river road you would never notice that spot, but there are big columns of limestone in the river which create huge whirlpools and you can see how the land changes with the faultline there.

The river used to jump channels a lot, too, particularly in the South as it neared New Orleans. Today there is a whole industry of containing the river, though sometimes we chuckled at the river trickling through the re-vetments, knowing that the Army Corps can't quite do it. . . .

I was in awe of the river before I went, and I was really in awe of it when I got done. But meeting people also became a major focus of the trip. A lot of people travel from the Twin Cities to New Orleans on big houseboats, but they don't stop in the little towns and talk to people very much. Talking to people and finding out how they felt about the river as we went along became one of the purposes of the trip. I hadn't had the skill of just going up to anyone and chit-chatting—my family didn't do that. But Janet would just engage people so that we constantly had people talking to us. I started enjoying small talk more than I ever thought I would.

What surprised me the most was not so much how friendly people were, but how interested they were in us, and how generous. We kept running into other teachers – I don't know if it was fate or what. In southern Iowa where we were having real trouble finding a place to camp, we came to a house right on the river and asked to camp in the yard. The owner was an eighth-grade teacher who had to go back to school for a PTA meeting, but he told us, "Here's a key to my house. There are towels, take a shower, whatever you want." People were really nice like that.

There were the women we met at a laundromat in Greenville, Mississippi. In laundromats, we would wear our bathing suits and then just strip down. So there we were, taking off our clothes, when this woman came over and asked us what we were doing. She owned the laundromat and went next door to get her sister and started telling us their story. They grew up in a huge, poor, fatherless family outside of Greenville. Both had married drunkards, and had tons of kids. One day they decided they didn't want to live that way so they moved into Greenville and bought the laundromat together. They never went back and don't care what their husbands are doing. They let us wash our clothes for free.

Most of the time, though, we found that men responded to us more positively than women. One of the disappointments of the trip was our lack of contact with women. Some of the women in small towns were leery of what we were doing, and weren't quite as willing to talk to us.

We met mostly men right along the river – men working barges, ferryboats, locks and dams. They understood our fascination with the river and were very generous and willing to help out. It was hard to find places to camp in Louisiana so one night outside of Baton Rouge we pulled up to a place where we knew the towboat guys come, hoping we could put up our tent in the parking lot. They not only let us, but invited us to a huge shrimp dinner. Then another towboat pulled up and invited us to dinner. We didn't know quite what to say, but there was an obvious competition going on about who was to host the girls. So we ate again. The next morning, the first towboat crew came over at 6 A.M. and fed us a pancake breakfast. I don't think we ate for three days after that.

People were so generous. It was incredible. They constantly gave us things – dry plastic bags, fresh garden vegetables. We were invited to a dance and a family reunion. A man came over to our camp one night and started telling us about how his life was dead-ended. He thought what we were doing was wonderful, so he gave us two dollars and told us to buy a catfish dinner and enjoy our freedom.

We did have some pretty funny things happen. I'm 5'1" and Janet is shorter than I. By the time we were in southern Illinois and had been on the water for two months we were really tanned. We also had gotten real short haircuts. About nine one morning, mid-October, we were walking

170

through town and a truant officer chased us down. I was 30 and Janet was 25, and it was all we could do to convince him that we didn't need to be in school!

People constantly asked, "Do you have a gun? Are you worried?" That happens a lot when I travel with women. We certainly thought about meeting people on the river. I had done enough camping, both by myself and as the adult in charge of Girl Scouts, to know there are places where you have to be careful. Coming through big cities it would probably not be smart just to camp on the riverbank.

Since we were sponsored by Grumman Canoe, we got lots of local news-paper coverage. In fact, by the time we got as far as St. Louis we were big stuff—people had talked about us up and down the river, read about what we were doing. But we made an arrangement with Grumman that no pub-licity would precede us to a town and that they would wait four days after we left before putting out any publicity. We just didn't want word to get out that we were there. We ended up having no real trouble, but I do think it was good that we took those precautions.

As we met people along the river, it seemed they were just doing their thing and we were doing ours. The ones who were the most *impressed* were the men who wrote sports columns. Our least favorite was the man in Memphis who wrote about the "two girls who gave the Mississippi a pad-dling."

We had a contract with an outdoor magazine to write a story for them, but I just couldn't do it. They would call me up and say, "Didn't you tip over or have anything dangerous happen?" Well, we didn't and we just never approached the trip that way. I didn't know how to write in that ad-venture mentality.

The Mississippi trip wasn't just a vacation, it really became a lifestyle. What we were doing was affecting everything in our lives, though I don't think we had any idea of the impact until we came back and tried to live in the city again. Janet went bonkers, just went nuts living in four walls. And driving—it took weeks before I wanted to drive a car—you go so fast. And there were always demands—people wanting me to be somewhere at a cer-tain time. We had been so used to calling the shots—we'll do it when we damn well please, thank you very much! It was hard to get back to other people telling me what I could do. I could do anything I want—I'd been on the river for four months!

The Mississippi trip has continued to influence my life. For one thing, it started me doing other long journeys. In 1983, I took a six week trip on the

Back River in the Northwest Territories with three other women. I didn't have the same feelings with the Back. We didn't see it from the very beginning so I never got that sense of growing with the river. The Back didn't change as much, wasn't as dramatic as I felt the Mississippi had been. And the whitewater was so consuming, so incredible at some points that it was hard to appreciate other aspects of the river. Sometimes I'd just realize, "We're all still alive, we made it." The Back River was more a vacation. I made the trip in the summer and I was still teaching, and I knew I was going back to a teaching job.

Then in 1985 I did a month-long backpack trip on the John Muir Trail in California. Being in the mountains felt so civilized compared to the Mississippi or the Back. I felt like I was walking a trail where people had always walked, and we saw people constantly.

The Mississippi still feels like the most important trip I've ever done. It showed me that I could set a goal, make all the preparations, and attain that goal. The Back was a much more challenging river; I certainly felt I was more in danger on that river than I ever was on the Mississippi. The backpack trip was physically harder—the altitudes and carrying a heavy pack. I was tired a whole lot more. But with those two trips I already knew that I could do what I set out to do. Whereas on the Mississippi there was always that sort of anticipation—"Yes, we *said* we're going to do this. . . ." Then, wow, we made it to the Twin Cities and then we got to St. Louis, and then to New Orleans. Plans went like we wanted them to, or they didn't, but we kept figuring out what we needed to do.

More than anything, the Mississippi trip made me very aware that one line I'd been handed as a good middle class person is not true—that if you don't continue in your profession terrible things will befall you. I learned that I could take a year off and use the time to figure out what I *really* wanted. I ended up going back to teaching in the same school system for four more years, but ultimately the trip made me a lot more willing to make a job change. If I hadn't taken a break at that point, I think I would still be plodding along doing the same things.

The trip made me aware that there are other aspects of teaching. I had always known I wanted to be a teacher, but I assumed the only way to do that was in a classroom. Now I became aware that I was also a teacher when I was a camp counselor, or when I was talking to people along the way and doing slide shows afterward. For three summers after the trip I worked guiding in Minnesota and Ontario for Woodswomen. I don't know if guiding is something I would have thought I could do before the Mississippi. And then when I got my present job at an outdoor store, I realized a salesperson could be a teacher, too. The trip broadened a lot of my horizons. It showed me the falseness of the idea that you had to stick to a career plan *or else.* I don't know what the "or else" is, but it has never happened.

PART FOUR:
The Very Poetry of Travel

Ojibwe women gathering wild rice, Leech Lake, Minnesota, 1896 (E. H. Bromley)

Marie Sarkipato Ericson, Wilderness guide on Big Lake, Minnesota, 1930s

"*A well-known Canadian author, writing of canoeing, gives women the following sphere: 'In the canoe the paddler is at the stern, facing the way he would go. The passenger looks at him instead of at the changing landscape. There is nothing to divert her attention from the skillful fashion in which he wields his paddle. Her business is solely to talk to him, or listen to him, and let him take her whither he will. It is exactly the arrangement which all men, and most women, probably, prefer. It even partakes of an ordinance of nature.' Fortunately, this ordinance is not of nature's making; the great, good mother was never known to encourage such a thing in all her long, sweet life.*"

Leslie Glendower Peabody, "The Canoe and the Woman," *Outing,* 1901

Canoing Ladies: An Introduction

JUDITH NIEMI

About 1900 there was a great burst in the popularity of canoeing as a sport, in the circles whose doings are noticed in print. Among the people with the leisure to practice canoeing simply for recreation, wilderness was beginning to be an attractive idea, and fitness was valued. Suddenly magazines were full of articles on how to canoe, where to canoe, why everyone should canoe. Canoeing became quite fashionable, for ladies as well as gentlemen. Silver cigarette cases were made with silver ladies in high-necked dresses paddling across the lid; canoe manufacturers' catalogs often pictured women paddling together.

Unknown canoeist, probably 1910–1920

175

Ladies insisted on being allowed into the boat clubs, which really spoiled the drinking scene, one approving outdoor writer noted, since men could hardly be permitted to imbibe if unaccompanied ladies were present. The ladies, however, weren't hanging around the club as spectators, but enthusiastically out on the water, "handling the craft as well as their brothers." (Leonidas Hubbard, "Paddling Your Own Canoe," *Outing* magazine, 1904.) And they wrote articles encouraging other women to take up this terrific sport. Some of them were awful snobs about it.

"Everything about the canoe is light, compact, graceful, delicate, dainty, serviceable – that is to say, thoroughbred. The canoe is the biggest little boat in all the world. It has a great heart, a thoroughbred soul." So wrote Mrs. Emerson Hough in "Canoes Seem Made for Girls" (*Ladies Home Journal*, 1915). And canoeing provided a great setting for a woman's charms. Not so long before, a lady was supposed to look pale and wan – now athletic chic was in, and naturalness was the thing. Mrs. Hough advises that a canoeing costume "is not more than will mitigate the process of sunburn. The glory of a girl is in her tan. Indeed this is the most pictorial of all sports, as any wise woman will not be slow to realize."

That's one of the worlds that Leslie Peabody and Isobel Knowles in this chapter lived in. Even Ms. Peabody, certainly an uppity advocate of women's equal rights in a canoe, notes "parenthetically," that canoeing puts a woman "without artifice, in a charming position. Kneeling at either end of the canoe she can be a veritable princess of the azure hour."

But the remarkable thing is how far some of these princesses went beyond the world of the boat clubs. Their enthusiasm is boundless, the list of places Ms. Peabody and Ms. Knowles paddled is impressive – and where *did* Isobel Knowles learn the whitewater and camping skills she writes about rather nonchalantly? When a lady says things like, "How sweet it is in the languishing days of summer to be removed from the strident noises of the city and the brutal struggle of its life," it can be hard to remember that she's not writing about a pleasant stay at an Adirondacks resort. She's talking about a two-week canoe trip on a wilderness river, paddling a stout twenty to thirty miles a day.

Clearly, the rather tame canoeing of the canoe clubs was "the parent of a more virile offspring," as Leonidas Hubbard had written; "canoeing with parasol does lead one to the sort that the voyageur knows." But it can take sharp eyes to find the women in the canoeing picture, even when you know they are there. Hubbard's own adored wife travelled with him on the wilderness Missinaibi, but is barely mentioned in his travel stories, except briefly as "Madam," whose "latent explorer spirit" was fired. She doesn't appear in any photographs and is not credited when she's the photographer. (Mrs. Hubbard's later travels, when her no-longer-latent explorer spirit took her to Labrador, are described in the last story of this chapter.) Historian Reuben Gold Thwaites, a scholar and energetic vacation canoeist, advised readers to go "with your best friend as messmate and explore the nearest river from source to mouth." His pal and messmate was his wife Jessie, but in his book (*Historic Waterways: Six Hundred Miles of Canoeing Down the Rock, Fox and Wisconsin Rivers,* 1890) she appears only as "W—." Together they muscled a canoe under 21 barbed-wire fences one day on the Catfish, and zipped through fast water with bystanders on shore yelling and cheering. Probably there were a number of other fun-loving canoeing couples like the Thwaites, other independent women like Isobel Knowles. But if it was unladylike to go dragging canoes around in the muck, it would be even more unladylike to say so in print, to put oneself forward and have one's name or photograph in public. (Endless travel books to much more socially acceptable destinations were signed only "By a Lady.")

But the growing popularity of canoeing was bound to bring changes, a new freedom. There was the matter of clothing. Just as early lady mountaineers were warning others of the foolishness of endangering one's life with wide skirts and corsets, Leslie Peabody tells women to feel the full stretch of their muscles and throw away "the trammels of conventionality"—stays, tight waists, and patent leather shoes. The women who felt they had to stick to long skirts somehow managed to keep them out of the mud of portage trails, but dresses were on the way out. Women bicyclists had smoothed the way by popularizing bloomers (and scandalizing part of the public). New articles on how to improvise an appropriate outfit for the outdoor life (including some by Kathrene Pinkerton, who appears in Chapter Two), usually recommended knickers or riding breeches. "No woman knows, until she tries it, what a relief it is to travel in the woods without a skirt and without big baggy bloomers to catch on everything." (Rena Phillips, in *Outing,* 1904.)

And many of the canoeing women enjoyed feeling a bit rebellious. They liked to refer to "gypsy blood" and to Indian ways of doing things. It was a period when the supposedly "vanishing" people were much romanticized, and every Indian a writer knew was called a "princess" or "chief." Still, some of the women who did travel with or among Indians (like Mrs. Hubbard or Kathrene Pinkerton) found in their life much that they genuinely admired and enjoyed. And when Leslie Peabody sees a canoe and writes, "All the Indian in me went out to meet it," it's a sign of how much the canoe represented to them not just a fashionable sport but an escape from fashion, a way out of the bonds of their own civilization.

Toward the Twenties, the canoe craze wore down, at least in terms of media attention, although probably there were just as many people canoeing as ever. Several articles in this chapter suggest the ways that women went on learning to love canoeing and the wilderness – family tradition of outdoor life; best friends; girls' camps, which often encouraged more competence in women than the society at large valued. And the "Women's Sphere," as they used to say, was not just as canoeing companion, but as independent adventurers and as guides and teachers. I spent a fine afternoon once, surrounded by doilies and braided rugs in a Lake Superior cabin, listening to two old women, sisters, reminisce and correct each other in the gentle way of old companions: "No, dear, that wasn't Hanson Portage, that was the Cherry Lake Portage, by the swamp – *you* remember." They had learned canoeing as children, in a family of settlers and explorers, and had spent several decades introducing young nieces and nephews and grandnephews and Eagle Scouts to the canoe country, one of the many women-run informal canoe schools around the country.

An interesting question to consider in most of the stories in this chapter is at what point a woman canoeist is accused of Going Too Far. Mrs. Hough in 1915, who found the canoe such an elegant thoroughbred craft, drew the line at whitewater. "Canoe stunts," she sniffed, "are better left to the heroines of fiction, who do not need to come back to superintend anything so prosaic as a dinner." Kathrene Pinkerton advised women (at least *other* women) to stay in the bow position for years. There are girls' camps that send children on quite adventurous trips, but hire only male canoe counselors; apparently it might be crossing some line to have female "role models," who would suggest that it was OK to go on doing canoe trips in adulthood. Ruth Schellberg's article presents an interesting switch – usually women do a lot more than ever appears in print, but in this case a magazine photographer wanted to make Ruth and her girls *appear* terribly competent and adventurous, but they were prevented from actually doing much.

The women here don't write too much about the complex mixture of admiration, hostility, envy and disbelief with which women canoeists have sometimes been greeted. They say very little about how they felt about it, just as they generally don't say much about their personal lives. We're just happy that nothing stopped them from doing the trips that they wanted, and that a few of them have given us some written record of their experiences.

The Canoe and the Woman

LESLIE GLENDOWER PEABODY

In the changing iridescence of early morning on the edge of a Florida bayou, I came upon my first canoe. All the Indian in me went out to meet it and the beguiling shape of the thing took complete possession of me. If you are to become a canoe enthusiast this subtle taking hold of you by the little princess of boats will be a thing beyond power of resistance, the fever will burn on, a fever from which there are no immunes. The canoe that I found waiting for me was painted a bright blue; a double-bladed paddle lay along the bottom – this and the fact that I was in my bathing suit was proof enough that the fairy finger pointed auspiciously. The idea of ownership was a technical point of butterfly importance.

My paddling that morning was unscientific and precarious, but I soon learned that the only thing a canoe really demands of you is a nice sense of poise, and a getting back to those antique laws of equilibrium, laws that get lost in the hurrying world of today. This knowledge is about the only luggage your brain need take; your muscles respond intuitively to the stroke of the paddle. The innate rhythm of the canoe is in you somewhere and the two come together in a great harmony. It is only for you to follow the lead of instinct, the greatest thing in the world, as any animal will tell you.

The silence of the ancient bayou clung round me. Strange eyes looked up through the shifting water; the "fragile people of the sea" were unafraid of the human that came so silently. The marvel of the turquoise shadow was unfathomable, and I was alone in the tangled depths exploring old, old water, heavy with the years. My identity was big and supreme. I paddled hundreds of miles into the very heart of alchemistic morning. After a long time, a great red sun came over the gulf to meet me, and I saw that a new day lay out on Santa Rosa Island.

My real introduction to scientific canoeing was in very different water,

(Excerpted from Outing, 1901)

179

on the coast of Maine, high under the polar star. Our canoe was fourteen feet long, built of canvas and as lithe and light as heart's desire. I soon got into the habit of paddling long distances without getting tired, changing the paddle from time to time.

If a woman wants to feel the glorious stretch of muscles from the top of her head to the tip of her toes, she must leave behind her "the tie that binds," the twelve and a half inch laundered collar, the nineteen inch waist and the size three and a half patent leather shoes – the trammels of conventionality. She should wear, if possible, moccasins, or soft-soled tennis shoes and she should let her waist muscles have a chance to respond to deep breathing; and because her throat is a delicate structure of fine nerves and muscles she should give it freedom too. The slightest pressure will spoil the great swing of the paddle and a woman will soon turn round and talk to the man at the other end of the canoe who will be waiting for just this to happen, relying on his well trained deductive faculties the while. To me, being told to sit still and enjoy myself is logically incompatible. To be a part of the active, alert life of the canoe, to see the new water waiting on ahead, to steal close to a prosperous porpoise or a lazy fisherman, or to feel the intimate leaning of the shore – all this is to know a great, good thing.

If you look through the interesting shelf of canoe literature you will find women mentioned rather vaguely as creatures to be stowed tenderly forward – if it be a pleasant day! One author says that a canoe affords a man "many an hour's enjoyment near home, perhaps of a summer's evening when she consents to accompany him, sitting forward most comfortably posed within easy distance of his place aft, where the paddle is plied."

This is the heart of the trouble and the wrong position for a woman to take. She should be just there herself, "aft – where the paddle is plied," and know all about that subtle turn of the wrist near the end of the stroke that keeps the little Romany steady. She should know how to handle the different paddles, and how to help carry the canoe, or to slip it carefully into the water at the treacherous time of launching. The lightness of the sport puts it easily into woman's kingdom. All the movements are to round the body out and forward, and to expand the lungs at every stroke. It is splendid training for the muscles of the arms, back and waist. The insidious seed planted and guarded over by our grandmothers – the idea that physical development coarsens a woman – is still bearing fruit in stray places.

Perhaps nothing was ever more misunderstood. The old lost truth is that all muscular training reduces the waist, poising the figure by distributing its force. Canoeing lifts the figure off the hips and puts the power in the arms and shoulders. The training is rhythmical and natural, asking less of a woman than the insistent golf ball. Above all things, parenthetically, it ought to appeal to a woman's vanity, for with horseback riding and swimming it puts her, without artifice, in a charming position. Kneeling Indian fashion at either end of the canoe she can be a veritable princess of the azure hour.

A well known Canadian author, writing of canoeing, gives women the following sphere: "In the canoe the paddler is at the stern, facing the way he would go. The passenger looks at him instead of at the changing landscape. There is nothing to divert her attention from the skillful fashion in which he wields his paddle. Her business is solely to talk to him, or listen to him, and let him take her whither he will. It is exactly the arrangement which all men, and most women, probably, prefer. It even partakes of an ordinance of nature." Fortunately, this ordinance is not of nature's making; the great good mother was never known to encourage such a thing in all her long, sweet life. It is of man's make, and it takes a good stiff five-mile stretch to paddle it out of him—this idea of nature's ordinance. There are many records of woman's achievement nowadays in the realm of boats, but I think we all suffer inconsistently from the folly of the one woman who stands beside a boat with a bunch of fluttering petticoats in her hand, and asks frantically where she shall step. That she often chooses the gunnel for her resting place is an old sorrow. . . .

From the enthusiast's point of view, there is everything in favor of canoeing, and nothing to be said against it; but this enthusiasm is often met by the cold questioning of the unmoved and uninterested listener, and then it is labor lost to try to prove anything. It must be in the blood—a strong love and lead— just as some men are magnetized by the North Pole, and cannot live their days until they are off after the finger of the compass pointing a due N. And again the vagabond paddler has to endure the definite and continuous existence of the individual who insists that canoes were only made for racing or for doubling the face of the globe.

It is for each one to get his happiness as he may, and if "you were born for deep-sea faring," you will hear the far summons, and follow after in any boat you find available when the waters are loosed and summer is on the land. Surely no woman with a drop of adventure in her soul will remain on shore. She will join the sea migration, or follow the first river that comes along. If she is a wise woman she will choose a canoe as the companion of her days. A short paddle will take her into a merry world all beyond the frustration of daily human life. She will be sunburned and lighthearted, playfellow of the summer wind.

The canoe is as old as time, and has never wandered very far from the primitive idea. Alien-hearted, it takes its place in the busy water world of today. Man has turned to it in his extreme need, and has found it in one form or another at the far North, on the equator, and in the southern seas, and it has given him, in return for proper management, the staunch-hearted comradeship asked of it at any imperiled moment. Rightly handled, the canoe is perfectly safe. The light draught and the buoyant resultant upward rise to the seas, and the perpetual demand of perfect poise, make it a thing for the finer intelligence, and keeps you alive to the need of the moment. An old and picturesque character who had canoed on many waters told me that he had fared well on all voyages until his canoe had "scented a rapid," and then no man could hold her. Breaking loose from all spirit of control, she was off after that falling water, even taking a daisy field cross lots in her tumultuous race. His fabulous story holds a grain of truth.

Each canoe you handle has its own temperament and there must be a period of adjustment between you. First of all, show that you have no fear, for there is a heady willfulness often times in that beautiful curve of the bow, something of the animal nature that needs a quick understanding and a short curb of power.

As far as my experience goes I like open stretches of salt water better than rivers or lakes for mere paddling. A river is generally a sweet, placid thing, talking in its sleep to the lazy trees along its shore, or an overwrought, bad-tempered stream crisscrossed by every impossible and erratic current known to water. But in the wide push of the sea, making for some sheltered length of beach in the face of the challenging slap of salt spray, you get more excitement and a wilder joy. It takes a short, stiff staccato stroke of your paddle to get through such water, but once in under the lee, you can dream unmolested dreams with a book, or, rarer than even a book, a comrade.

And night paddling is a new wonder. I remember a jeweled passage in this same high latitude. We paddled out from shore about two o'clock in the morning, and took the broad band of Jupiter's reflection as a course. There was no wind and mystery lay close against the heart of the northern night. Deep in under the shore the phosphorescence caught and held the blade of the paddle, but out in the open, starlight and diminished moonlight lay broadcast. It is only a canoe that can give you these noiseless intimate hours when you listen to the breathing of the world and become a part of the vibrating mystery. The always uppermost quality of stealth and secret adventure in a canoe come out to meet the night hours, and it is well not to let your mind get too far afield, or you will find your canoe buccaneering off on its own account after the lost Pleiad, and it will take more than Sagittarius to get you safely back home.

I have always believed a canoe half in league with the electric currents of the unburnt air since a trip across to the mainland one September. We started from a far outreaching point before the winds, in the twilight of early morning, the gray half tones giving way to the active light. The wooded islands loomed big and austere. We were miles ahead of the sun, but off in the eastern garden of the sky the glory was imminent. We paddled very quietly, and spoke little in that imperative silence of dawn. The sea on the outer reefs was busy with her old secret under that lighthouse that burned orange in the far gloom. It is seldom that we bathe our eyes in the tincture of new day. It gives a rarer vision. When the sun rose, we took a sudden vertical sheer into the midst of a mirage shot through with color. Towered cities came down out of the sky, inverted but veritable.

Since then I have not believed the step into the next world such a long one as it seems when life is bounded by a cable car. When the sea is piling cobalt out on your horizon, and the morning is in your veins, and the great negation is swept clear by a strong tonic wind straight from the misty mid-ocean—then it is that you get very near the gods, or they get near you. Anyway, I know I have mixed kingdoms with my paddle out there in the wide blue.

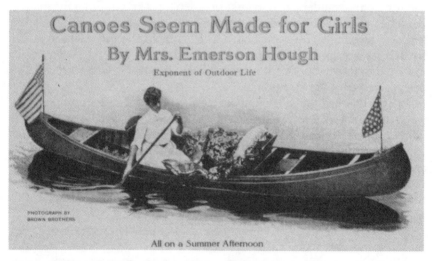

Canoes Seem Made for Girls
By Mrs. Emerson Hough
Exponent of Outdoor Life

PHOTOGRAPH BY
BROWN BROTHERS

All on a Summer Afternoon

(*Ladies Home Journal,* 1915)

Two Girls in a Canoe

ISOBEL KNOWLES

I am an experienced canoeist, but those rapids on the upper Gatineau caught me unawares. We had been paddling for mile after mile through comparatively sluggish water, when a sudden narrowing of the channel brought us to the head of a gorge down which the river tossed and roared angrily like a living thing.

We were two in the canoe, and we had passed the rapids on our way up the week before, but did not recognize them now that we approached from the opposite direction. Then we had portaged around them, carrying the canoe on our shoulders, over trunks of fallen trees and through the matted branches of the brushwood. Since that time we had seen much of river scenery, seen hills rising beyond hills till lost in the distant haze, great silent forests of spruce and pine, and placid sheets of crystal lake, and now, toward the close of our two week outing, we were two days' travel from the nearest outpost of civilization.

So stealthily had the swiftening water above the turn carried us on, that we were going at a ten mile-a-hour gait before I realized our position. Then the sudden leap of the canoe, the roll and pitch of the water under us, warned that the time to land had passed. There was no turning back against a ten-mile current, no making for either side, where the broken ripples on the surface showed jagged rocks only a few inches below. Down the middle of the channel lay our only course, and the path of the wave was narrow and the rocks harder than birch bark.

Quickly I changed places with my companion, crawling cautiously over the camping outfit stowed in the bottom, while she crept as carefully backward. In a rapids the bowsman guides the canoe, and I was the more expert. But this maneuver nearly brought disaster. A treacherous eddy just before the first pitch whirled our canoe around and we struck broadside on a boulder, where we hung, held fast by the rush of the current at

(Excerpted from *Cosmopolitan*, October 1905)

Then we pushed the canoe again into the water (*Cosmopolitan,* 1905)

the bow and stern. The edge of the canoe upstream began to settle, the water grew quickly up the side, and we avoided a spill by jumping over-board, almost up to our waists.

This, however, was only a beginning. Pulling the canoe to one side and holding it headed downstream, we stood on the rock for a breathing space while we surveyed the river, above so gentle in the sunlight, around and below so wild with the new spirit which had possessed it. Making a quick entry, with difficulty, from the rock, we again started down, steering our way where the comparatively smooth water showed the rocks well covered, working our arms till they seemed pulling from their sockets. Below us, the dashing spray, the circling eddies, the increasing clamor of the torrent, seemed to lure us as the call of a Lorelei to destruction.

The excitement of the course filled us with an ecstasy of abandon; but a sudden dash of water over the bow into our faces brought us quickly back to a sense of the danger which a moment's relaxed vigilance would bring. With every nerve alert, and guided by my previous experiences with Canadian rapids, I picked the way down the channel, my companion in the stern keeping the canoe straight with the current.

Thirty yards of fairly smooth water intervened between the upper and lower pitches, and here, somewhat awed by the spectacle of the leaping white caps farther down, we attempted a landing. Swinging the canoe across the current and heading for the shore which promised best, we applied our whole force to the paddles. But we had no more than half covered the distance when the futility of the effort became apparent, and we quickly turned and made in the opposite direction, where, we now discovered, the main channel lay.

Even the excitement of the adventure did not blind me to the peril which now faced us. On the lower side, as we bent our paddles to reach the channel, a row of partially submerged rocks grew ever nearer as the current drew our canoe toward them. Should we fail to reach the channel before striking, nothing human could prevent an upset, and, so far as I could see, nothing human could prevent a drowning. Although a good swimmer, I could not hope to breast such waves and, escaping them, avoid the whirlpool at the foot.

With all our strength in our paddles, we lifted the light bark canoe over the water, and just as the farthest rock grated our side we swung into the channel and boiled down between the boulders, the current sweeping us on at a rate of fully fifteen miles an hour. But as we swung, my maple paddle had snapped from my hands, caught in a fissure of the rock where I had jabbed it to keep from striking.

In impotent despair I looked around at my companion. Until the present trip she never had been in a canoe, and her only knowledge in its management had been gained by my coaching and by less than two weeks of practice. But plainly the river and the forest were now in her veins, and the craft of the paddle had come by inspiration. The hesitation of the city-born was dispelled, and with skillful stroke, scarce noting my discomfiture, with eyes fixed on the winding channel ahead of us, she steered safe through the boiling waters of the second pitch. With a whirl of spray at the finish—for the rapids keeps its greatest waves for the foot, as an orator his fiercest invectives for his peroration—we brought up in the eddy below, gasping from our effort yet thrilling with the joy of it.

That was the incident of our canoeing trip which I am likely longest to remember. There were three inches of water in the canoe when we reached the foot of the rapids, which had come in over the sides as we bowled through the last big pitch. We went ashore and bailed it out, and had a view of what we had come through from a safer point than the rock in midstream.

"No more rapids for me today," said the helmswoman who had steered us so safely. Now that the excitement was over, all her bravado was gone, and but for the remembrance of the flashing eye, flushed cheek and rigid muscles which had confronted me when I turned to look back after losing my paddle, I could have fancied her again the city girl who stood hesitatingly with a bunch of skirts in one hand when I first invited her to step into a canoe.

A few miles below the rapids, we landed for dinner. It was only eleven o'clock, but we called it noon. It was noontime with our appetites. Bored mortals of the city, where we had turned the millstone of work and so-called pleasure, we were transmigrated into new bodies, endowed with fresh sensations and a marvelous hunger. We lit a fire of twigs and drift-wood, between two logs placed side by side, over which we bent a shar-pened pole, with one end driven into the ground. On the pole we sus-pended a kettle filled with water, into which we thrust a good-sized fowl, purchased from a chance habitant near where we had spent the previous night. With carrots and potatoes, no city-prepared turkey, skewered and stuffed, ever tasted so delicious on costly porcelain as this on our tin plates.

We spent an hour for dinner, and another reclining on the shaded bank, lying upon our backs, looking dreamily into the ether of the heavens, which showed in little patches through the leaves. Then we pushed the canoe again into the water, crossed a lake with scarcely ruffled surface, and emerged once more on the river, paddling for miles through an avenue of poplars.

How sweet it is in the languishing days of summer to be removed from the strident noises of the city and the brutal struggle of its life. Care and worry slip from us on the river as the water slips from beneath the canoe. In the little bayous, the pond lilies, caressed by soft zephyrs and kissed by the sun rays, sparkle in the half shadows of the trees. Above us the marvelous clouds float distantly, lifting the gaze to the ineffable skies.

The canoe is the primal form of water craft. It goes back to the Indian, and all the Indian in me, all the instinct of revolt, bubbles forth as I paddle away from civilization. The wild abandon of nature nowhere is so im-pressive as from the level of its lakes and rivers, and the canoeist, riding over its expanses centaur-like—for the canoe and the paddler are as one— feels a part of the great outdoors. The unutterable sound of the waters, and of the trees and the grasses beyond, speak, in the strange sweet voice of nature, and I hear and understand. The friendly branches reach out and caress me, the rippling wavelets patter a musical babble, lapping my hand as I dip the paddle over the side, and no voice of discord mars the sweet harmony.

Thirty miles a day was the average which we had set for ourselves on our downward journey; twenty miles a day was all that we had been able to make on the trip against the current. The country through which we passed was almost uninhabited, only at infrequent intervals a clearing of the trees, a whitewashed cabin of hewn logs and a barn proclaiming the dwelling place of some isolated backwoods farmer. Here we would wave a neighborly salute, the goodly-proportioned form of a matron would appear in the doorway, filling it, and three or four small children would squeeze past and stand in the doorway gaping. The passage of a canoe was an event of importance.

We encountered two more rapids before we reached the end of our journey, one of which we braved by running, but the other caused us to land and portage. We carried the canoe over our heads, inverted, with the paddles on our shoulders for supports. The portage is the one unpleasant feature of a canoe trip in a wild country. Through the moss and ooze of the swamp the way may lead, over giant rocks and the tortuous trunks of trees, or along steep precipices where a careless step might send us plunging into the swirling river. The camp outfit, too, and the provisions have to be carried, in packs slung over the shoulder, bound together by tumplines.

I have canoed on Florida lagoons, on the deep running waters of Maine, on the shallower streams of Connecticut, on the Hudson and Delaware Rivers, on the mountain encompassed lakes of New York and New Jersey, but nowhere have I enjoyed the sport as on the wild forest rivers of Canada. The panorama of scenery which changes from the pastoral calm of unruffled river and lake, fit mirror for the yet unscared dryad of the woods, to the torrents which whirl great trees like playthings and the cascades leaping in silver shafts from the precipices, is not surpassed in grandeur in the world.

"Through the moss and ooze of the swamp the way may lead . . ." (*Cosmopolitan,* 1905)

188

The Passionate Paddler

MARY WICKHAM BOND

Passionate paddler Mary Wickham Bond is a Pennsylvania-based writer and traveller. She founded a local newspaper, has written a number of books including a collection of poetry, and has contributed poetry, short stories, and nature and sport articles to Ladies' Home Journal, Reader's Digest, *and other magazines. She has travelled widely with her ornithologist husband, James Bond.*

Seventy-two years ago I was shown how to step into the bow of a canoe and sit down in the middle of the seat. I was handed a paddle, instructed to tuck my left leg under the seat and extend my right leg in preparation for paddling on the left side of the canoe, the reverse position for paddling on the right. I was told to stretch the upper arm straight out, dip the paddle cleanly into the water and draw the blade backwards parallel to the canoe. The canoe counselor was seated in the stern.

All of this occurred at Pinelands Camp, a summer camp for girls on Squam Lake, New Hampshire. I was fourteen and I can still remember the feel of the canoe sliding over the surface with a quiet burble, all so much more delightful than rowing and fussing with oar-locks or catching crabs. I spent four summers at Pinelands as a girl and two as a junior counselor, with canoe picnics my favorite sport. Indeed, there was the beginning for me of a whole new world of pleasure and adventure which has lasted me a lifetime, and a long lifetime at that.

In my twenties I had an absurd adventure paddling a canoe on the Thames River in England. In my thirties and forties I shot the rapids of the upper Delaware River from Margaretville down to Port Jervis half-a-dozen times and got dumped only once. Then with my husband and my three stepdaughters, I began a yearly summer trek to our camp on "the backside" of Mount Desert Island, Maine, in those days far from the giddy life of Bar Harbor and Northeast Harbor.

189

Here I have had summers of canoeing and paddling a kayak for forty-six years, playing games alone in my kayak with loons and porpoises; trying to lure seals to my side with a mouth organ (seals are said to love music); teasing cormorants and gulls off their favorite ledges, and terns off their favorite lobster pots; constantly invading the privacy of great blue herons in quiet coves, thus stocking my memory with wonderful snatches of the songs of the winter wren or hermit thrush or the olive-back.

The Thames River episode was ridiculous. When travelling in Europe in a small group, properly chaperoned, just after the first World War, I met an Englishman in Nice with whom my chaperones permitted me to go out to tea. When our group reached London some weeks later, I was pleased to have another invitation from the "nice little Englishman," this time for lunch. I got all dressed up in a blue silk dress with lace sleeves (ruffled at the wrist), a large blue hat to match, white gloves, fancy silk stockings from Paris, and high-heeled patent leather slippers.

He drove me in a tiny car out of London to a restaurant somewhere on the Thames, and told me what I couldn't believe – that the river flowed in one direction on the outgoing tide and reversed itself on the incoming tide. If I didn't believe him, we'd take a canoe and he'd prove it. The restaurant provided punts and canoes and I couldn't resist the latter, but felt like a fool sitting in a canoe all dressed up like a French doll.

We floated down river and secretly I was not pleased with his paddling. He scraped the gunwale of the canoe frequently and paddled with a bent elbow. No style at all! After awhile we tied up at a little island, waiting for the tide to turn; at least he'd had the timing all worked out.

But, alas, on our return to the canoe, although the tide had turned as expected, my nice little Englishman had tied up the canoe much too close to the branch of a tree, and to my horror the bow was almost under water. My paddling pal didn't seem to know what to do, so I lost no time and scrambled into the canoe, kicked off my patent leather slippers and cautiously crawled over the thwarts and paddles to the bow. Lace ruffles and silk dress or not, I plunged my arm down into the water but could not reach where the rope was tied. I visualized the bow being drawn down under, the canoe swamping, and both of us struggling for the shore while the current swept away my handbag with my passport and money inside! If *only* he hadn't tied us up so tight!

Sheer luck got us out of trouble. A length of free rope surfaced and I grabbed at it, hoping to pull us closer to the branch, but the knot came apart and we were free! We were both rather quiet on the trip back and I wasn't sorry to arrive at last at the restaurant's boathouse.

Mary Porcher [Mary Wickham Bond], Thames River,
London, 1922

Shooting the rapids of the upper Delaware was a very different story.
Sometimes our party consisted of four or five canoes and we took two and
a half days to do it, spending one night on the Pennsylvania side, and the
next on the New York side, ending up at Port Jervis where we had left our
automobiles. There were no motels in those days and we stayed at what
was then called "Tourists Accommodated." Our favorite place was Ruby
Gore's (believe it or not, the butcher's wife), a red-blooded woman indeed
who gave us marvellous Pennsylvania Dutch dinners, the table cluttered
with platters, plates, teacups, and little china bathtubs full of a variety of

edibles. We once counted 137 pieces of china on the table all at once.

Marvellous days! Warm companionship! Thrilling episodes! Lacka-waxen, Cochecton, Big Cedar! Ah, Big Cedar Falls—the scene of our downfall! My partner and I on that occasion must have been careless, for midway through Big Cedar we shipped a wave, another, and a third threw us over. It was a raw, overcast day in April and the river full of ice-cakes. Our duffle flowed fast ahead through the turmoil of white water and hungry rocks. But we managed to hang on to the canoe and came through without harm. We were dragged ashore, and even our paddles and duffle were saved. If I'd thought the water was cold, the air was even colder. By good luck a new road was being built and a concrete mixer was running in a shed. There the shivering paddlers put on dry clothes provided by sympathetic companions, but I confess that once we were back in our canoe, my knees shook all the way through the next falls. I couldn't help remembering a former trip when one of the canoes had upset. The paddlers, waist deep, had watched it catch broadside on a huge boulder where it snapped in two as both ends filled with the force of the surging current.

In my fifties I paddled one morning in Switzerland on the Silsersee, a small lake in the Engadines, borrowing a kayak from a young Frenchman. It was a slick little craft made of dark blue canvas with red trim and very short paddles. I spent some heavenly hours exploring the coves of the Chasté Peninsula with its huge rock on which was engraved a line from a poem by Nietzsche, and caught glimpses of the delicate roebuck in the woodlands while listening to the low intimate calls of the cuckoos calling to one another across the lake.

In my sixties, on an unforgettable ornithological expedition among the Venezuelan islands, I paddled an Old Town canoe through secret and mysterious lagoons inside quiet water behind the reefs. On one occasion our canoe startled a school of fish which leaped clear across my lap, some falling into the bottom of the canoe and flopping unhappily around my feet. We tossed back as many as we could.

And now, past my seventies and in my eighties, I have continued my adventures in a modern streamlined fiberglass kayak, although my excursions have become limited to a tiny section of the North Atlantic coastline. Even in so short a distance as from the Ellsworth Bridge south to Duck Cove (Mount Desert Island, Maine), many adventures can be found. For example, try pitting the tide against the wind! A good place for this is over the sandbar between the Paine Camp and Moose Island. Pick an hour when the water is about three feet over the bar and the twelve foot tide is coming in, with the wind blowing against it. All at once the kayak is "in irons" and you're deadlocked over the bar, sitting there as cosy and comfortable as if languishing in a chaise lounge. A heady sensation, this—a taming of the elements!

Another sort of thrill is shooting the Pretty Marsh rapids—very tame compared to the upper Delaware, but tricky nevertheless. You idle about the upper basin, just below the road to Somesville, waiting for the tide to turn. At last the moment comes when you must deliver yourself to the heavy current now pouring over the ledges and down the narrows. You are quickly at the point of no return and a chill runs up your spine as you slide down the all too short flouncing, boisterous white water into the calm, smooth pools below.

Perhaps my only real claim to bravery was one day when I met a tidal bore travelling fast and relentlessly across the harbor between me and our float. I had come down Bartlett's Narrows as far as West Point to observe a snakey-looking line stretching from Hardwood Island past West Point. I knew I must not let it catch me broadside, so I took a deep, brave breath, paddled straight into it bow on and—went through it like a knife in soft butter!

Sloops, catboats, ketches, yawls, rowboats and outboard motors—all have their charms. But there's something about canoe and kayak that creates for the paddler a profound intimacy with tides and changing winds, with remote coves and endless hours of quiet happiness. One of my favorite moments is to paddle up the glittering path of gold that stretches on clear summer evenings from our float across the harbor to the dark silhouette of Bartlett's Island against the evening sky. When the last glint of the setting sun rolls over below the jagged outline of trees and the glittering path is gone, I turn about and paddle home quietly under the soft afterglow.

Quetico-Superior Honeymoon, 1925

HAZEL RICE

While gathering material for this book, we received a letter from Mrs. Hazel Briggs Rice of Madison, Wisconsin, recounting a month-long honeymoon canoe trip with Alfred Briggs over sixty years ago. We have included most of the letter for its picture of canoeing before the days when hundreds of manufacturers provide thousands of lightweight "necessities" that we modern canoeists take for granted. We have also included a poem Hazel wrote to her close friend and paddling partner, Elizabeth Brandeis.

Hazel Rice was born in Toronto, Ontario in 1896. She went to school in New England and in Germany and returned to this country during World War I. "Not until I came to the University of Wisconsin in 1921 did I have much opportunity for outdoor activity and then I grasped at it eagerly." She still loves canoeing, and would like to do it more. Since retiring she has been writing fiction and poetry.

July, 1984

Dear Miss Niemi,

It all took place, as you can see, long ago. I am now eighty- eight years old, but I must admit that this and other trips Alfred and I made have not entirely faded from my memory.

Alfred Briggs and I were married on July 30, 1925. It had been our plan to make an extensive canoe trip during the month of August. We had learned how to handle a canoe from our close friend, Elizabeth Brandeis, and by the time Alfred and I married, we were excellent paddlers, although our actual experience was only of short duration on the lakes of Madison, Wisconsin. I was never a stern paddler, largely because I am small and not very strong, although amazingly hardy.

In preparing for the trip we got what information we could from all sorts of sources. We ordered a tent from somewhere, I suppose Abercrombie and Fitch. It was a very small tent and was bat-shaped—wide at the entrance with two sort of wings. The material was a waterproof lightweight canvas. We could sit up in the front of the tent—hardly in the back—so we lay with our feet to the back and our clothing packed neatly in the wings.

From all we could gather, we had to make "food bags"—heavy individual cotton bags, large and small. These we sewed ourselves (or had done, I can't remember which), and then they were dipped in candle grease to prevent moisture from getting to the food.

We had three large packsacks made here in Madison. Our bedding consisted of a number of army blankets. We each had a poncho to wear in case of rain. We carried plenty of rope, a folding candle lantern, a waterproof match container, and an ax. Each of us also had a knife case which fitted into our belts.

Nesting cooking pots from Abercrombie, a grate, utensils for eating, etc., were all packed not only in the packsacks but in their own cloth (candle wax dipped) containers.

We carried no canned food except what was then known as KLIM, a dry milk powder. We had dried fruits, bacon, flour, pancake mix, oatmeal, cornmeal, no eggs or egg powders (there were none), and beans. When my grandchildren who go camping hear about our food and equipment, they say, "Grandma, how could you ever carry all that stuff?"

Naturally we also carried some fishing equipment—spoon hooks and fishing line. No rod. We trolled the line from the back of the canoe and caught all the fish we could eat. We threw back all but walleyes and had a large fish meal every single day.

Now as to clothing: I had a pair of boy's twill woolen knickers—very elegant, I thought—a number of blouses and a suede leather jacket, woolen knee socks, sweaters, and a canvas hat.

Our canoe, a 17-foot Thompson, was very heavy. We did not have life jackets (there were no such things). We carried no swim suits because we planned to swim naked (no one, no one, was ever around.)

I think Alfred had a large map from which he was able to devise some sort of circular program. Our plan was to put in at Ely, Minnesota, and follow the Basswood River into Basswood Lake and then to go westward through portages and connecting lakes back to Ely, all by compass. Somehow we did accomplish this. There were innumerable portages, which we found not by posted signs but by tree slashings. On one of the big portages we fortunately met a forest ranger and he drew a map for us to finish our trip. Unfortunately, he left out one lake, which caused considerable dismay and confusion.

Our main insect problem was black flies and this was extremely hard to cope with. Just before we left we had bought a newspaper and had taken it along. This we made into sort of puttees which covered our legs up to our knees, below which we were most vulnerable.

We were gone a month. The weather was marvellous and we found that paddling early in the morning, if there was much wind, was by far the safest. We tried to take no chances and if the lake was very large we did not go directly across. Nonetheless, looking back, I now think we took too many chances. With just two people alone, if anything had happened to either one of us, it would have been disastrous

During my marriage to Alfred, we spent almost every summer on a canoe trip somewhere—to the Adirondack lakes, to the Rainy Lakes District, to Vilas County, Wisconsin, and once back to Quetico for an anniversary trip. After Alfred's death in 1936 lengthy canoe trips were not possible, but I continued my paddling on local lakes with my good friend, Elizabeth Brandeis Raushenbush.

Elizabeth, to whom this enclosed poem is written, was my close friend for over sixty years. We saw each other almost daily and as long as she was well and strong we paddled in her canoe constantly on Madison's several lakes.

Elizabeth was the daughter of U.S. Supreme Court Justice Louis Brandeis, who was a devoted paddler and taught his daughters how to handle a canoe. I spent many summers with Elizabeth and her family at their summer home in Chatham, Massachusetts, and we took long trips into the bay, sometimes rather hazardous ones.

For many years Elizabeth was a professor of economics at the University of Wisconsin. My poem was written for her when she was too frail and too forgetful for much communication. She was a wonderful woman.

Lament

Do you remember
A very special day
long, long ago?
Some would say almost a lifetime
but for me it is as yesterday.
We called it special then—
a day we both looked back to many times.

On a hot summer morning in July
we took the Oldtown canoe
down the Yahara
and into the swamp's tepid water —
a trip we'd never made before.

We took the Oldtown into the swamp
down where the lily pads
lay glistening in the sun
and their lush white blossoms
smiled at us through teardrops
from our splashing paddles.
We moved through the swamp,
past fallen logs, past driftwood
and all sorts of water weeds
that brushed against the sides of the canoe.

We talked of nothing,
really nothing
in your life or mine,
but of the sun hot on our backs,
the shadows on the water,
the small blue heron
standing on one leg among the reeds
and the joy of being out, free
and together.
Best friends
our children always said.

Do you remember none of it?
How we beached the canoe and waded
through the algae covered water
to a tiny spit of land
with daisies growing and damp spongy moss
soft underfoot?

You don't remember
the unhulled strawberries in the mason jar
whose sweetness came directly from the sun?
Nor the bite into the dark rye bread
spread thick with cheese and juicy pickles?
Nor the rosy radishes
that snapped between our teeth?

You don't remember
that we rolled our slacks
above our knees and sat like youngsters—
indeed, like our own children
whom we'd left at home—
and splashed our toes in the tepid water?

And when I tell you all of this
or any part of it
you don't remember?
There's no one left
to share this memory with me.

What do you see, old friend,
as you sit with vacant eyes
gazing wistfully out the window?
You are more gone from me
than that hot summer day
so long ago.

Out of Stereotype by Canoe in 1942

RUTH SCHELLBERG

Life *magazine, July 1941, carried a rather surprising photo essay, "Two Midwestern Girls Canoe Down Old Voyageur's Highway." (We weren't surprised they had done the canoe trip, just to see it in* Life.) *The girls are photographed running rapids, paddling topless, bathing in waterfalls, curling their hair in the tent at night. They also caught and cleaned their own fish, pitched the tent, and cooked their own food, the article says. Guides and a chaperon were vaguely mentioned. We got the real story of that trip from the chaperon, Ruth Schellberg of Mankato, Minnesota, now retired from a long career as a professor of physical education, and still canoeing. In a 1986 interview with Judith Niemi, Ruth shared this story and her 1941 photo albums — part of the great collection of canoeing artifacts and mementos that fill her house.*

It was as a chaperon over forty years ago that I became convinced the guide role was the interesting and exciting one. At the urging of the Minnesota tourism department, *Life* magazine sent a photographer, Wallace Kirkland, to Minnesota to photograph college women on a canoe trip. The members of my canoeing class at Macalester College were ranked in order of their photogenicity (mostly even-ness of teeth), and two were picked for an eight-day wilderness trip. In 1941 this would be an unlikely story (two co-eds out with a male photographer and two male guides) so I was asked to go along as chaperon.

Eight days and 400 pictures later, Penny and Flo and I decided that the males had all the fun. They paddled in the stern, carried canoes, caught fish, cooked over the open fire. We were relegated to the bow positions, dishwashing, and blowing up air mattresses.

It wasn't that I didn't know *how* to do those "male" things. Growing up, I had spent my summers at Camp Fire camps, learning to paddle canoes, build fires, and travel by map and compass. These activities carried no "tom boy" connotation in our girls' camp world, and to attend camp was quite the "in" thing to do. For a dozen summers later as a counselor I taught these skills and conducted trips on nearby lakes and rivers.

As a camper and counselor I had dreamed of paddling in "The Far Northland" that we had sung songs about. No women I had ever known had done such a trip. Now, at last, the opportunity.

At Border Lakes Outfitters in Ely, Sam the head guide showed us the hats of 42 people who had drowned on canoe trips in the last 18 years. He kept them hanging around the room as it made a good story. Mr. Kirkland said that was just one of Sam's yarns. Then the men got to talking about plans that we weren't supposed to know about, so we went off to find out what kind of food was sent along on the canoe trips.

Ruth Schellberg, Minnesota/Ontario boundary waters, 1943

We took off from Ely with each of us in the bow of a canoe, the photographer and the two guides in the sterns. Bow paddling was the woman's lot and only the thrill of being in Canoe Country balanced our disappointment in being assigned bow seats.

The guides would show us on the map at the day's end which way we had come, but were very secretive when we started each morning about where we were going. We loved to cook out-of-doors, but this, too, was forbidden, as we might burn the kettles and the guides would have to clean them.

There was one time when we almost erected a tent (the photographer was taking pictures of us and guides were not permitted in the pictures), but the photographing was over too soon so we were sent off to blow up air mattresses. Canoes we could carry if we were posing for pictures. If not, we carried paddles and the guides' fishing rods. Once Penny and Flo did get to paddle together on the Basswood River, while the photographer shot upstream toward Wheelbarrow Falls, so it would look like they were running the rapids.

When *Look* magazine got wind of what we were doing, they sent out a photographer too, and at Basswood Lake we met the *Look* party, with two models fishing from the pontoons of a plane. Later, when a plane came down to deliver to us some rolls of film and a deck of cards, Penny and Flo stood on the pontoons, imitating the *Look* models. I really do have some respect for the authenticity of the story in *Life*—we did at least make the trip, although we didn't get to do too much.

Sometimes the men claimed their sleep was disturbed by the giggling going on at night. We were laughing about all the tall tales Mr. Kirkland and the guides tried to make us believe during the day. The "Dog and the Pipe" and "Moose and Canoe" were voted the best.

At the end of the trip I made plans to become a guide. I would paddle stern, determine the route, cook, fish, set up tents *and* blow up air mattresses, starting the very next summer. There were only three women students on my first trip. (Many more weren't able to obtain parental permission to go without a man.) We had a wonderful time. We followed the international border along the historic and scenic voyageur's route, caught some very large fish, swam in crystal clear water, and found we were adequate in the wilderness.

My next 71 trips have been very popular. Mothers were not as reluctant to let their daughters go, though for many years I was receiving the "thank you for bringing my daughter home alive" type of letter. Students who had been with me became guides. I had become their role model.

For over forty years, Ruth Schellberg has devoted most of her summers to leading canoe trips for college classes, for her colleagues in physical education, and for the staff of the Camp Fire camp that she directed for several years. In 1984 and 1986, members of her 1947 camp staff held reunion trips, paddling the same routes, with "Miss Ruth" still in the lead canoe. In the summer of 1987, when she is 75, Ruth will complete her 75th canoe trip.

Woman of the Boundary Waters
JUSTINE KERFOOT

Justine Kerfoot is one of many women who have chosen to live in wilderness areas, and for whom canoeing is part of their livelihood.

When she first came to northern Minnesota in 1927, the Gunflint Trail was a rough road following an old Indian winter route, a narrow corridor into what would later become the Boundary Waters Canoe Area Wilderness. Her mother was buying a small summer fishing lodge, but during the Depression the family made the Gunflint their permanent home, and Justine learned the skills of self-sufficient life in the North—trapping, canoeing, fixing generators and bush telephones. For the next 50 years she operated Gunflint Lodge, and was one of the first canoe outfitters and guides in the area.

Her autobiography, Woman of the Boundary Waters: Canoeing, Guiding, Mushing and Surviving *(Grand Marais, Minnesota: Women's Times Publishing), was published in 1986. The following brief excerpts tell of her choice of the wilderness life, and an early experience as a canoe guide in a country then not well mapped.*

A LOVE AFFAIR

I don't know when I first knew I was in love with this sometimes harsh and demanding land. Did I fall in love in winter, when the snow is cold and crunchy as one pads along on snowshoes? When in the early morning the rising sun reflects on the hoar frost and each separate branch and tree in the woods stands as if covered with jewels? Then the fairyland is both cold and disinterested, yet somehow soft and beckoning.

Or did I fall in love when the change from winter to spring begins, and one hears the sound of the first gentle rain on the roof, running off in rivulets? Mist rises from the ice on the lake, an impenetrable barrier that becomes a sheer veil moments later. Treetops on the far shore are suspended in an ethereal horizon. The ice rumbles, and a few sea gulls talk their way across the sky, looking for a patch of open water.

As the days lengthen, a lead opens along the north shore of Gunflint Lake, and shallow bays throw back their winter cover. The sun melts the snow on the ice field, creating puddles that filter through the porous ice. The river melts little estuaries into the lake, allowing the wind to move in and push the monolithic covering, undulating, at first mere inches. The ice gives in, disintegrating into crystals or breaking into sheets that gain momentum as they move. Like miniature glaciers, they pile onshore, standing docks on end or brushing them aside.

Justine Kerfoot (Charlotte Merrick)

The snows melt. The sunny hillsides are loaded with small, sweet, wild strawberries. The blossoms of moccasin flowers past their peak of bloom hang limp and brown like tiny pieces of chamois, interspersed in the woods with vivid red teaberry. Bunchberries gather in clusters, holding their white blossoms snugly against the leaves. Coral root stands stark and naked, leafless like Indian pipe, but showing a series of look-alike flowers that resemble minute orchids. The blooms of bush labrador tea cover the marshy areas with a blanket of white. Red devil's paintbrush waves abundantly along the roadside. Ground pine spreads along the forest floor, holding its evergreen twigs erect in an effort to compete with its small, colorful neighbors. In secluded parts of the woods, hidden by overhanging flowers and large leaves, nests woven of twigs hold mottled brownish eggs. The evening grosbeaks, feeding on seeds and bugs, flash yellow among the dark spruce and balsam.

As fall approaches, leaves start to turn haphazardly, as if a child were dipping a brush in pots of yellow and red paint and dropping a plop here and there. It is the rutting season of the moose; bulls are in a restless mood as they search for mates. A flock of geese, chatting sociably, passes overhead at little more than treetop level. The mushrooms that come into being overnight carpet the woods floor with browns, yellows, reds and whites. Beaver accumulate fresh food piles of aspen branches before their houses. Their nearby trails lead to trees chewed partially through, with fresh-smelling symmetrical chips at their bases. When the trees are felled by the first heavy wind, tiny chisel marks are left on the stumps.

Mountain ash is now a mixture of yellow and orange. Aspen and birch tipped with yellow and the deep red of moose maple are accentuated by the somber dark green of the pines. This is autumn's defiance, an orchestra reaching a crescendo, before the silence of winter descends.

I don't know when, but the fact remains that I did fall in love. An infinitesimal speck in the cosmos, I stood on the shore of Gunflint Lake beneath a great white pine—matriarch of a fast-vanishing tribe. And I knew I was home. I was 21. The year was 1927.

LEARNING TO GUIDE

Gene [Genevieve] Bayle, my friend from Grand Marais, taught me the proper way to handle a canoe. After a week of practice, up and down rapids and in the wind, I became comfortable as a stern paddler. This new art served me well, for in the struggle to pay our bills, I worked into a guiding routine of paddling a canoe load of guests the sixteen miles (including four rapids and eight portages) to Saganaga Lodge and picking up a return group to go back the six miles to Gunflint Lodge via two rapids, a portage and across Sea Gull Lake where we were met by the lodge truck.

At times, as I heaved a heavy canvas-covered canoe onto my shoulders at a portage making this round trip, I thought, "There must be an easier way than this to make a living."

Many of my days were spent guiding fishing parties on Gunflint Lake. The fishing parties were mostly men, but on a few occasions there were couples. On one rare occasion I took two women on a week canoe trip. We took a route to the southern arm of Knife Lake and planned to take a short-cut, which I had used once before, over a few hills and lakes to Otter Track Lake.

Maps were quite inadequate at this time, and portages were unmarked except for a few faded blazes on scattered trees. I had a compass and a sketchy map I used to check off the landmarks as I paddled. In spite of all the attractions, birds and beaver houses that I pointed out to the two women, their one desire was to see how rapidly they could go from one portage to the next. They kept a diary noting times consumed over each lake and each portage traversed.

We crossed the Eddy Lake portage and turned to paddle east to Knife Lake bay. When I reached the end of the bay, I suggested the women wait in the canoe while I hunted the blaze marks and found the trail to the next lake. I left my compass and map in the bottom of the canoe since I would be gone only a moment.

I found a path which could be the portage. It seemed familiar and yet a little different from the one I remembered. I went further and came to a large pond which didn't look right either. Thinking the trail was further to my left, I searched in that direction. Then I turned to head back to the canoe. I found myself hopelessly lost in unfamiliar country, on an overcast day, without a compass.

Momentarily I was overcome with utter panic. I felt nauseated as thoughts whizzed through my mind. No compass, no matches, no protection from the elements. Gone for a week so no one would make a search for several days, plus the unpredictable reaction of two novice canoeists for whom I was responsible. It took all my will power to calm down.

I was in a stand of large jack pines whose limbs obligingly extended to the ground. I climbed to the top of one jack pine and thought I could see a hidden valley between two hills which could contain the waterway where I had left the canoe. I shouted from the top of the tree but there was no answer. A light spot momentarily appeared on the horizon. When I climbed down I blazed the tree on four sides with my knife and marked the initials N, S, E, and W.

I used this large jack pine as my anchor point and headed south, which I thought was the right direction. I broke twigs to mark my path, constantly sighting back, first toward the tree and then down my straight line of broken branches. In about an hour I came to the exact jack pine from which I started. I had completed a large perfect circle.

Once more I climbed to the top of the jack pine and with two fingers whistled a shrill whistle. Way off in the distance I heard an answer. Then it was clear that I had become entangled in a series of small ridges. I started toward the whistle and after every two or three ridges I crossed, I climbed another jack pine and whistled. Each time the answer was closer. When I reached the canoe, I discovered the women had not stirred. They sat all those hours visiting. My relief was unbounded.

We paddled out of this bay, went around a point and into the next bay to the north where I found the portage easily. It was over a year before I would step any distance into the woods without a compass.

1500 Miles Down the Saskatchewan

AGNES LAUT

"Sas-katch-e-wan! . . . What word in the glossary of rivers surpasses this in the virility of its sheer sound?" proclaimed Mr. Emerson Hough in the pages of Outing magazine in 1907. "Let us have rivers for young men, men thin in the flank and hard of leg." Undeterred, Miss Agnes Laut, a small woman then in her late thirties, and her companion Miss Simpson canoed down the Saskatchewan River in 1908, with only one guide and paddling their own canoe (not always the practice of white explorers of the period). They seem to have thoroughly enjoyed themselves.

Agnes Laut gives us almost no personal information, as is typical of women's travel writing of the time, nor does she say what made them ready to undertake such a strenuous trip. (They were certainly not the only curious and adventurous ladies travelling the rivers of the Northwest and Alaska in those years.) Her article does make clear that they travelled with an interested eye on modern progress and development along the river, and with an even keener interest in the romantic past. Miss Simpson was a grandniece of the most famous governor of the Hudson's Bay Company. Agnes Laut was an author who between 1899 and 1932 contributed to many magazines, often writing on the history of the Northwest and on women's issues. She also wrote historical novels of fur trade life, these and many magazine articles appearing only under her initials, A. C. Laut.

Outing magazine (in a brief profile in January 1906) asked this "soft-voiced, slender, essentially feminine woman" about her experiences gathering "her virile material." She replied matter-of-factly, ignoring the supposed contradiction: "My facts were not gathered at all. They were soaked in unconsciously during a lifelong residence in the Northwest, at Winnipeg. My lungs went to pieces while in college, and in the camping and horseback pilgrimages that restored my health was developed or germinated the passion for the out-of-doors which led me into new trails."

(Excerpted from *Scribner's*, April 1909)

Most of the 1909 Scribner's *article is included here, omitting several sections on settlements and missions.*

It is a curious sensation, that—canoeing down a vast river whose waters sweep an area equal of half-a-dozen European kingdoms and at every bend reveal shifting vistas of new peoples and new regions.

Every paddle dip, every twist and turn of your supple craft to the rustle and splash and gulp of the live waters under the keel brings out some new caprice of the river's mood to which you must pay court or penalty. The waters begin to roil and your canoe to lag. You must catch the veer of the current, or you will presently be out to your knees shoving off sand bars. Over there, the bank is cut sheer as masonry; and you bump off the shallows back to the swift flowing deeps with a gurgle of laughing waters that is zest of pure joy in the scheme of things. You begin to understand why Indians regard all rivers as living personalities and make the River Goddess offerings of tobacco with the words: "Here, Granny, take this! Now give us fair wind and good luck!"

*

"When you leave Edmonton, you are going to jump off somewhere," Sexsmith had answered when I asked our head guide why we could not rent our camp outfit instead of buying it. "When you leave Edmonton you aren't just going to the woods on a picnic. You are going somewhere. You buy your outfit because you are going to be away so long you will wear it out. Edmonton is the jumping-off place for a lot of long trips. There is down the Mackenzie north. There is up the Peace west. And there's down the Saskatchewan east—that means from 1500 to 1800 miles, according to the place you stop down on Lake Winnipeg."

It was down the Saskatchewan we had decided to go, partly because all the romance of the most romantic era in the West clings to its banks, partly because its snaky winding trail half the width of a continent marks the last trek to the last frontier of the last West.

It was up and down this broad stream—*Kis sis katchewan Sepee,* the Indians called it, "swift, angrily flowing"—with its countless unmapped lakes and countless unmapped islands, that the war canoes of the Cree long ago flitted like birds of prey to plunder the Blackfeet. It was up the Saskatchewan the French explorers came wandering mazed in search of the Western Sea. Along these high, steep banks, where you almost break your neck trying to get dunnage up to a level camping place, the voyageurs of the old fur companies toiled, "tí-í-ing, tí-í-ing" in monotonous sing-song

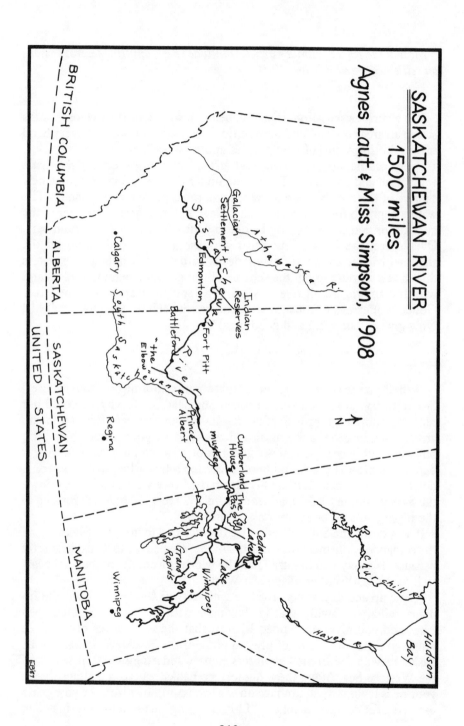

SASKATCHEWAN RIVER
1500 miles
Agnes Laut & Miss Simpson, 1908

BRITISH COLUMBIA

ALBERTA

SASKATCHEWAN

MANITOBA

UNITED STATES

N

•Calgary

•Edmonton

•Regina

•Winnipeg

Athabasca R.

Galacian Settlement

Saskatchewan R.

Indian Reserves

South Saskatchewan R.

Battleford

Fort Pitt

"the Elbow"

Prince Albert

muskeg

Cumberland House

The Pas

Cedar Lake

Grand Rapids

Lake Winnipeg

Hudson Bay

Churchill R.

Hayes R.

day and night, tracking all the way from tidewater to within sight of the Rocky Mountains. Then, up these waters with rapids so numerous you lose count of them, galloped at race horse speed little Sir George Simpson, doughty governor of the Hudson's Bay Company, with the swiftest paddlers the West has ever known.

You can make the Saskatchewan trip in three weeks. That is—you can if you race like Sir George Simpson, travelling day and night; but if you want to camp near the new settlers each night and see how they are making good away from the immigration agent; if you want to wander over the sites of the old historic places and ramble to the Indian reserves where you can meet natives still uncontaminated by the whites—better make your time limit six weeks. You could profitably spend twelve on the trip.

Our outfit consisted of a big Klondike freight canoe, twenty- two feet long and wide enough in the beam to take a small steamer trunk crosswise, a tin grub box proofed against the marauding huskies, cooking utensils, food enough for five or six weeks, with a margin of rice and flour over actual needs (in case of delay from high winds when crossing wide lakes), a small tin tent stove, and three tents. The canoe we chose in preference to a York boat or scow, because it could be handled by one man and ourselves with an extra paddler for the roughest rapids only; whereas a York boat would require a large crew, and a scow at least three men.

Curiously enough, my camp companion is a niece of the little governor who used to race up and down this river. At four o'clock on the clear sunny afternoon of August 5th we shoved out from the bank near Edmonton on the roily flood of the Saskatchewan, swift here as a mountain stream and still silty with the grind of the mountain glaciers. Our canoe could easily have carried twenty people; and Miss Simpson and I had intended to take two men paddlers along with an Indian woman; but the old timers advised us to take only one thoroughly competent head man and to pick up a second paddler only where we needed special steering through dangerous rapids. The time has long passed when any one man knows the Saskatchewan River from end to end. Today you can hire only men who know the river in sections; so it came that we did the first 800 miles of the river with only one man and the help of the other two big paddles wielded by ourselves.

Morning call at six, breakfast at seven, on the water at eight—that was the daily routine, with variations earlier when mosquitoes prevented sleep, or later when the weather forbade setting out; but that programme does not tell you anything about the mice running over the tent roof between you and the stars, or the Northern Lights setting weird shadows dancing, or the lonely bark-bark-bark-yapping howl of the coyotes, or the first pink cart-wheel shafts through the morning mists as the sun came up

211

over the water horizon. By the time you have encountered a dozen families of ducks sidling and sailing to the current through the hiding of mist with babies scrambling over the water half-wobble, half-scuttle, not sense enough among any of them to be afraid – by the time you have encountered that and felt the great soft white sun-shafted peach of the quiet morning, you begin to wonder what it is all about down there in New York, anyway, where men hound one another with wolfish zest for a thing that is not and never will be happiness.

We had been plying down the current the second day, watching Galician and Russian women washing linen at the river brink and noting how islands dotted the widening expanse like a second St. Lawrence or Georgian Bay, when a sound of rushing waters came from the fore and our canoe began to pick up her pace like a horse taking the bit. The river was swirling along in corrugated runnels too swift to spread out from centre to shore, and we were bouncing through our first rapids almost before we knew it. With high water and a good steersman (and we had both) the sensation is one of sheer delight, with far less risk than you run taking a motor down Broadway.

Well-intentioned advisers had strictly warned us "to portage *all* rapids." I wonder, did they know some of those rapids were twenty-two miles long? How many there were on the whole trip I don't know. We lost count after the twentieth. As the big canoe rose and fell to the buoyant swell with the ease of a sailboat climbing waves, it seemed perfectly absurd that log booms had jammed the size of a house and scows gone to wreck on these rapids. I asked two Indian steersmen whom we picked up for the worst water what the trick of running rapids was; and they both answered the same thing – to catch the drive of a current that will carry you away from the angriest spots; having done that, not to work too hard, but to let her go quartering to the wildest rush. To catch the drive at just the right moment of just the right swirl to miss the angriest rocks is not always easy.

Beyond the Galician Settlement for a hundred miles you are traversing a wilderness primitive as the day when white man's boat first penetrated these lonely wilds. Hawks shriek from topmost boughs of black poplars ashore. Whole colonies of black eagles nod and bobble and scream from the long sand bars. Wolf tracks dot the soft shore mud; and sometimes, what looks like a group of dogs, comes down to the bank watching you till you land, and when they lope off, you see they are coyotes. Again and again, as we drew in for nooning or supper to the lee side of some willow grown island, black-tail deer leaped out of the brush almost over our heads and at one bound were in the midst of a tangled thicket that opened a magic way for their flight. Early one morning, a little fawn came trotting down to the shore of a long island and ran abreast of us, unconscious of danger for half an hour; and one night when we drew into a lonely bank for camp, we found the mud heavily tracked by large footprints like cattle; but there were no cattle within a hundred miles; and from the dew claw, it was apparent the tracks were of moose.

From the Galician Settlement to Lake Winnipeg, a distance of almost a thousand miles, with the exception of the section round the Elbow, a good hunter could keep himself in food summer and winter with small labor. As to mosquitoes, I was so long a resident of the West that I must have become immune; but when they are so numerous and so big they darken the outside of your tent, there is no denying their existence, though I do not know what it is to be bitten by them. A few Chinese joss sticks set smoking and stuck up in the sand inside our tent kept the unwelcome pest out.

Down to the weed-grown site of old Fort Pitt the north bank of the Saskatchewan is flanked by Indian reserves. More ideal hunting ground could not have been chosen. In the valleys nestle lakes literally black with wild fowl.

Fort Pitt for a hundred years witnessed scenes of daring hunt and high wassail. Furs to the value of millions of dollars were brought here from the North and rafted down the Saskatchewan. Here paused Governor Simpson on his mad pace across the continent to race his thoroughbred "Fireway" against all comers along the mile track, which you can still trace across the river front. Hither came hunters with ponies and dogs gay in ribbons and a-jingle with bells for the week's racing. Fort Pitt also witnessed the most stirring scenes of the '85 Rebellion, when bad management by flunkeydom brought about a clash of arms that was at once tragic and criminal. Of the old fort there exists today not a vestige but the cellar holes.

Between the Indian reserves and Fort Pitt you pass from the Province of Alberta to Saskatchewan, and begin curving round that three-hundred-mile bend in the river known as "the Elbow." Very slack water it is, wide as a lake and shallow, with such numbers of sand bars and islands you lose yourself trying to keep the current. Shallow water sounds easy for canoeing. Take my word for it, and choose the deep!

For a hundred miles from Fort Pitt was not a single settler. It is lonely, high-rolling, sheep-ranch country, with no population that we could see but the coyotes and eagles. The tempest days of heat and wind were usually followed by calm nights, with the river gold in the evening glow, and the clouds sweeping down the lonely valleys like gorgeously clad spirits in a realm of mist.

On the afternoon of August 15th the river was once more winding through homesteads, and a sudden bend brought us to the little town that was the capital of the Northwest in the territorial days – Battleford. The tide of progress has rolled past her door, but now immigrants are beginning to come to the old capital and it is the most frontierish looking town north of the Boundary. At the street corners you may see as curious a medley of humanity as any place in the world. Doukhobor women with bright handkerchiefs round their heads, big Galician men with cowhide boots half-way to the waist, ruddy-faced Germans, soft-spoken Norwegians, French rivermen now turned lumberjacks, Cree Indians from the near reserves, American settlers from Iowa and Nebraska – jostle along the board walks or hold animated conclave over some newcomer's prairie schooner.

Leaving Battleford, the river takes a great bend to the north to Prince Albert, a trim little city on the south bank with one main street facing the river and a great wealth of trade in furs and lumber. Recently discoveries of gold quartz and copper ores in the Lac La Ronge district 220 miles north toward the Churchill River have set the little city dreaming of another kind of wealth. I confess the wealth that interested me the most there was the wealth of legend about the Old West. Here dwell many of those delightful and vanishing types of old-timers who have seen the West transformed from a boundless hunting field to a checker-board of barb wire fences. They have lived the kind of things that other people read about – these old frontiersmen – and some of their experiences make the finest spun inventions of fiction seem very flaccid indeed.

Beyond Prince Albert the Saskatchewan takes a great swing northeast through the true wilderness primeval. The rough water below the town is the first of twenty-two rapids round as many sharp bends in the river, some mere riffling of the current more noisy than dangerous, others good bouncing water long as sixteen miles.

The night of August 29th we camped where the Saskatchewan breaks from its river bed and, flowing up the old channel of Sturgeon River, breaks again eastward through Muskeg River to Cumberland Lake – lengthening its course by 150 miles. We were now in the country of pure muskeg – quaking silt, soft as sponge, overgrown with muskrat reed and goose grass. There were not even *low* banks. There were *no* banks at all. Your canoe was on the level with the land, and the reeds lined the aisled water channels sixteen feet high. You could stand on prow or stern of your canoe, and far as eye could see were nought but reeds and waterways, waterways and reeds. This muskeg covers a region of about 70 by 200 miles, in wet seasons 300 miles.

Mighty glad were we on the morning of Saturday, August 20th, to see the tuft of a lone lob-stick rise above the mist marking the site of Cumberland Lake fur post. With a rasp of the keel on the pebbles and a howling welcome from the husky dogs in all the keys of a grand orchestra gone on a drunk, we landed in a storm of rain that almost blew us off our feet. The fort is built on an island that runs out like the fingers of a hand. We had landed on the point farthest from the Hudson's Bay House. A tramp through the woods did not lessen our sopping wetness, though it was impossible to add to it—like the sponge, we had reached our full absorptive limit. Dripping from hats to boots, we entered the little Hudson's Bay store and presented our water-soaked letters of introduction to the management.

Guests at a house three hundred miles from anywhere, without warning of mail or wire, are no light consideration for a housekeeper where help cannot be hired; and a child had been born that very morning in the home of the manager. I begged the bookkeeper to tell Mr. Rosser not to bother about us, but just to assign to our use one of the empty houses where we could spread our camp kit to dry. Do you think that easy way out appealed to the Hudson's Bay Company fancy? The mother heard that two women had arrived and could not rest till we came across to the house. Two hours later, dry and glowing warm, we sat down to such a dinner of wild game as money could not buy in the hotels of New York or London.

Having swung north for 350 miles, the river now turns southeast for 200, winding amid banks of heavily forested swamp round great bends where the current coils in glassy pools known as big eddies.

The Pas or Pasquia Mission lies seventy miles south of Cumberland House, on a limestone knob of rock that sticks up through the interminable muskeg for all the world like the fist of a drowning man. It is the centre of a big Indian Reserve, and by virtue of its position along the route of the new railroad that the Dominion Government is building to Hudson Bay, it is the newest city in Canada.

Toward night, the second day out from the Pas, it became apparent that the chart had led us astray. We should have been at Cedar Lake, and we were not. The banks had fallen even lower than at Cumberland House. A spot of dry land the size of one's bootsole we did not see mile after mile, though reeds grew on both sides in feathery ridges lining interminable swamps. There was an angry sunset across the marshes with a heap of black cloud-drift coming down on us before a high wind. We had been paddling a back-breaking pace and betting last boxes of raisins that the next twirl would bring us round to Cedar Lake Post. All afternoon the ducks had been whistling overhead so low you might hit them with your paddle, and the old ganders did not bother to honk a "get-up" when we came on the big flocks bobbing and wading among the reeds. Suddenly all three of us gasped and dropped our paddles.

"What in *thunderation* is that?" someone asked.

I have heard old-timers' tall stories and lived many years in the West, but I had never heard what I now saw with my own eyes. It seemed like the dream or delirium tremens of some old hunter. I thought it was a shallows of small drift. Then the sticks began to move.

"There are millions! There are millions!" exclaims Sexsmith. "I've lived twenty years in this country, and I never saw anything like it."

We drifted close to the hiding of the reeds and—looked! Then, someone hit the water with a paddle, and the whole surface lifted—a live mass of wild fowl, ganders honking-honking in confused circles, white ducks, black ducks, young teals, old mallards—the air was aquiver with a whistling of wings; and the creatures did not know enough to be afraid. It would not have been sport; it would have been slaughter to have hunted there. You could have waded out and caught them in your hands. Apparently, our stray wanderings had brought us to secluded and unfrequented haunts of northern wild fowl.

At noon, Saturday, September the 5th, we rounded a high rocky point of a lake-like expanse as if we had been shooting the chute, and at the same moment once more struck the roily lost current of the Saskatchewan. The banks were pink granite—*cedared!* That was enough. We were on Cedar Lake—the only cedared forests of the whole Saskatchewan. Then, at a turn, there loomed on the crest of a high hill to the fore—Indian huts. Close ashore we saw the red-doored, white-log store of the Hudson's Bay Company.

What with its wonderful game haunts and forested pink granite islands untrodden by man and unrun by fire, Cedar Lake down as far as Grand Rapids—a distance of sixty-four miles—is bound to become a great summer resort in the North. Sunset in a crimson sky set the lake on fire. The wind lulls at last, the first time, I think, since we left Edmonton five weeks ago. The willows are no longer green, but gold. Clumps of brush have turned deep purple in the frost. There is a tang of winter chill in the air; but it is ozone that goes through your blood like champagne. At Cedar Lake there was only one white family, that of the company manager, Mr. Hooker, an Eton man, stuck at this Back of Beyond.

"Isn't it lonely and dangerous for your little family so far from a doctor?"

"Oh, yes, it *is* lonely," he admitted, "but not dangerous in case of illness. Why, last winter, when my little boy was ill, I had to take the dog-train only fifty-five miles for a doctor."

The last night out we camped amid the cedars under a Turner sky—all bronze and gold mist with a blood-red sun, burnt umber shot with fire, a wild scud of tangled purple clouds above, red bars like brush strokes across mid-heaven, and the quick-silvered lake deepening to lavendar. The sunset boded ill for next day, and we set out in the morning to a piping wind with a Cree sail, rigged of our canvas, and two sapling trees. The lake gradually narrowed to a sharp bend between banks of gold willow, and about mid-day of Monday, September 7th, we swirled out to the main river again. Swift eddies warned of the Little Rapids just beyond the Narrows, a mere riffling of the current, but they bounced the canoe about in fine shape, giving prelude of what was to come in Grand Rapids. At this point, the company has a storehouse to receive cargoes above the Big Rapids.

Where the waters of half a continent become hemmed in between rock walls not a third of a mile wide with such steep descent over huge boulders and rocky islets that it could not be any steeper without being a cataract – I can promise you that things are doing in the river. We heard the far wh-u-sh; then the wild roar; then the full-throated shout of triumphant waters! You think your blood will not run any faster at that sound after having run more rapids than you can count? Try it! We sat up from our sluggish easy postures. Then the river began to round and rise and boil in oily eddies and the canoe to bounce forward in leaps without any lift on our part – then a race-horse plunge; and we are in the middle of the furious tumult! The Indian rises at the stern and leans eagerly forward. Even the cool Sexsmith admits, "This *is* a place where the river really does things, isn't it?" But the Indian is paddling like a concentrated fury. Sexsmith drops to the bottom of the canoe to lower weight and prevent rolling. Then we shoot forward into a vortex of whirling sheaves of water.

"She – strong – she – *ver'* – strong rapid," shouts the Indian as we swirl past one rock and try to catch the current that will whirl us past the next. "Pull-pull-pull – a strong paddle," and we rise to a leap of wild waters, plunge into the trough, and are climbing again before someone can remark, "Say, I don't like ever sidling to rapids."

There is a rock ahead about the size of a small house, where the waters are breaking, aquiver and white with rage. The Indian had risen again. "Stop," he yells, "don't paddle! Let her go!" but he, himself, is steering furiously as we gaze past out to the bouncing waves! So we run the Big Rapids for about a mile, then ride a third rapid in a long easy swell, and swerve into the north or left side where a tramway of three miles leads past the last and worst of Grand Rapids. Only a riverman who knows this last rapid as other men know their dining room will conduct parties down. As we did not care to risk our expensive canoe, the Indian went overland to the Hudson's Bay manager asking for the tramcar to convey our kit across to the lake.

217

A walk for three miles over punky logs along that very foot trail which the fur brigades used to follow of old brought us suddenly to an opening on the high cliff commanding the Big Chute. It is a wild scene—the wildest of any rapids I know in America. The river bed is scored and torn to tatters with rage. Huge rocks split the torrents and throw them back in furious turmoil. These are the rocks where so many countless craft have come to grief when the crews failed of strength or nerve for the big lift past the undertow. Great rocks of spray rise above black pools with deafening roar.

None of us said very much; but we had decided to run those rapids by better light next morning and were walking back to our camp when a wild "yahoo" through the woods hastened us. While we were at the Big Chute, half-breed boys had come with the horse and cart to convey our traps across, and they shouted that the last steamer on Lake Winnipeg for the season was leaving Grand Rapids in an hour. A moment later we had jumped in the canoe, which was strapped on the tramcar. I think we were fairly well content to leave the Big Chute for the next trip.

Following Mrs. Hubbard Through Labrador
JUDITH NIEMI

Labrador was a place that fascinated readers and adventurous travellers at the turn of the century. Medical missionaries had made the name familiar, and there it lay—a bleak, beautiful, vast, still-unexplored wilderness, stretching from the St. Lawrence River north to Hudson Straits, from Hudson Bay to the Atlantic. People were beginning to notice there wasn't much wilderness left on this continent, and Labrador was close enough to be accessible to east

coast canoeists and gentleman adventurers. Bowdoin College boys went there; William Cabot made many trips, trying to meet the Naskapi Indians. Ladies went too: Martha Craig apparently made several summer trips into the interior with the Montagnais Indians; in 1908 Steven and Florence Tasker hired two of Mrs. Hubbard's guides for an ambitious trip across the peninsula (Florence did not enjoy it). The most publicized and controversial of all the explorations were the Hubbard expeditions.

Mrs. Mina Benson Hubbard got to be an explorer the way

". . . there came a sense of unspeakable relief in thus slipping away into the wilderness." (*A Woman's Way Through Unknown Labrador*, 1908)

219

women sometimes get to be politicians—she married one, and he died. She was an independent Canadian woman with a career in nursing and unmarried until she met Laddie at 31. Leonidas "Laddie" Hubbard was an outdoor writer who hoped his exploration of the Naskapi and George Rivers would establish his reputation. He got lost in the wrong rivers, and starved to death. Mina Hubbard channeled her intense grieving into another Hubbard expedition, which she carried out successfully, always emphasizing she was only completing her husband's work, for his name.

"... many times I found myself wishing I need never have to go back again." (*A Woman's Way Through Unknown Labrador*, 1908)

But, in spite of herself, she also had quite a wonderful time in Labrador. She wrote the story in A Woman's Way Through Unknown Labrador. (*New York, 1908, reprinted by Breakwater Books, Newfoundland, 1981. Other sources of information are listed in the Bibliography.*) *When I read her book, the obvious thing to do was follow her route, to get to know her and Labrador. Jesse Ford's story in Part One ("What Did Flies Matter When You Were Free?") is about our 1982 trip; this is about Mrs. Hubbard's journey, as I see it, and in many of her own words.* ★

A lady explorer was standing next to the roaring river in Labrador, wearing a long skirt over her knickers, her moccasins gripping the wet boulders. Rapids fascinated her. "I wanted to be near them and watch them all the time," she wrote. "They were so strong, so irresistible. It made one wish that it were possible to join them and share in their strength."

Her alarmed guide came up the trail. "Mrs. Hubbard, you must not do that. You will get dizzy and fall in." "But I do not get dizzy," she protested. George Elson was adamant. That was one of the problems of being a lady

★ See accompanying map on page 8.

220

and an explorer in 1905. Chivalry. Even in wildest Labrador, Mrs. Hubbard was in some danger of having no adventures at all. Much as she liked and appreciated George, she confessed that she found it sometimes irksome to be so well taken care of.

Seventy-seven years later when a group of Minnesota canoe women followed her trail we wore the clothes we thought she'd have been more comfortable and safer in: neoprene rubber wetsuits, layers of wool pants, lifejackets. In our indestructible plastic canoes, we got to run the rapids she had to walk around. We wanted Mrs. Hubbard to be with us in spirit and brought along one outfit for her: an ankle-length wool skirt and Gibson Girl blouse which we took turns wearing, although not very often.

And we wondered what camping life must have been like without the wonders of modern technology (no DEET in the bug dope! No plastic bags!). Labrador was called by early explorers "The Land God Gave to Cain." Gale winds and icy rain dripping down your neck. What an uncomplaining and enthusiastic spirit she had. As we re-read her book around our campfires, we realized that the significance of her journey was not just that in 1905 there had been a woman explorer who made an amazing trip. It was that a spirited woman had, briefly, found a way to step out of a civilized world that didn't fit her very well. For she came to really love this wild country and her life here.

For Mrs. Hubbard, this trip had begun in grief, and in bitterness. Her poor dead husband, lost and starving on the wrong river, had been fond of quoting Kipling: "Something lost beyond the Ranges, lost and waiting for you—Go!" A small man, with a Teddy Roosevelt moustache, Laddie Hubbard was an incurable optimist. Wandering around carrying a canoe through rough country with no water in sight, he still talked of a "bully trip." Even when staggering from hunger, eating moldy flour and his own moccasins, he was saying "We can and we shall." His companions Dillon Wallace and George Elson loyally followed his charismatic leadership (George often offering some realistic pessimism and foresight), and very narrowly escaped with their lives.

Mrs. Hubbard did not forgive Wallace for outliving her husband, whom she idolized, nor for describing him as the poor brave homesick boy he was at the end. Wallace was planning a return expedition, so she also decided on a trip to Labrador "to complete my husband's work." There was not much precedent for being a lady explorer, but the role of grieving and dutiful widow could be understood by the public. She financed the trip herself. Laddie's Scots-Cree guide, George Elson, readily agreed to go with her.

What a difference in style, and outcome, there was between her trip and her husband's. Or between hers and Wallace's rival expedition, which was on the Naskapi and George Rivers at the same time. For one thing, she really listened to George's suggestions, and brought enough provisions, not counting on "living off the land," where local people often feared starvation. Her book has no boisterous lines from Kipling, and none of the woodsy language of outdoor books of her time; nobody shows true "grit" or eats "grub." There are no heroic poses in the photos.

The Hubbard-Elson expedition and Dillon Wallace's set out the same day, same place. (Not that either ever mentioned the other in their books!) His photo caption: "Our lonely perilous journey toward the dismal wastes had begun." "All were eager to plunge into the unknown and solve the mystery of what lay beyond the horizon." Even the weather seemed to co-operate: "As if to give us courage for our work and fire our blood, the leaden curtain was drawn aside and the deep blue dome of heaven rose above us."

Mrs. Hubbard's leave-taking is told with less drama. She was, after all, travelling with Indian guides who lived in a rather similar place and called it not a perilous waste, but home. The horizon was less mysterious since the Labrador boy with them knew people who trapped up the Naskapi River. "It did not seem strange or unnatural to be setting out as I was on such an errand," she wrote. "Rather there came a sense of unspeakable relief in thus slipping away into the wilderness."

She soon developed a friendly, bantering relationship with George and the other guides whom he had hired. "Every day my admiration and respect for the men grew. They were gentle and considerate, not only of me, but of each other," she wrote. "They had jolly good times together," and she enjoyed listening to them sing "Lead, Kindly Light" or an Indian paddling song. They treated this unusual white lady with chivalry and friendliness. The boy Gilbert Blake blew up her air mattress each night (Mrs. Hubbard observed, sensibly, that without a good night's sleep she would lose her nerve); the shy Cree Job Chapies who "loved to pole up a rapid or hunt out a trail just as an artist loves to paint," slipped her a plate of pancakes, cooked up just the way she liked them. Joe Iserhoff rigged up a trolling line for her. In a while Mrs. Hubbard was enjoying the trip so much she felt almost guilty, and was forgetting her grief.

At least that's how we read it, as we pored over her book, getting some practical tips about the route as well as a sense of history. We joined her trail halfway along it, at the top of the Labrador plateau, skipping the long upstream haul on the Naskapi, which had taken Mrs. Hubbard five weeks. The Naskapi has been dammed—one of the main concerns of modern canoe travellers—and would be a better backpacking route. Train and plane bring a canoeist to Lake Michikamau (now the Joey Smallwood

222

Reservoir). But as soon as you shake off the speed and noise, you are in a place where not much has changed since Mrs. Hubbard's time.

Right away we could locate sites from her book. Here's the deep channel they poled up. Here's the hill where Mrs. Hubbard almost ran right out of her moccasins, excitedly chasing caribou with her cameras. George teased her, insisting that to catch them she should sprinkle salt on their tails. The caribou are still there, and we shared their enthusiasm. "The country was literally alive with the beautiful creatures," she wrote. "The enjoyment of the men showed itself in the kindling eyes and faces luminous with pleasure. All his long wilderness experience had never afforded Job anything to compare with this day. He was like a boy in his abandon of delight."

They did shoot an occasional caribou for food, of course. Mrs. Hubbard hated to watch, but she found it delicious, and appreciated the security of extra provisions. But they did not need more food at the time they met the biggest migration. "I am glad I can record that not a shot was fired at them. Gilbert was wild, for he had in him the hunter's instinct in fullest measure. The trigger of Job's rifle clicked longingly, but they never forgot that starvation broods over Labrador." For days the group simply enjoyed stalking caribou, trying to photograph them, sometimes racing after them.

Hard portages and dangers counted for little in a country that was filled with caribou, and rainbows, and beautiful rapids. One evening at the riverbank Mrs. Hubbard asked pensive George what he was thinking of. "I was just thinking how proud I am of this river," he said.

"How little I had dreamed when setting out on my journey that it would prove beautiful and of such compelling interest," she wrote. By the time she reached the upper George River, she was in love with the country. "Weariness and hardship I had looked for, and weariness I had found often and anxiety, which was not yet past. But of hardship there had been none. Flies and mosquitoes made it uncomfortable sometimes but not to the extent of hardship. And how beautiful it had been, with a strange, wild beauty, the remembrance of which buries itself silently in the deep parts of one's being. In the beginning there had been no response to it in my heart, but gradually in its silent way it had won, and now was like the strength-giving presence of an understanding friend. The long miles which separated me from the world did not make me feel far away—just far enough to be nice—and many times I found myself wishing I need never have to go back again."

But the question of when, and how, this expedition would end did begin to intrude. Still in the upper George River, Mrs. Hubbard and her group made almost no progress for a week because of early August snowstorms. If they did not arrive at the Hudson Bay post at Ungava Bay by the end of the month, it was likely they would miss the only supply ship of the season. How could she support her crew over the winter? What other route could they use to return? And she had no way of knowing whether it would take ten days or two months to get there. Her men were willing to go on, but was turning back the only responsible thing to do?

Windbound on those boggy riverbanks, feeling "rather desperate, and sick with disappointment," she spent a restless night, and seems to have resolved the question intuitively. "My tent was sweet that night with the fragrance of its carpet of balsam boughs, and a big bunch of twin flowers, but it was late before I slept. Perhaps two hours later I awoke to find a big moon peering into my face through the open front of my tent. I was startled at first, and instinctively reached for my revolver, not knowing what it was; but when full consciousness had returned, whether it was the effect of the moon or not, the question had somehow been settled. I knew I should go on to Ungava whatever the consequences might be."

Resolution Lake, she named a wide windy lake she came to the next day. It was a glorious morning, "rather shivery, but I loved it," and she met the first Indian camp, on a high hill which overlooks miles of water. There are still piles of caribou antlers there, gold with lichens, and long silvered tamarack poles lie on the ground, left from the tents of the Montagnais that Mrs. Hubbard met. The Montagnais women were afraid, until George spoke to them in their own language, because all the hunters had gone to Davis Inlet on the coast for winter supplies. The camp was poor in food. If only we'd known how close the Montagnais were, Mrs. Hubbard thought, we could have easily brought them some caribou. According to the Montagnais women, it was still very far to Ungava.

More unknown river for them to find a way through. "The river drops rapidly round many little islands of pink and white rock by a succession of picturesque falls and rapids and chutes, and here a number of short portages were made." Picturesque, we grumbled one exhausting day. *She* could talk, she wasn't carrying her own damn packs! Mrs. Hubbard realized how easy the trip was being made for her. A photo in her book of George and Job loading up packs is wryly captioned, "The white man's burden."

But she was busy and productive. One day she took advantage of the men's being busy portaging to get an entire afternoon to herself, happily ranging far and wide on the hills, scouting. She was rained on, and flies bit her till the blood ran down her neck. "Still what did flies matter when you were *free,*" she thought. We found her descriptions of the route an accurate guide of what to expect in the rapids.

Finally they reached Mush-au-wau-ni-pi, the Barren Grounds Lake. (Indian House Lake on maps.) It was a landmark that Mrs. Hubbard had

224

been waiting for. Sixty miles of no rapids and no portaging! You enter a "great magnificent corridor," the narrow lake stretching away to the North with 500-foot hills on either side. From the gravel ridge at Naskapi Point you can look miles down the lake. The ground is covered with bearberry and crowberry, and the place is full of the kind of presence you feel where people have lived for a long time.

Mrs. Hubbard found the Naskapi camped here. They were so little known in her time that even her own guides from James Bay, whose language was close to theirs, were afraid of what the encounter might bring. They had a reputation among the English for being "intractable" and unreliable – that is, they preferred not to become dependent upon the Hudson Bay Company and white man's food. This was wise of them; Mrs. Hubbard learned that their hunters had just returned from Davis Inlet, where they had found the post empty – the supply ship had not come. They had been unable to get food or ammunition from the English.

It was, in spite of George's worries, a very friendly meeting. They invited Mrs. Hubbard up the hill to their camp (where she went, of course, noting that George would have preferred that she didn't), and they exchanged gifts. The people seemed more care-worn than the cheerful Montagnais. "Even the little children's faces were sad and old in expression as if they too realized something of the cares of wilderness life." The old women, she thought, "seemed the brightest of all and were apparently important people in the camp." She noticed with enjoyment that one of the handsomest young men, with the reddest leggings, was casually trying to make an impression on her. This kind of friendly interest was not always typical of travellers of her time. "In a way which I had not in the least expected," she reflected, "I found these people appealing to me, and myself wishing that I might remain with them for a time."

From the Naskapi Mrs. Hubbard heard good news – Ungava was quite near, only five sleeps if she travelled very fast. But expressive hand gestures told of the steep rapids and waterfalls they could expect all the way. The sun, for once, smiled on her journey, and they sped down the long lake in only two happy days, with a tailwind, once even catching an unwilling caribou for a brief tow. At the outlet of the lake begin the 130 miles of almost continuous rapids that Mrs. Hubbard said were "like a toboggan slide."

Mrs. Hubbard calls this part of her trip "the race for Ungava." There was ego and reputation involved in her unacknowledged race against the Wallace party, and very practical consequences involved in her race to catch the supply ship at the post. Still, they did not rush, and we thought they set a good example for careful wilderness paddlers. "The travelling day was a short one during this part of the trip. I often wondered how the men stood the strain," she wrote. "Once I asked Job if running rapids did not tire him very much. He answered, 'Yes,' with a smile and look of surprise that I should understand such a thing." They ran close to the shore, occasionally cutting out around ledges.

Leadership was flexible. Mrs. Hubbard had decided the expedition would continue to Ungava; to George she left the day by day management of the journey; all of the men took part in route finding. Now Job, as the most experienced whitewater man, had the biggest responsibility. When he was feeling unwell, Mrs. Hubbard asked him, "Too many rapids? He smiled and said, 'I don't know,' but as if he thought that might be the trouble."

Job woke one morning from a troubling dream of their being entrapped in rapids and carried over a fall. "He told his dream, and the other were warned of danger ahead." They took extra care that day, spare paddles in easy reach. What a pity, we thought, that Mrs. Hubbard's husband had not been able to pay similar respect to George's intuitions. On that dreadful return trip George had a vivid dream directing them down a new route. Had they been able to follow the river without a mishap, it would have brought them to a settlement. It was only a dream, said Laddie. They went the other way. Well, speak no ill of the dead, we thought, but if The Leader Laddie had not been so boyishly arrogant. . . .

Well, then of course his widow would not have found her way to this incredibly beautiful place. "Splendid mountains," as she had told us, rise a thousand feet above the river. "We are in the midst of scenes which have a decidedly Norwegian look." Another "very, very fine mountain reminds me of an Egyptian pyramid. The river grows more magnificent all the time. I took one photograph of the sun's rays slanting down through a rift in the clouds, and lighting up the mountains in the distance. I am feeling wretched over not having more films. How I wish I had brought twice as many."

Her observations were so precise that we learned not to be surprised at seeing a porcupine right where she did. But once poetry seems to have outrun the facts. "More weird and uncanny than wildest cascade was the dark vision which opened out before us at the head of Slanting Lake. The picture in my memory still seems unreal and mysterious, but the actual one was as disturbing as an evil dream.

"Down, down, down the long slope before us, to where four miles away Hades Hills lifted an uncompromising barrier across the way, stretched the lake and river, black as ink now under a leaden sky and shadowing hills. The lake, which was three-quarters of a mile wide, dipped not only with the course of the river but appeared to dip also from one side to the other. All seemed motionless as if an unseen hand had touched and stilled it. A death-like quiet reigned and as we glided smoothly down with the tide we could see all about us a soft, boiling motion at the surface of this black flood, which gave the sense of treachery as well as mystery. As I looked down the long slope to where the river appeared to lose itself into the side of the mountain it seemed to me that there, if anywhere, the prophecy of Job's dream must be fulfilled. Cerberus might easily be waiting for us there. He would have scarcely time to fawn upon us till we should go shooting past him into the Pit."

That is not the kind of place a careful canoeist can admit to looking forward to; still, it's just a bit disappointing to get there and find no sign at all of the sideways slant, of the treachery and mystery. Different water levels? "Maybe she was feeling PMS?" we suggested, disrespectfully. But a wilderness trip can have those days when the place, the mood, the weather conspire to create that kind of foreboding. With no topographic maps to tell them the river did not go crashing into a canyon, with no safety equipment to make a capsize seem an acceptable possibility, they must have been under enormous tension. Looking back into the rugged Bridgman Mountains they had just come through, "George said, with something of awe in his tone, 'It looks as if we had just got of prison.'"

"I shall be glad for everyone, and especially for Job, when we have left the rapids behind," she wrote in her journal. There was one near upset, and several times Mrs. Hubbard was asked to get out and walk around a dangerous place. Though they never talked of the rapids as sport, there's no doubt the men – and Mrs. Hubbard – did enjoy the excitement. "Sometimes after passing a particularly hard and dangerous place we ran into a quiet spot to watch Joe and Gilbert come through. This was almost more exciting than coming through myself."

We wondered sometimes if Mrs. Hubbard wouldn't have made a fine whitewater paddler. For a while I felt quite righteously indignant – what a pity it was that she never did get to paddle at all, even in calm stretches. But that wasn't just because she was a woman: up to Mrs. Hubbard's time a number of male canoe explorers travelling with Indian guides had also not paddled their own canoes.

On the day that they approached the end of the trip, however, Mrs. Hubbard found sitting still was almost impossible in her anxiety. "I did wish that the men would not chat and laugh in the unconcerned way they were doing. If only I might reach the post and ask about the ship! If only I might fly out over the water without waiting for these leisurely paddles! And now, from being in an agony of fear for their lives, my strong desire was to take them by their collars and knock their heads together *hard*. This was not practical in the canoe, however, and I was fain to control myself as best I might." The men were amused at her impatience, and teased about drinking up for lunch the little bottle of tea she was keeping as a souvenir. And she admitted, sheepishly, "Quite out of harmony with the still dignity of the day and the scenes of desolate grandeur was the mind within me."

And suddenly they were there. The Eskimos and Mr. Ford, the Hudson's Bay Company agent, welcomed them. They were in time for the ship, and ahead of Dillon Wallace. (He would arrive six weeks later, after many adventures and misadventures.) She might have felt relieved. Triumphant. She didn't.

"There are times when that which constitutes one's inner self seems to cease. So it was with me. My heart should have swelled with emotion, but it did not. I cannot remember any time in my life when I had less feeling." Numb, she noticed that "Mr. Ford was asking me to come with him to the post house and looking at my feet. Then George was seen to rummage in one of the bags and out came my seal-skin boots." She does not remember what they talked about, only that Mrs. Ford had very blue eyes, and they "shone like stars as she took my hand and said, 'You are very welcome, Mrs. Hubbard. Yours is the first white woman's face I have seen for two years.'"

But her men were still sitting at the canoes, not having been invited up to the post. "Suddenly I realised that with our arrival at the post our positions were reversed. They were my charges now. They had completed their task and what a great thing they had done for me. They had brought me safely, triumphantly on my long journey, and not a hair of my head had been harmed. They had done it too with an innate courtesy and gentleness that was beautiful." She went immediately back to her men, to thank them, and they came up the hill to make camp. "As I watched them from the post window busy about their new camping ground, it was with a feeling of genuine loneliness that I realised that I should not again be one of the little party."

Any intense trip may end with times of disorientation, saying goodbye to friends, wondering how to hold on to a reality that is already beginning to slip into unreliable memory. But when we sadly left the George River, we knew we'd be able to re-create this life. We'd see our paddling friends back home, we would try to bring our Labrador selves back to the city, and we would soon be planning more wilderness trips. Mrs. Hubbard could probably see no way to do any of that. It was over. The beauty, and excitement, and the easy-going life with her guides. All that must have seemed totally unconnected to the world she'd be going back to.

We thought about that a lot. Maybe she should have done something rash, like marry George and go live in Missinaibi or Moosonee? That wasn't a totally far-fetched fantasy. They were warm and admiring friends, who had in common their dedication to Laddie's memory. In the National Archives of Canada are Mrs. Hubbard's and George Elson's unpublished diaries. George mentions how much Mrs. Hubbard had encouraged his aspirations, his idea of writing. She was like the dearest sister to him, "my best friend in the world." Mrs. Hubbard for some reason was nervous enough to ask the men to sign statements that they all had behaved like Christian ladies and gentlemen. She did have public opinion to consider.

But what if she hadn't thought it was her duty to go back to New York and write a book, and get her husband's (and George's) name on maps? Could she right then have jumped out of her upbringing and even *considered* chucking it all and going to live in the woods? Probably not. Anyway, she didn't. She wrote her book and went to England on a book tour, where she married and had children and was later divorced. As quite an old lady she walked onto railroad tracks and was killed.

But once she did make a return trip to Canada, in 1936. No details are known of this, just the barest facts: she was 66; she looked up George Elson, living in Moosonee, Ontario. And they went on a canoe trip.

PART FIVE:
Listening

Turtle River, Ontario (Judith Niemi)

Martha Craig (*Cosmopolitan*, 1905)

"When the rivers are freed from their icy chains, the innermost depths of my being respond to the call of the wilderness. Tell me where anything comes from, and I will tell you whither it is going. Things animate and inanimate move in circles. In their course they change their identity from time to time, but each change is only a step on the journey back. I go back to Nature because that is where I came from, that is where we all came from. We are all on the way back, but at different stages in the journey."

—Martha Craig, "My Summer Outings in Labrador,"
Cosmopolitan, 1905

THE CANOE TRIP is travel in physical space, and in mind and spirit, although the geography of those travels is less easy to describe than portages and campsites. Wilderness travel can be a deliberate or half-recognized quest, from which, as Lady C. C. Vyvyan writes, "the serious traveller can never return home unchanged." These essays—and others in this book— are by women who see canoeing as a significant part of their lives, who try to listen carefully, and who reflect on some of the places to which rivers have brought them.

232

Bear Story

HEART WARRIOR CHOSA

Heart Warrior Chosa lives six months of the year at her family cabins on Basswood Lake within the Boundary Waters Canoe Area of Minnesota. She picks up her supplies at Ely, 22 miles away and across two lakes and a four-mile portage built by her grandfather in the early 1900s. Her father's people are Ojibwe whose original village was on Basswood Lake, and her mother's people are Métis of the Turtle Mountain Reservation in North Dakota. She studies spiritual teachings from many sources, as well as traditional Indian medicine, and is a sun dancer. She sews Hudson Bay blanket capotes, in line with her Métis heritage, and at her home on Basswood Lake offers historical workshops and campouts with women's medicine talks from a native American perspective.

In 1987 she published Seven Chalk Hills *(Ely, Minnesota: Bearhand Publishing), book one in a projected autobiographical trilogy,* The Heart of Turtle Island. *The following story is an excerpt from the third book. "It was a time of realignment," she wrote, "of withdrawal from the dominant culture after I earned my B.F.A. I was offered an Indian TV news program, and scholarships to continue for a master's degree, but instead went back to the home of my ancestors to reacquaint myself and replenish my spirit. My task on this particular canoe trip was to become at ease with nature and purify from city life."*

In June of 1974, I went on a canoe trip alone into Canada. My son had returned to the cities and was staying with his grandma. My intention was to camp and canoe for a couple of months in the wilderness. Consequently the canoe was overloaded.

The first day out was innocent enough. There were no portages, so I easily covered twenty miles with the wind blowing strong against me. That's when I really enjoy canoeing. Calm days when the lakes are like

Heart Warrior Chosa (Judith Niemi)

glass are beautiful, but not as invigorating as rolling waves, cool spray and a good struggle. That evening I camped in a secluded spot, hanging the Duluth packs high in the trees so hungry bears wouldn't get them.

I heard the bears were getting used to campers and often raided campsites. They were especially active that summer. I overheard the camp guides telling funny stories about how the bears were smarter than the tourists. They usually were loners, but with the number of canoers and camping people coming into the area the past few years, the bears had started working in groups raiding camps. Otherwise they were never seen in the woods. They never came around my cabin.

The second morning at dawn after a hasty breakfast, I struggled with the two huge packs plus my drum and books. I balanced, ever so carefully loaded, with the last pack on my back held by only one shoulder strap, and one foot in the canoe. The weight shifted, the canoe tipped, and everything ended in the lake, soaking wet.

After my gear was dry and neatly packed into the overloaded canoe, I shoved off. By then the early morning mist that usually floated across the top of the lakes was gone. There was no wind and it was a sultry day, the lake like a mirror. On such days my canoeing isn't as ferocious. The canoe glided silently. Soon it seemed effortless, and my mind wandered to the clouds above, or trailed through life's events, or watched the beauty of the water and how it seemed like oil sometimes, deep and mysterious.

Most canoers recommend staying close to the shore, but I always like going right down the middle of the lake to get the total view and make faster time. The canoe would float if it should capsize, and in a good wind you would eventually be carried to shore. So I never felt afraid of the water. But the woods had taken more getting used to.

* * *

Only a few summers before, I met a biologist and took a two week canoe trip with him and his students. He had a real love for the woods and it was from him that I learned all the herbs in the woods and their scientific names. It was on this trip that I felt I was really initiated into the woods. We plunged through every type of habitat on the land. There were so many beautiful spots and different land formations, with small rivers, bouncing sedge mats, and rushing falls, each creating a world apart.

I have so many memories of that first camping trip with the biologists, that it is still like a dream. The group was always awake and completing breakfast with the dawn. As the sun hit the horizon we silently stole out onto the still waters and paddled in the mist that lay upon the lakes during the first half hour of the morning. The cool stillness of the damp air was invigorating.

I was the official interpreter of the red rock paintings we came upon a week out on the trip. Scientists have not been able to figure out the type of paint used, for it is thousands of years old. These paintings are on the sides of cliffs near the water's edge. One particular bunch of them was located near an island that was one gigantic rock. Once on top of that rock you could see for endless miles in any direction. The Indians used to call it Warrior Hill, and from the rock drawings it appeared to be a holy vision quest place. It's about a forty mile canoe trip from our family cabins and near a Canadian Indian village of people who used to make their camp with our family years ago during wild ricing time. It must have been where my great-grandma sat when she first made it back home to this area after her escape from her captors way to the North.

There are special places where we lunched or camped that were holy. The atmosphere would change as we neared these holy grounds and would provoke such a quickening that at one place everyone felt it. We had arrived one afternoon at a small island with raging falls on both sides of it. Everyone was drawn to a silence carried suddenly inward. The intensity of that place cut our lunch break short, as it was more than most of us were prepared to stand.

I found another exquisite and holy sight when I had run off alone from a campsite to locate a secluded spot for my sweat lodge. Every night when we stopped and made camp, I took a sweat. I went alone, as it was a private thing in the Indian Religion. The teacher knew I did this, but the others knew nothing about it.

Thick green moss covered the forest floor as I searched further into the woods. There lay a huge flat waist-high rock. The energy of the rock was of an altar. Colored rays of the setting sun shone through the trees. There, on top of the rock, was growing one of the rarest and most delicate flowers natural to that area. Its stem is made of interwoven white petals and is shaped just like a peace pipe. That's why this flower is named Indian Pipe. Next to it lay some feathers, as if set there by a bird. It was an altar made by nature.

The altar campsite was towards the end of the trip. That evening I had just completed giving an astrological reading to the professor and we sat talking. Suddenly storm clouds were crashing and a torrent of rain and hail plunged to the earth. None of the hail hit us but it sank at least six inches into the moss-covered earth. Lightning displays followed, and the professor and I watched for a long time. In the cloud formations could clearly be seen a man and a woman talking. With each crash and change of flashing light the silhouetted figures appeared to move, nodding their heads and gesturing with their hands. It was like a copy of us talking.

*   *   *

Now, out here for a long trip alone, I paddled along, steeped in memories of that time – first real trip canoeing and camping – and flashed on the many people who had never had this experience with nature and who were afraid of it. Even many Indians today who are raised in cities never have had these experiences. It is always healing for me being here. I was alone and prepared to camp out under falling stars with plenty of notebooks for recording the vivid dream life that sleeping right on the earth seems to bring.

The canoe glided effortlessly along in the still unmoving waters of the hot afternoon. I neared U.S. Point and climbed out on the jutting flat rocks for a break and soon fell asleep in the hot sun, like a turtle lying on a log. I awoke with a start, worried about losing too much time.

Coming up the lake was a group of canoers. I decided to scootch in with their formation because I intended to go into Canada without a pass and a plane flies above checking campers. A tight watch is kept and only so many passes are issued a summer for tourists. Since our family are the only people allowed to live in the Boundary Waters except for an old woman to the east of us, we don't need passes, unless going into Canada. Of course, the Jay Treaty made long ago gives border Indians the right to go back and forth, but the government never lives up to these treaties and Indians are too poor to fight them on it.

The lakes went many different directions from that point and after we were inside Canadian waters, I cut off alone toward the northwest into waters I had never been in before. Soon a huge wind came up and blew the canoe into shore. I hastily jumped out and pulled the canoe up on land, turning it upside-down. I was sure a storm was coming, as it was rare I couldn't handle the canoe in the wind. Soon the tent was up with the rain tarp above it. There was one skinny tree too small to hang the Duluth packs on and one huge tree too tall to hang them on, so I put them between the tent and the canoe. I dove into my mummy sleeping bag, waiting for the downpour. Nothing happened. After awhile I came out and ate a cold lunch and sat on the flat grey rock that jutted out over the water.

This is a wasted day for making time, I muttered to myself. First I swamped the canoe, then fell asleep on U.S. Point, and now got fooled by the wind and made camp too early in a place I'd never ordinarily choose. It was obvious I'd brought too much junk along, and the portages coming up would have to be crossed four times each before I got all my crap across. Dejectedly, I scraped the ground with my foot.

The campsite was very small. On two sides was water. Behind was a sheer rock cliff and on the other side a swamp with a little river running through it. The site was inaccessible except by water and that thought made me feel safe about any bears bothering me. Ah heck, I might as well read and record notes. I had brought a notebook and was keeping an eye on the Mars transits in particular and had an ephemeris along that told where all the planets were each day. Again I dozed off unexpectedly.

Four loud splashes on the water woke me. It was twilight and the air had cooled off. I flashed back to a camping trip my son and I went on when he was about five, and how one campsite was across from a beaver lodge and how the beavers slapped their tails on the water right next to us as they swam by. That must be the sound of beavers, I thought, then was snapped out of my reverie by the most stinking odor.

Oh no, only one thing can smell like that. Bears! It was too late, as I lay pinned in the mummy sleeping bag. One sat on the left side of my little one-man tent and another was on the right sniffing, while another sniffed further out and the fourth ambled along and fell upon the food pack. "Ho, ho, ho," he roared in deep throaty laughter. The closeness of his delighted laughter to human sound startled me stiff. That was followed by the screeching rip of a pack and happy snorts and grunts. I visualized him finding the gallon glass jar of honey, a gallon glass jar of peanut butter, the dates, raisins, nuts, and blueberry and raspberry jam!

The other bears didn't seem to join him and the one to my left side sat there the whole time, periodically scratching himself. After a while my terror subsided a bit and I shimmied out of the mummy bag, quietly so as not to alarm the bears. I wasn't aware they worked in groups now, and surmised it must be a mother with yearling cubs. Everyone knows the only dangerous bear is a wounded one or a mother with cubs. If she knew I was there and I made any sudden moves, I'd get clawed or trampled to death. There wasn't that much room on that little island. Ee-gads, I thought, there's no escape. Foolishly I had placed the food pack between me and the canoe, and all there was in the tent was some rolled up maps, a book and a flute.

Being a person who has to act in an emergency, I picked up the flute, if only to keep from panicking. I was afraid, but also reasoned the bear was one of my clans and so I shouldn't be afraid. It seemed hours that I talked to them through the flute. They listened attentively and quietly. When finished, I sat still, listening to them and they sat quietly unmoving also. Their silence seemed to have a question in it. Perhaps they thought I was a big soft musical rock.

After another hour I grew claustrophobic – I've got to bust out of here. I reached for my boots. The slightest rustling noise brought them scurrying close to the tent with long deep tokes and sniffs. When I pushed them on the nose they scrambled backwards. This went on a while till I was dressed and sent a message, "I'm coming out no matter what." After a long silent pause, I crashed through the door, jumped over the packs, grabbed the canoe and dove into the water with it, and paddled furiously out into deep water.

I floated out there and found I couldn't see one inch in front of my face. It was the dark of the moon. Everything in me was strained from hearing the bears, smelling them, but not being able to see them.

Actually, by averting one danger, I had landed in another. It was five miles back to the campsites at U.S. Point, via twisting unfamiliar waters which eventually opened up to a huge expanse of water that went in four directions, all dotted with smaller islands. I couldn't see the shore lines with only the starlight; besides, the front of the canoe pointed up because of my weight at the stern. The slightest wind could have pushed me off course or over into the water, and I only guessed where I might be. Never had my sense of feel been so much called into play.

Soon I arrived at the great body of water which seemed several miles to cross. U.S. Point was the only familiar landmark I knew, but around its shores were boulders sticking out of the water so the approach had to be careful even in daytime. Luckily I found it and paddled around the rocks. Earlier that day I had passed a campsite a quarter of a mile down. Guessing the spot, I hollered into the night, "Help, help, is anyone there?" After awhile a male voice answered.

By the time we sipped the steaming hot coffee around the campfire, the sun was on the horizon. They turned out to be a group of eight men from Chicago on their first fishing trip in the Boundary Waters. They had everything but the kitchen sink including motor boats, which have since been barred from the lakes there. They gave me a ride back to my camp. The bears, it appeared, had not eaten anything, but had run off with the cooking oil and a box of powdered milk. The peanut butter was smeared all over the ground and a full teeth impression was sunk into my cook pot. One pack was ripped open but the other was intact. Either the bears weren't hungry or the garlic bulbs prevented further investigation.

I packed up the canoe and decided to paddle back to my cabin for a good night's rest. The next day, still shaken from the experience, I picked up a book a friend sent me, not knowing what it was about. This will relax me, I assumed, sitting in the captain's chair propped next to the long window I had set into the frame of the door that used to lead out onto the porch.

The book turned out to be prophecies from around the world from Nostradamus, the great pyramid, Hindu astrology, Edgar Cayce, etc., all on one subject—the end of the world. Not a relaxing book. I threw it down, leaned back in the chair and turned to press my nose against the window pane and peer out into the waning day. At the same moment a bear on two legs, with paws on the window sill, peered in with nose also on the window pane. Our noses met exactly on time. "Ahhhhhhhh," I yelled jumping up on quivering legs. "Ahhhhhhhh," yelled the bear as he flew into the woods.

Ever since then I've never been afraid of bears but have a healthy respect for them.

A Way of Life

VALERIE FONS

Valerie Fons has made canoeing her way of self-discovery and her career, paddling many thousands of miles in the last five years. Her book, Keep It Moving: Baja by Canoe *(Seattle: The Mountaineers, 1986), tells of the personal transformation that took place during her first major trip, 2400 miles on the ocean in a solo canoe. She is listed in* Guinness Superlatives *for the world record in paddling the Mississippi River (2348 miles in 23 days). With Anne Renaud she won the women's title at the World Championship Au Sable Marathon in Michigan. She is one the few women members of the prestigious Explorers' Club; she writes and gives slide programs on canoeing, finding that sharing her experiences with others is the "blessing of adventure."*

The following commentary on some of her experiences during her unusual career is assembled from her previously published writing and from several letters from Valerie, since she has once again gone canoeing. She and her husband, Verlen Kruger, are away for two and a half years on a Two Continent Canoe Expedition.

* * *

"I left home to go canoeing," Valerie says. That was in 1982, and she hasn't been home since. Or rather, a canoe has become her home.

She had been a casual canoeist, just learning to love the fast movement of racing canoes, when she met Verlen Kruger as he passed through Seattle on his 28,000-mile Ultimate Canoe Challenge.

Something about his energy and the spirit of that trip drew her. She asked to join, although she had almost no sea paddling experience. A few weeks later when Verlen called to see if she could accompany him on one leg of that trip, the dangerous 2400-mile trip around Baja California, she didn't hesitate. Within three weeks, she had rented her home to strangers, quit her job, sold her car, and outfitted herself for paddling on the Pacific Ocean.

240

The journey took them three and a half months, paddling down the western coast of the Baja Peninsula, then north up the Sea of Cortez. Often they had to paddle all night to reach protected harbors. In this excerpt from her book Keep It Moving, *Valerie describes one crucial incident of that trip, being caught in a* chubasco—*the Spanish word for high winds reaching hurricane force.*

My sheltered upbringing in the suburbs of America had defined gale warnings as rain drops on the outside of the windowpane. Hollywood movies educated me on the blues of stormy weather with a vision of Lena Horne standing on a bright lighted stage torching her popular song. My favorite television weatherman declared atmospheric disturbance with a wave of his hand-held pointer.

The reality of a storm was vastly different as I sat at the water line in my small canoe. We were literally sailing northwest. Putting paddle in the water did little good, since there was no water to draw—it was all scooting under the boats from the force of the wind machine at our backs.

We were flying, but not on course. The wind was pressing us toward shore, and the coastal land there was a low flat plain with sand shoals and breakers off the lagoon openings heading to the main channel of San Ignacio. Both of us paddled maniacally, turning the canoes sideways into the wind, quartering the force against us, trying to work our way into open water.

The canoes were making no progress west in the sea of constant motion. Waves climbed like angry fists punching toward the sky. We could not judge the reef systems—the entire ocean was erupting. Pointing the bows directly away from land, we headed west against the blast that was pushing us shoreward.

"We can't turn north yet, Verlen, I see breakers over there," I cautioned.

Steering judgment was now more critical than ever: we were in danger of losing control and being shoved on a northeast angle positioning us between an evident reef break and the frenzied surf beating onshore. The collision course became unavoidable. Breakers crashed fore and aft and ahead a crest tumbled forward, falling in a mass of foaming white water. A nightmare was made real in the storm.

"Keep your bow pointed straight into it," Verlen was yelling. I had never hit an explosion head-on. The angle of direct confrontation was crucial if we were to stay upright. Light blue water and bubbles of violence cascaded over our bows, smashed our faces and covered the sky. I was buried in a rush of water that pressed my arms and paddle flat to the deck of my canoe. In an instant I recovered my motion and kept paddling as we punched out and through.

The scene would soon repeat, and we had only a moment to clear the space before another swell arrived for its disintegration. Precisely as the jaws shut, we had slid through a space between the front incisors, and were spit clear from the force of the reef.

Terror has a limit. There on the reef, where Verlen and I escaped with our lives, my fear died in the battle. The miracle of coming through brought a humble acceptance of the work to be done: we would have to paddle without letup to avoid being swallowed in the storm.

They paddled all night, past exhaustion, often just holding the bows into the wind. Finally they saw the lights of a harbor, and at dawn were able to land through the treacherous surf. Twenty-seven boats had been overturned by the sudden storm. With only a few days' rest, they set out again to complete the voyage.

Later, Valerie reflected on her entire Baja experience. "I had learned to survive, but I had also learned how to live. The experience had transformed me. It had developed within me a durabilty that was not something I would say goodbye to. I would live with this blessing the rest of my life."

Asked how she had decided to do a trip that involved such risks, Valerie said, "I chose to go because I couldn't do anything else. I couldn't ignore the strong feelings I had about breaking out from my life and experiencing the world of nature. I wasn't running away. I had a lovely home, many good friends, and lots of activities, but a door of opportunity came and I knew I had to take it. I remember that a teacher told my mother once that I had lots of energy, but what I needed was direction. The movement of the water spoke to me and I discovered a direction."

Valerie next decided to compete in the 1983 World Championship Au Sable River Marathon in Michigan. In the thirty-six year history of the race, no women's team had finished the race in qualifying time. She called Anne Renaud and asked her to be her partner. "At first she would not even return my calls. She thought the idea was impossible—two women racing against the men. But I didn't want to race the men, I just wanted to be the very best I could be. And Anne agreed with that principle."

Valerie first moved to Montana to train with Anne, and a month before the race they drove to Michigan to scout the course. "Many news stories said it was Anne and I against the river but that couldn't have been further from the truth. We were two women working with the river. When we arrived at the Au Sable, we sat on the bank and put our hands into the water, making friends with the river, knowing we would work with the current every foot of the way. We were on the Au Sable River to do our best and as we entered the Men's Pro Division, we became two good paddlers, not two women."

They finished the 240-mile race in 16 hours and 50 minutes, in tenth place, ahead of twenty other teams.

In April 1984 Valerie and Verlen took on the Mississippi River Challenge, a race down the full length of the Mississippi, competing against the previous world record of 42 days, held by a British Royal Air Force team.

In her "pre-canoeing life" Valerie had developed a love of quilting. Her quilted Christmas banner packed away in its waterproof bag had accompanied her on the Baja trip, surviving two efforts to lighten the load by eliminating all unnecessary equipment. Now while preparing for the Mississippi race, Valerie calmed her uneasiness and anxieties by beginning a Mississippi Quilt with her sister-in-law, Marianne Fons.

Our success in the canoe race would depend on our commitment to the finish, a commitment built on motivation that grew from desire and intensive preparation. Every detail of the race was figured in advance. Like a colorful quilt, our race was a vision even in the planning stage.

I began to sew. As I hand stitched each block, I tried to visualize the race itself. With needle and thread in my hands and my mind attending to creation, I began to feel the strength and peace I needed. I knew that when the race started I would be required to paddle like a machine. The womanly parts of me found expression in the makings of the Mississippi Quilt blocks. My part of the challenge was now under control.

Valerie and Verlen finished in 23 days, 10 hours, and 20 minutes, beating the British Royal Air Force record by 19 days. Valerie also used the Mississippi River Challenge as an occasion to raise pledges of $10,000 which paid for the training of a guide dog named Missi for a blind student from El Paso, Texas.

Besides her races and publicized expeditions, Valerie has found the time, and the need, to travel alone. Her first solo trip was on Lake Superior, following the Minnesota shore from Grand Marais to Duluth. It was October, when the lake is often very rough. "My one real problem was knowing when to get off the water, gauging my reactions and trying to understand how far my fear would allow me to go before good sense took over to tell me the water was too big and I should head for shore." At the end of the trip she sat out a storm for three days, waiting for the surf to calm, before she finally gave up and went home to try again during calmer months.

Valerie considers her most successful solo trip to be a 200-mile trip across Iowa on the Des Moines River.

"Heart's Desire is the fourth block of my Mississippi quilt. The record for racing the Mississippi was previously held by the British Royal Air Force. We were out to beat the best of the men and knew a commitment of determination was necessary." (Valerie Fons)

I had the necessary equipment and a good base of experience. I took the correct food and I went knowing what I wanted to accomplish, and it worked. The river was not beyond my skill level and I was able to concentrate on reading the river and paddling toward my goal. What a great experience!

But once again my problem became fear. At night after paddling forty-some miles, I would be tired and my imagination would get carried away about being alone in the middle of nowhere without the security of another person. I tried to find security within myself and within my faith in Jesus, but I was plenty scared at night, wondering what the sounds were outside my tent.

I found, though, that the situation was what I had sought, what I wanted—a confrontation with myself, a woman in the wilderness—that would enable me to grow and become more capable of pursuing my happiness.

In 1986 Valerie and Verlen Kruger were married, and in June, when the ice went out, they left from Inuvik, Northwest Territories on their Two Continent Canoe Expedition. It's a 21,000-mile voyage of discovery, from the Arctic to Cape Horn, in which they are observing and documenting the land, peoples, and water quality of the western hemisphere.

Just a couple of weeks before leaving on this expedition, Valerie sent us a letter telling what canoeing has meant in her life:

Canoeing has helped me to achieve my goals. I used to try something and not succeed right at first and so I would quit. Canoeing has helped to teach me what the rewards are when I don't quit but stick it out..By challenging myself and pushing myself to reach my goals, canoeing has helped me grow up.

Please say that women can be explorers. That is what I am becoming – a canoe explorer. And I love it!

Celebration

SUE SHERROD

Sue Sherrod is a physician practicing anesthesiology in Dallas, Texas. Since 1976 she has been an active whitewater paddler, making annual canoe or raft trips on the Rio Grande, Snake, Colorado, and Nantahala Rivers. In the last few years she has also been exploring the world—trekking in Nepal, volunteering in Ethiopia, and "wandering around" other parts of Africa. "I've had a glimpse of my mortality," she says, "and now if there's anything I want to do, I don't put it off."

In the summer of 1982, she and three other Texas women (six for the first part of the trip) canoed nearly 2000 miles of the Yukon River from White-horse, Yukon Territory, to the Bering Sea.

Why am I so afraid? Why can't I "get a grip" as Beth, our trip coordinator, would say? Is our situation really as dangerous as it seems? Things have really stacked up on me today. First, a maddening early morning upstream paddle, then an all day paddle in a hellish wind, and now at day's end there is no place to lay my weary head. Every one of my muscles aches. Of course, I'm angry too. Jude, my canoe partner, has pushed for days to finish this trip, is still pushing, and I'm screaming, "Go where? There is nowhere to go!"

The desolate Yukon River bank stretches as far as we can see, unchanging, inhospitable. We've already tried to stop three times. The shore slopes at a 60-degree angle, up some 15 feet to what we hoped was land, but was very unsolid tundra brush, muskeg swamp, and mosquitoes. We can't even sit down and rest on it, let alone pitch a tent. I worry about Beth and Evelyn—we lost sight of them miles back. They tend to paddle slower, an advantage today. I hope they found a campsite and are now off this treacherous river.

We are tired, bone weary, but there is no way we can rest. For either of us to put our paddle down even for a few seconds means the wind takes the upper hand, wrenches us around broadside and begins its destructive work of dumping wave after wave of frigid Yukon River water over our gunnels. We are carrying a heavy load and the possibility of swamping is not far from our minds. How cold would that water be? How long would one have before hypothermia rendered one senseless?

For that very reason we hug the shore, hoping we could swim if we had to. The waves seem a little smaller and less angry near the shore—or is it just a feeling of comfort we get from being near land? Of course, there are dangers here, too. A particular characteristic of the Yukon is its tendency to undercut its banks, which then sometimes fall into the river in great hunks, with a sound like a cannon shot.

For some reason I blame it all on Jude. She is young and strong and seems to react to everything with an enthusiastic "Let's go!" The big white-capped waves are pounding us, battering us; I don't know how we keep going.

As if by magic, and just in time, the wind dies, the waves calm. We have time to ferry across the powerful current to an island, a solid tent-pitching, head-laying sandbar. Now I find the sunset becomes a thing of beauty instead of fear. The sandhill crane call is music to my ears, and Jude is once again a fine warm person. Even the vast, flat tundra has its charm. I see its scrubby bushes bathed now both in sunset hues and in autumn yellows and reds, for it is late August.

We have spent the whole summer, 74 days so far, canoeing nearly 2000 miles of the Yukon River. In these difficult remaining days on the lower river we often ask ourselves why we came here. I know why I came—to celebrate life. Reluctantly I think back on my last year, remembering the feelings vividly, the days of fear. . . .

*　　*　　*

Cancer. The word recurs like the chug-chugging of a locomotive gradually accelerating. Cancer. My mind has got to stop reeling. I have to stop this train of events, which seems like a runaway, with no engineer. Instead, there are just a lot of would-be drivers milling around, giving advice, all knowing they could drive this train given a chance and yet glad they don't have to. It all seems to be leading down a tunnel which narrows and ends in a huge black hole of fear, of desperation, of nothingness, of death. Cancer.

I have glimpsed down the tunnel, have tried to look in the face of fear, but I can't sustain it. I quickly turn back toward the light, the known, the comfortable, the routine. Still, the train accelerates. Cancer. If I don't do something quickly, when will the journey become irreversible? Has it already?

I try to break out of the paralysis of fear. It feels very much like a dream when one's legs just won't move, they're too heavy. In this situation my mind is too heavy, sluggish, reeling from the shock of it all. I am trying to get a grip between disbelief on one hand and that big black hole on the other.

I force myself to look at it, just a moment, and then look at reality. They may not be the same track. I can't see the convergence, so there is hope. If there is hope, there is decision—I can alter the course of this train. I have some control and many resources. I can fight this thing. I can use every switch available and turn this hurtling train toward the light, toward life.

These are my feelings as I pick myself up from the diagnosis of cancer and start the battle to live. My plan is to attack cancer from every front, use every method that makes any sense, to battle this disease. Conventional medicine, surgery, and radiology are major weapons but even these I plan to use differently. It is me they are working on and I can help run the show. I don't want to be herded around like a helpless sheep. I have a sense of direction now and the train is beginning to turn.

What else can I do? What about the mental aspects of cancer? The emotional? If I can get these areas of life in better order won't I be more able to fend off this dread disease? I have a therapist and a group. We practice visualizing, seeing our body's defenses kill the tumor cells. We practice taking care of ourselves and our own needs.

My friends are incredibly valuable. They set up a support group and come talk with me every week to help me over the rough spots, to make suggestions, to let me talk. My friends go to chemotherapy with me. My friends go to the river with me. We all laugh at my bald head and celebrate life. We talk of cancer and the continuing nausea of chemo, but also of the good things and everyday things.

On one of the river trips Beth mentions that she will be doing the Yukon River next summer. In a flash I recognize this is a perfect opportunity to end a year of total immersion in the battle against cancer. I could step off the train, at the end of twelve long months of hurtling along, racing to treatments, to work, to group meetings, to therapy sessions, and to doctor's appointments. I could finally rest. On the river, which has always represented peace for me, I could stop thinking about cancer. I immediately say to Beth, "I want to go."

My next step is to present this relatively wild scheme to my housemate and canoe partner. Jude is not as adventurous, not given to abandoning the usual on the spur of the moment. However, it is supremely important that she see the need for and beauty of this trip, for if she doesn't go, I won't go either. Jude has become the most important friend in my life. Through all my work against cancer she has been there, has picked me up every time I fell, has been there to lean on, to live with, to travel with. Our lives are so intertwined that even the Yukon would not be complete without her.

Once again she is there for me. She will go. She worries about mosquitoes, bears, not having a hot shower at least every now and then, and me. Will there be any medical facilities? Should I be where I can get checkups, X-rays, lab tests? I don't give it a second thought. Not that I don't worry about the occasional crazy bear who might give us trouble. But the Yukon will give me the means to look beyond cancer. I can see the good times, the adventure to come, and the fear of disease fades. The dark tunnel that frightened me so has become the bright river that calls to me to escape that weary world and live for a while just for the moment.

*　　*　　*

And this summer on the Yukon I have lived at the river's pace. We have learned to take the weather and this world as it comes.

We started where the Yukon flows free, below the dam at Whitehorse, Yukon Territory, June 9, 1982. There were a few days when the sun was the only object in a bright blue sky and the air felt clean and crisp. The clear warmth encouraged easy paddling or just drifting, sometimes shirtless, watching multicolored bluffs and mountains go by, dazzled by contrasting brilliance of wildflowers, and coolness of crystal mountain streams tumbling down into the silt-laden Yukon.

Our first two weeks on the river are not only a big water experience, they are a historical experience. We are following the route which gold rushers frantically travelled back in 1898, escaping a depression in the lower Forty-eight to look for gold in the Klondike. I'm also escaping, to look for a different kind of treasure.

We think of the gold rushers as we hit Lake Laberge. Did a three-day squall blow them, as it does us, to the right shore? We barely find a place to eke out a home between dense dark woods and cold, rocky beach and anchor our tents in the roaring wind.

We think of the gold rushers as I lead our group through Five Finger Rapids where the river has carved four passages through the bluffs. The roar and size of the river are awesome, all to narrow down and smash through the four channels with hundreds of yards of standing waves and turbulence. My years of whitewater canoeing pay off here, as we run the right passage. We know a bit about boat handling. They did not know. How many were lost here? There are no records, but we hear that only last year several canoeists drowned. One German couple drifted into the treacherous left channel; their aluminum canoe was found later with a basketball-size hole in it.

We think of the gold rushers as we pitch our modern, lightweight tents every night and crawl into our warm, fiberfill sleeping bags with Therma-Rest pads underneath. How much could they have lightened their loads if they had the nutritious, dehydrated foods that we have taken three months or more to prepare? Did they sing, as we do, sometimes rowdy, sometimes lonely songs? Did they think about bears at night as we do? Did one or two of them even move on down the river as we do one night after finding a huge, fresh grizzly print? Did they thrill as we do to the sight of moose, beaver, foxes, wolves, Dall sheep and bald eagles?

History is alive in the people we meet on the river. We see Sybil Britton canoeing alone one evening on Lake Laberge, and invite her to dinner. "Best offer I've had all day," she says, then tells us about herself, her love for the area and the people who live on the upper river. She has lived here long enough to know most of them. They all share the paradoxical struggle: how to remain free and yet make a living in the harsh demanding land. "You take any job just to stay here—I've worked more jobs in the last few years than I have in my whole life before that," she says exuberantly.

We spend a raucous Saturday night in Dawson, a town preserved in museums, dance halls, theaters, buildings, and spirit much as it was in 1898. We drink a beer or two and gamble a dollar or two at Diamond Tooth Gertie's. There really was a Diamond Tooth Gertie and she really had a diamond embedded in her front teeth.

We paddle on into Alaska. We stop at the beach in front of any town and start talking to whoever happens to be near. Not only are we outgoing, but the river people, whether Indian, Eskimo, or Anglo, are almost always friendly. They are eager to help, eager to talk, to share a cup of coffee or a salmon they have caught, or to just be amazed at anyone silly enough to get out on the Yukon in boats without motors.

As we journey down the river we pass fish camp after fish camp. In the summer salmon season the people disperse from the towns to these camps. Their dependence on the salmon is nearly absolute. If they catch what they need (and most wouldn't catch more than they need), it will be a good year. If not, many will go hungry because few can afford the food prices. The salmon run hasn't been good this year—not only that, the weather hasn't been good for drying them.

The weather turns bad one day in mid-July as we head for Rampart, a little village more than half way down the river. The wind blows and the rain falls continually. We camp in Rampart (we usually don't camp in towns) and wait for the rain to break. We wear parkas and long underwear. As it turns out, we better get used to this outfit for we hardly take it off the rest of the trip.

Three days later there is no sign of better weather, so we move out in the wind and rain and waves. Carefully. The changes in routine that this prolonged storm means for us are profound.

We can no longer drift easy in the balmy weather, reading and writing in our journals. We have to paddle, to keep our bows into the waves and to keep moving downriver. Before, we could cover thirty miles a day easily with some paddling; now twenty miles is difficult.

And what about meals? It's tough to sit around a campfire in gale force wind and drenching rain. It's tough to cook. It's tough to even see what we have to cook because we hate to dump out a food sack in the rain. Our system doesn't function well in thirteen straight days of such miserable weather. We do not have fast foods.

In a while, we also do not have dry tents. Or dry sleeping bags. Or dry much of anything for that matter. Waterproof bags become a joke, although we are rapidly losing our sense of humor.

One evening we camp on a barren sand bar, even though it would offer no protection from the wind. But it has been a windless day and we have paddled forty-five miles and are tired. In the middle of the night we wake up. Our dome tent is flattened against our faces. The stakes have blown out. The wind is howling and so are our fellow campers, although we can barely hear them. Next morning we learn that Beth's tent blew down completely. She crawled, tent and all, over to Evelyn's and yelled to be let in. Evelyn responded, "You'll have to let yourself in. I'm holding up the tent." That sand bar is home for two days while the wind plays havoc.

On these days, and others like them, Jude and I fill the weather-enforced tent time with scrabble and reading, but often those little nylon walls begin to close in. I start thinking again of this past year and my battle with cancer and that pervasive fear of death that I lived with for so long. I realize the fear has been absent this magical summer. Out in the wilderness time has been suspended, and it has often felt like nothing could happen to me, that I am safe here.

The howling wind seems to be warning us to leave the north country before an early winter sets in, so we push on, despite the unyielding weather.

And finally, we are nearing the end of this big river. It is as if the sun approves of our finishing, for on the last two days it shines on our smiles as we approach Emmonak, the last village. Here, surrounded by Eskimo

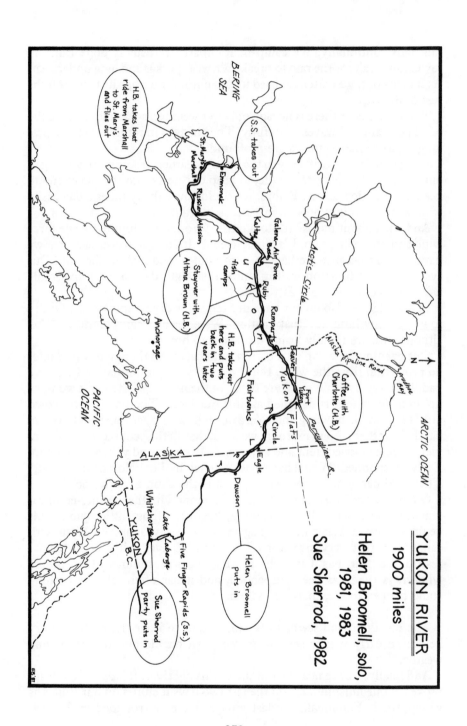

YUKON RIVER
1900 miles

Helen Broomell, solo,
1981, 1983
Sue Sherrod, 1982

ARCTIC OCEAN

N

Porcupine Bay

Arctic Circle

Alaska Pipeline Road

Porcupine R.

BERING SEA

St. Mary's
Marshall

Emmonak

Russian Mission

Galena—Air Force Base

Kaltag

Ruby

Koyukuk
fish camps

Rampart

Beaver

Fort Yukon

Yukon Flats

Fairbanks

Circle

Eagle

Dawson

Five Finger Rapids (S.S.)

Lake Laberge

Whitehorse

YUKON
B.C.

ALASKA

Anchorage

PACIFIC OCEAN

H.B. takes boat
ride from Marshall
to St. Mary's
and flies out

S.S. takes out

Stayover with
Altona Brown (H.B.)

H.B. takes out
here and puts
back in two
years later

Coffee with
Charlotte (H.B.)

Helen Broomell
puts in

Sue Sherrod
party puts in

252

children, we arrange our final day: disposing of extra equipment, selling our sentimentally valuable canoes, buying plane tickets to Anchorage, and arranging a tow from the Bering Sea back upstream to Emmonak.

Excited, yet a bit weary and sad, we get into our canoes for the last time, fifteen miles to go. Finally, we smell salt air; we paddle around a sand bar and there it is, the open sea. I'm a long way from the world I left in Dallas last spring. We have paddled one thousand nine hundred sixty miles. It is August 23, 1982, 1:10 P.M., Bering Sea Time.

Solo on the Yukon

HELEN BROOMELL

In canoeing down the Yukon River alone, at 65, Helen Broomell was fulfilling an old dream. She began "a love affair with canoeing" as a child, spending summers in northern Wisconsin around the boys' camp her father had founded in 1904. In the 1940s she listened fascinated to the stories Alaskan sourdough Slim Williams told the boys. Finally, after her retirement as director of the same camp, she said, "I had to go there and find out if everything Slim said about Alaska was really true. It was true, and then some."

She paddled 600 miles on the Yukon in 1981, from Dawson to the pipeline road, and then spent four more months travelling around Alaska. Two years later she returned to canoe the remaining 700 miles of the river.* In 1985 she made a sea kayaking trip with Alaskan friends. (Helen Woodings tells about that trip in "It's All Old Ladies," page 38.)

Asked how she got to be so adventurous, Helen said, "I wasn't always this way—it's a fairly recent acquisition. I was a typical suburban housewife. I smoked for 40 years, I wore high heels. Being divorced in 1967 and running the camp with my son was the beginning of a change. I hadn't had confidence in my ability to organize, in my leadership skills. I did a complete about face. Now I can't imagine anybody not changing; if you don't change, you don't grow."

Does she mind being known as "the canoeing grandmother?"

"No," she said, "I don't get annoyed at anything. It amuses me. I did this trip with no thought of anything but having an adventure. So I was 65 when I did it—that's neither here nor there. I inherited some good genes."

To avoid letter writing, Helen sent articles from Alaska to her hometown newspaper, the Lakeland Times *of Minocqua, Wisconsin. (These have been collected in two small books,* Solo on the Yukon and Other Alaska Adventures *and* Solo on the Yukon Again.*) This story is condensed from those articles and an interview with Judith Niemi in June, 1986.*

---

* See map on page 252.

254

Within each of us there must be, at least occasionally, a desire to simplify our life and reach out to new and challenging experiences. When I decided to canoe the Yukon, I didn't think much about the fact that I was going alone. But as I look back on it, I realize that in my whole life I had never been all by myself for any length of time. There's a 25-year span between the youngest and oldest of my children, so that's 40 years of taking care of kids. And after they grew up, there was the camp. So I never had been alone. It was high time!

I approached the Yukon trip as an expedition, not as a journey of self discovery. But I found out that I enjoy my own company and that it was very good for me to talk with myself for awhile.

But I also enjoyed meeting people along the river and spending time with them, finding out how they live, about their children. I didn't know if that would happen, if I'd be welcome, but I was. I learned a lot from the Eskimos and Indians and gained a deeper insight into my own nature. My appreciation goes out to all the new friends who now have become old friends, whose warmth and help along the way made it all work. The entire trip flowed from one experience to another in much the same positive manner as the mighty Yukon, and with about as many meanderings as I encountered paddling through the Yukon Flats!

1981

It was a sunny Saturday afternoon on June 27th when I launched the canoe in Dawson, Yukon Territory. The Yukon is one of the great rivers of the world. It carries the glacial silt from thousands of icy peaks, which accounts for its milky appearance and the strange, soft tinkling sound one hears in an aluminum canoe. The shores, particularly the outside curves, show the damage done at break-up when blocks of ice weighing tons come crashing downstream, demolishing everything in their way. Bark is stripped from trees 30 feet above the river, large boulders are shoved along the shore, and entire trees of all sizes are carried away, some as far as the ocean. There the Yupik Eskimos live in a land barren of trees, but with a seemingly endless supply of timber.

Young people in this day and age seem to be more into whitewater canoeing. And it *is* terribly exciting; I enjoy the whitewater when it comes along. But I don't like going out just for the thrill of the moment. I like to *travel* by canoe — it's a totally different feeling and attitude. To be on the river is to be in a world apart. Complete isolation, with no sight or sound of another human being for many days. It's something to cherish and enjoy to the fullest.

The Yukon at Dawson is about a quarter of a mile wide, with a current of six or seven miles an hour, which is just fine, and explains why excursions on the river are called "float trips." After only five days of paddling I arrived in Eagle, Alaska—110 miles, as I measured it on my map with a flexible plant stem. That's an average of 28 miles a day and it was easy, except for a strong head wind one day which brought white caps with it. Best not to "float" under those circumstances.

Helen Broomell at home in Minocqua, Wisconsin (Judith Niemi)

Eagle is about the friendliest town I've ever visited. I had invitations to be the guest of two charming girls who are living in a teepee just outside of town; an elderly gentleman who is a CB radio freak; and the two women and their four boys who own the general store. I chose the latter and was almost forcibly invited to remain another couple of days for a steak dinner and a salmon feast.

The Yukon flows free. With the exception of one dam fairly close to its source, there are no man-made obstructions in its way to the ocean. In the "Yukon Flats" the river widens, forming many channels, called braiding. Choosing a course is often a problem, as I proved by missing the town of Circle completely. Rain and high winds combined to conceal the village until it was too late to get to shore across the current. The decision to go ashore must be made about a quarter mile ahead of time, as there is no possibility of canoeing upstream! I was sorry to miss Circle, known during its brief heyday (1890–1899) as "The Paris of the North."

I spent several nights on gravel bars, and with a change in the weather to steady rain for almost three days, I was glad to have a good tent along. One night an old prospector's cabin furnished a roof over my head, while I slept on the table, the only flat place inside. The tin roof flapped all night and the thoughts of former occupants filled my mind.

As I neared Fort Yukon it was essential to do some careful navigating – I didn't want to miss another village. The islands are confusing, but by correctly figuring the current I came out suddenly facing what at first seemed to be two fifty-story skyscrapers. Nothing on the maps indicated this, and I felt as if I had been transported to some science fiction setting. Later I found out that the strange sight was the Early Warning System of the military.

Fort Yukon is located at the confluence of the Porcupine and Yukon Rivers, and is the air hub of northern interior Alaska. It was founded as a Hudson's Bay trading post in 1847 and is the largest native village on the Yukon. It's a surprise to find about fifty cars in a town with only eight miles of roads!

I found it very easy to meet people, travelling alone – that's why I turned down so many people who wanted to travel with me. Being alone, and a person my age, I have so many advantages. I don't pose a threat to anybody. I often was lucky to be included in local activities. A highlight in Fort Yukon was a trip by outboard about three miles upriver to check Bill Black's fish net. And in the evening I was invited to join four young people who are part of a group whose aim is to bring a recreational and water safety program to the children in outlying villages. As a retired camp director, it was interesting to hear of their problems and talk about the program. Some good conversation and a good location for watching the sunset-sunrise all at one time, as the orange-flowing sun moved around the horizon without falling out of sight.

Back on the river again. As a result of the junction with the Porcupine River, there was even more debris floating by. All sizes and shapes of trees, logs and branches slid by, looking like sea serpents and dragons. Because of recent rains the water level was high, and more and more mud banks were ker-plopping into the current. I watched a 30-foot spruce slowly topple in and be carried away, complete with moss and ferns growing among its roots. These trees travel at a great rate of speed in the current, and several times I've hitched a ride for many miles with a friendly tree.

In these weeks my paddling experiences went from one extreme to the other, from carefree floating to really working. I had sore and tired muscles from trying to cross the current one day when the river narrowed, the speed picked up and the wind did, too. I had no choice but to ride out the stretch of two-foot waves. It was exhilarating, to put it mildly.

I stopped in the village of Beaver for fresh water, and the postmaster was anxious to have me meet his mother, Charlotte. We enjoyed an hour or so of good talk and good coffee. At 75 she leads an active life, after raising ten children alone following the death of her husband. She says, "No hunger here. Hunger everywhere, but no hunger at my house in the old days."

Two more canoeists turned up outside of Beaver. One a carpenter who had built a cabin I visited in Eagle, the other a painter at Prudhoe Bay, on their way back to Fairbanks. I shared a wild rice, onion and beef jerky stew with them. (The wild rice I cooked at home, then dried in the warming oven of my range, and presto! instant wild rice.)

The last two days on the river brought me out of the Yukon Flats and into faster moving water and more mountainous terrain. With the end of my journey came a real regret at having to leave the river. The ever-changing Yukon and I had become good friends, although I'll have to confess that after three weeks, many aspects of her personality still remained a mystery to me. If nothing else, she left me with a great respect for her changing moods. Docile and euphoric at one moment, and the next moment angry and turbulent beyond belief. Rather like temper tantrums that rarely last for any length of time.

Perhaps sometime I would return.

Helen finished her trip to the only road access on the Yukon in Alaska much sooner than she had planned, due to the fast current and her high energy level in the long days. Not expecting to come back, she left her canoe at the truck stop, saying, "Sell it and keep everything over $100." Then she spent the next four months in Alaska's mountains and villages, hiking, rafting, dogsledding, and meeting people. When she got back to Wisconsin in the fall, she says, "I *realized I* had *to go back. I frantically wrote a letter – 'Can you hold my canoe for me?'" In 1983 she returned to do the rest of the Yukon.*

1983

It was good to be back on the Yukon again. Like meeting an old friend, it seemed as if no time had elapsed since our last visit, and we started in right where we left off. Two rigorous winters hadn't damaged my aluminum canoe that "Dave the Certified Welder" had reduced from a 17-foot boat to a 15-foot one for me. Easier to handle and I didn't need the extra space.

The river was about one-half to one mile wide here. With the all-night summer light, and the fast current, there's no reason for not drifting on if a person has trouble finding a campsite, and good campsites are rare. Shorelines are a mix of cliffs or bluffs, cut-banks that are a tangle of fallen trees and muck. The good old gravel bars from earlier on the river were replaced by mud bars, making camping impossible in many places.

The weather was a bit of everything. At one time repeated thunderstorms brought lightning, and hail that bounced in my aluminum canoe like cannonballs and on my head like golfballs. Following that storm more of the riverbanks fell into the water, making a lot of noise. The skies were more beautiful than I remembered, with sometimes half the sky bright blue with fluffy, white clouds, and the other half black and threatening.

The first village stop was in Rampart, where at one time there was talk of building a hydroelectric dam. Fortunately for those of us who like our rivers natural, and for others whose livelihood was threatened, the project was defeated.

Down river a few miles, I met a young man who invited me to come visit his mother and a friend at their cabin. They have a permanent fish camp on the river. For supper I had my first meal of fish heads. It's a custom to eat the heads first, and with salmon there's quite a lot of meat, but I'll confess to passing on the eyes. It was comfortable sleeping on their sofa and I enjoyed visiting with them.

For the next hundred miles or so there was little activity and no villages. These were excellent days for observing wildlife. A young black bear ambled along the beach at the same speed my canoe was drifting. For about a mile I watched him playing in and out of the water. Ravens are plentiful. I began to understand why the raven played such an important part in the folk stories and lives of the early Alaskan Indians. Their voices have an almost infinite variety of sounds, some as clear and bell-like as a marimba note, and at other times a mix of gurgling, gargling and glurping. They seem always to be arguing with the seagulls over a dead fish, or protecting their territory, or possibly (I like to think) just talking with me.

259

When alone in the wilderness, I speak to anybody who comes along.

One of the largest fish camps on the river is operated by the Honea family of Ruby. I couldn't turn down an invitation to a lunch of moose roast, mashed potatoes and salad, with such charming companions, after helping them remove salmon strips from brine and hanging them to dry.

In the village of Ruby I looked up Altona Brown, the eldest of the Indian women in town. She was going strong at over 80 years of age, and on her third pacemaker. When Altona noticed that it looked like rain she suggested that I stay over and sleep on her sofa, which was just fine with me, as I was anxious to hear more of her life. She gardens, runs her own skiff, could easily shoot a moose or a bear, was tanning two hides, makes mukluks, does beadwork, and to top it all off, she looks and acts only 60. She also speaks her own mind, and obviously is a very strong woman. We sat up late (for me), talking.

People make such a big deal out of me doing this trip alone at 65, while in Alaska there are women doing so many things that are much more substantial and much more impressive and difficult. Women going out and building their own houses, living a subsistence lifestyle, running traplines—things that to me would be impossible.

I didn't stop in the next village because there is an Air Force base there and I was afraid it would be a let-down after Ruby, which really has to be the gem of the Yukon. I set up camp downriver from the village and was cooking dinner when my "friends" began warming up an F-15, I think it was, just the other side of a bunch of willow trees. Following that a dust storm almost blew me away. If there had been another such performance I would have moved, but fortunately there wasn't, and except for a very disagreeable odor, it was a quiet, peaceful night. The juxtaposition of the fighter plane with the fish wheel made me think of the difficult position of the native people.

The villages surprised me with their friendliness, and I was often tempted to stay over longer. In Kaltag the impression was one of busyness. They were building sixteen new homes, there was a fish roe processing plant, and the town was obviously in the midst of change. There were people living in the old landmark church and tractors in the streets and bulldozers eating up the earth. And no trees. There are changes going on everywhere in Alaska, but nowhere is it more noticeable than in the Indian villages. The clash of cultures brings problems, but on the bright side, the old languages are being taught, old skills are being revived, and the old cultures may be saved.

One day I did a funny thing because of not having a watch. It had been windy and rainy, so I was tired enough to just fix something to eat and go to bed. After a good many hours of sleep I heard quite a few boats go by and thought the men were on their way to start their fish wheels. So after a good breakfast I was on the water. The sky was overcast and temperature cooler, but it wasn't until I had been out an hour that I realized something was wrong. Suddenly I was aware of lovely sunrise and sunset colors in both east and west! It wasn't long before the rising sun took over with an awesome display, and I was left marveling at the wonders of the universe. And laughing at myself, realizing that the men I'd thought were going to work had been instead returning from a night of partying in town. Apparently I had gotten up at about 3 A.M.

Another day I was caught late in the evening with no campsite available and a high wind. I retreated to the shelter of a cut bank where large trees had fallen into the water, making a natural protection from the wind. Spending the night in my canoe didn't seem like such a bad idea with a waterproof and mosquito- proof sleeping bag cover. This was obviously the time to try it. With a foam pad on the bottom and the canoe properly tied, I was soon sound asleep, lulled by the rocking motion and sung to by the wind in the poplar trees.

And then came the surprise! An odd sound awakened me—a small black bear was standing in a tree about twelve feet right above me! He was looking directly down at me with what appeared to be great curiosity. I sat up slowly so he could see me, and then began to bang on the sides of the aluminum canoe to see if I could get him to retreat. I was pretty sure he wouldn't jump into the canoe, but preferred to see him on the bank.

After what seemed like forever but was probably only a minute or so, he retreated to the land. I very quietly got out of the sleeping bag, untied the canoe, and pushed away from the trees. Not satisfied as to who or what I was, he continued to follow me down the bank before wandering off into the woods.

There were indications that the river was trying to tell me something about when I should be thinking of leaving it. Weather became more unpredictable, with a lot more wind, and the river urged me ashore several times. Sometimes gently, occasionally not so gently. I noticed, too, that instead of the large flat-bottom boats, all the boats now looked like large skiffs designed for use on the rock-bound coasts of Maine.

I didn't have a map for the last part of the trip, but the people I had talked to in Russian Mission said I would have no trouble. The day wasn't very auspicious as I paddled away from the village to the accompaniment of many children who came to see me off. There was more beautiful country, with bluffs for a number of miles accented by large patches of lichens of brilliant orange, pale green, and several shades of grey.

But as much as I enjoyed looking at these bluffs, they were beginning to take on a more ominous character as the wind steadily increased. At several points where the sheer cliffs rose straight up from the river, there was no place to land, and with the waves approaching a size I no longer wished to deal with, I began to have my first qualms about further travel down the river. As soon as there was a slough that I could sneak into I landed, in the rain by this time, and put up the tent in a spot that I wouldn't choose under other circumstances.

At one point during the night I was so concerned about the canoe and the fierce wind that I got up out of my warm bed, dressed, and fumbled my way through the brush to the shore. The canoe was okay, but I pulled it all the way up the wet and muddy bank.

The next day was more of the same. The sound of the gale howling around the cliffs, and the waves crashing against the rocks made me grateful that I was safely ashore. I knew that if I got frustrated or impatient by having to wait out the weather, I would just be making trouble for myself, so I sat still and went into a kind of meditative state.

I slept less well the second night, as I had decided that whatever time the wind stopped, I would pack up and leave to get around the hazardous rocks before another wind came up. Sure enough, I woke suddenly to realize that the strange sensation that had come over me was caused by the lack of noise. I could see well enough to get everything stowed away and eat a brief breakfast before paddling out onto the barely rippling river. What a relief!

It wasn't long before I paddled off the map and was on my own, grateful for the unusual phenomenon of a tail wind. After many hours and only a few navigation decisions, I came around a bend to discover a good size town on a hillside several miles away. By the time I arrived, it was raining again and I stopped to inquire what town I was in, and what time it was. The town was Marshall and the time was only noon. I figured that I had been paddling about eight hours.

The thought suddenly came to me that it might be wise to inquire about a boat ride from Marshall to St. Mary's and the end of the trip, as there is no other village between the two. There was an uneasy feeling in the back of my mind about this last stretch of river, as well as apprehensions concerning time. If I were held up again by wind I would miss my airline connections. So, in my usual way, I followed my instincts. I traded my true and faithful canoe, which never leaked a drop in 1300 miles in two summers on the Yukon, for a boat trip 70 miles downriver to St. Mary's. I had not intended to paddle all the way to the ocean anyway—I take things kind of easy.

Returning from the second trip I found myself even more awed by what I had seen and much less awed by what I had done. Travelling alone for

700 miles by canoe brought me great exhilaration and great comfort, and I'm sure that the beauty of the country has become a part of me.

1986

I plan to go back to the Yukon when I'm eighty and canoe the whole river in one season. Crazy lady! But it's like going down the river in the first place—I just said I'm going to go, and then I had to do it because I'd told everybody. If you think about something hard enough, it will happen.

Then I can come back and retire, move out to my cabin. Just taking care of everyday needs—hauling the wood and water—that should be enough to do. Sometimes I think that if I decide it's time to go, a good day to die—the Indians often knew that—then I'd take a small canoe out into Lake Superior, in bad weather. But a friend asked me, "And then what would you do when you got across the lake, Helen?"

Building Your Own Fires

AUDREY SUTHERLAND

The following excerpt is from Paddling My Own Canoe *(Honolulu: The University Press of Hawaii, 1978) in which Audrey Sutherland describes her solitary journeys to the northeast coast of Moloka'i. Sutherland, a divorced mother of four living in Honolulu, first saw the spectacular waterfalls and coastal cliffs of Moloka'i by plane and knew she had to visit there.*

Unable to afford a charter boat, Sutherland decided to swim there, towing her pack. Following a harrowing experience in which she almost lost her life in the rough surf, Sutherland returned the next year in a nine-foot inflatable canoe. She found a deserted mining shack on one of the cliffs high above the ocean and returned, alone, year after year, to explore the rugged wild splendor of the Moloka'i coast.

And why did I always come alone to Moloka'i? I know why, but the telling is hard. Daily we are on trial, to do a job, to make a marriage good, to find depth, serenity, and meaning in a complex, deteriorating world of politics, false values, and trivia. But rarely are we deeply challenged physically or alone. We rely on friends, on family, on a committee, on community agencies outside ourselves. To have actual survival, living or dying, depend on our own ingenuity, skill, or stamina—this is a core question we seldom face. We rarely find out if we like having only our own mind as company for days or weeks at a time. How many people have ever been totally isolated, ten miles from the nearest other human, for even two days?

Alone, you are more aware of surroundings, wary as an animal to danger, limp and relaxed when the sun, the brown earth, or the deep grass say, "Rest now." Alone, you stand at night, alert, poised, hearing through ears and open mouth and fingertips. Alone, you do not worry whether someone else is tired or hungry or needing. You push yourself hard or quit for the day, reveling in the luxury of solitude. And being unconcerned with human needs, you become as a fish, a boulder, a tree—a part of the world around you.

I stood once in midstream, balanced on a rock. A scarlet leaf fluttered, spiraled down. I watched it, became a wind-blown leaf, swayed, fell into the water with a giant human splash, then soddenly crawled out, laughing uproariously.

The process of daily living is often intense and whimsical. The joy of it, and the compassion, we can share, but in pain we are ultimately alone. The only real antidote is inside. The only real security is not insurance or money or a job, not a house and furniture paid for, or a retirement fund, and never is it another person. It is the skill and humor and courage within, the ability to build your own fires and find your own peace.

On a solo trip you may discover these, or try to build them, and life becomes simple and deeply satisfying. The confidence and strength remain and are brought back and applied to the rest of your life.

I go on to Waikolu, to Father Damien's church, and to the plane at Kalaupapa, on to people and problems and coping. But it is all right. Always now, Moloka'i is there, it is part of me. I can return to the lonely splendor, and I am no longer afraid.

Echoes and Silences

LADY C. C. VYVYAN

In 1925 Clara and her friend Gwen Dorian Smith, at home in England, sat down with an atlas, discussing the wild places of the earth. Having previously found each other "adequately tough," they picked Alaska for their next travels, because a school friend had visited there in 1913 and sent back a volume of Robert Service poems and descriptions of vast desolate country. They learned of a route recently taken by professor Laura Frazeur of Chicago with two Indians from Aklavik: upstream from the Arctic Ocean on the Peel and Rat Rivers, over the Continental Divide and down the Porcupine River into the Yukon basin. "Sounds all right," said Gwen. "I do not remember what I said but I can never forget what I felt," wrote Clara. "Was the road to the Islands of the Blest opening before us?"

There were a few problems before the road opened. Although both women were over forty, their "very cynical" mothers strenuously objected. However, when a distinguished neighbor, an officer of the Hudson Bay Company, voiced approval, family opinion changed.

Then on the steamer trip down the Mackenzie River, Gwen strained her Achilles tendon. When they arrived in Aklavik, on the Arctic Ocean, a doctor prescribed a couple of weeks in a cast. "Good job I brought Eddy's army boots," she said. But surely they are far too big, protested Clara. "Stuff 'em with grass in the toes," replied Gwen.

A severe blow to their plans was their discovery that LaPierre House, where they'd been told to hire guides for the Porcupine section of their trip, had been abandoned. They would have to do over a hundred miles of the journey unguided. "Have you ever paddled a canoe?" Gwen asked Clara. No. Nor had Gwen, really. While Gwen's ankle healed, Clara found someone to teach her canoeing, and the two talked to the old-timers. Some said, "You'll be eaten alive by mosquitoes. No sane person would choose to travel up the Rat River for pleasure." Others were more encouraging: "The Rat ain't no asphalt pave-

ment laid for patent leathers, but there it is, 'tis a trail same as any other and you'll get over it all right."

Although Lady Vyvyan is the author of many other travel books, she did not write the story of this 1926 canoe trip until 35 years later, in Arctic Adventure *(London: Peter Owen, 1961). These excerpts are from that nostalgic book. "I see us as two human atoms in a vast country, paddling our canoe alone down a river bathed, at midnight, in golden sunshine. Paddling whence? Paddling whither? And for what purpose? Perhaps it was for the sole purpose of remembering always the silence of the Yukon."*

GREAT SLAVE LAKE

Their trip across Canada, and north from Edmonton to Aklavik by river is interesting in itself, partly because of her awareness of the women settlers they meet. At first she and Gwen find the men charming company, full of information, and the women dull. But some of them were charming alcoholics, she soon reveals, and their wives were understandably hopeless and depressed. She calls the North "the harbor of wrecked men."

Crossing Great Slave Lake by steamer she encounters another malady of the North — "horizon fever" — the sense of spaciousness that can take complete possession of a traveller.

We found ourselves moving steadily forward across a lake that was as still as glass. Our world was now only sky and water in which we could detect no solid object except one seagull flying like a wraith across our bows. Far ahead, dividing sea and sky, there was a narrow green line. We could not see any break in that line, as we scanned its length, looking for the opening where the Mackenzie River flows out from the lake on its northward course.

We are lost in a tenuously silken web of water below and sky above where a single feather-light cloud hangs overhead. The Slave River delta, through which we entered the lake, is out of sight and the green line of forest far ahead is rigid and unbroken. In any case, why should we wish to leave this lake? Why should we not float on forever in a world that is so calm and beautiful? The things that we have left behind are remote and unreal, those years of dreaming and months of preparation, discomfort of travel by sea and rail, busy hours at Edmonton, new faces on the river journey. Ahead of us the unknown, mosquito-haunted and perhaps malignant Rat has no importance. We are lost in a world of clear water and clear sky which have a strange impalpable look, as if they could bear no weight and had neither beginning nor end nor purpose; no origin nor any aptitude for change. Something has touched me here and now like music on

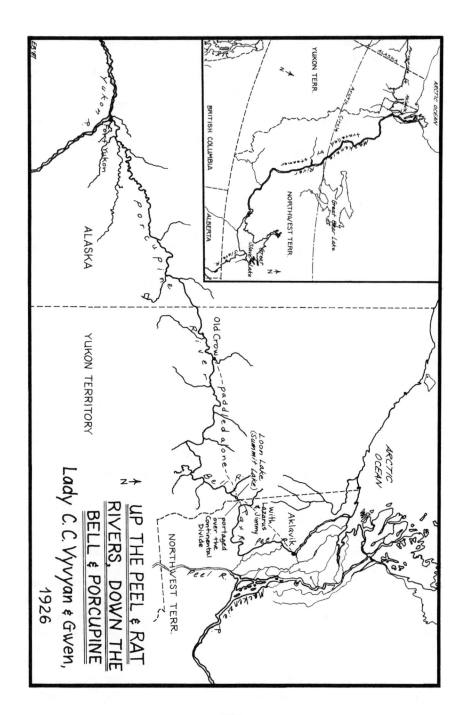

UP THE PEEL & RAT
RIVERS, DOWN THE
BELL & PORCUPINE

Lady C. C. Vyvyan & Gwen,
1926

muted strings. I have come home; back to that long lost home which, without plan or conscious purpose, I have always been seeking.

Suddenly a voice breaks in on my reverie as I stand leaning on the rail. It is a harsh voice, but the words are not harsh. "Isn't that just the quietest water you ever saw?" says a man standing beside me. The two tourists join us. One, a rough-spoken, hardened person, owns to having spent a sleepless night on deck, as if in spite of himself. "That blessed sun going down behind the spruces and the light in the blessed sky all night, it just got me," he says. The other man says nothing, but his eyes have the look of a child seeing something that is not there.

CROSSING THE DIVIDE

The most significant part of the trip in Lady Vyvyan's memory is their reaching the Continental Divide, crossing from the Yukon into Alaska, and the subsequent days of travel alone. In Aklavik they had hired Lazarus Sittichili and Jimmy Koe as guides to paddle and line the canoe up the Rat while the women hiked overland through the muskeg and mosquitoes. At the height of land the guides left to walk home, and the women paddled alone on the Little Bell and Porcupine, until finding more guides at the first settlement, Old Crow.

The Divide. The Height of Land

What romance and suggestiveness lie in those words, what a sense of continental vastness. They provoke thoughts of adventure and gold-seeking, of the Rocky Mountains and incredible feats of pioneers who were always driven by some nameless urge toward the sunset or the North.

I murmured the words over and over to myself in deep excitement, for we were actually nearing the Divide. All subsequent travels over cols and passes have been colourless by comparison.

We and our guides were nearing the Divide alone, having climbed thus far after days of muscular effort. Nor were there any landmarks by which we could direct our course in this illimitable country. There was only the position of the sun and direction of flowing water to help us in our journey to the Yukon.

We felt a heightened, perhaps rather childish, sense of adventure. This sense of adventure which comes and goes like gleams of sunshine in the traveller's overarching sky, was by no means often with us while we were pushing our way up the river. There were long spells when we thought only of how we could manage to put one foot before another, or extricate a boot from mud. The strange thing about those happy, sunlit moods is that they never may be summoned, nor commanded to stay. Such a mood may take possession of one for a whole plodding day, when there is nothing of spectacular beauty in earth or sky and it may desert one in the face of Niagara.

Half-way through the day we passed a big river flowing into the Rat – it was not marked on our inadequate little map. Over and over again we had to push our way through thickets of these scrubby willows or to wade across muddy side creeks which were now very frequent. How we managed to keep our feet in good condition I do not know, for they were nearly always wet and once we had crawled into bed there was no means of drying them. Perhaps their sodden condition prevented them from getting rubbed or sore; I only remember that one of my toes became so water-logged that, at a later stage of the journey, the whole skin peeled off like the sheath of an *Eschscholtzia* flower. Luckily, that was after the mosquitoes had left us and I could with impunity sit still in the canoe or walk about, shoeless, on sand or muskeg.

We lunched royally that day on the usual pemmican and pork, with Gwen's "Puftaloonas" for dessert. Just as the Indians craved for fresh meat, so did we crave for sweet food. But neither of us had any aptitude for cooking. Gwen, however, made up her mind to produce doughnuts and she set to work with flour and sugar. There may have been other ingredients but I do not now remember the exact recipe for that memorable dish, yet I can see her at work on it, in my mind's eye, to this very day. Her method was simple and forceful. She would take the ingredients in the palm of a very horny hand that had been hardened by rowing sea-boats since infancy; she would then weld them as if they were pieces of metal and she herself a blacksmith. Sooner or later, by hard pommeling the mixture became homogeneous, and when satisfied that it was solid as a cricket ball, she would cast it into the frying pan with a determined gesture. The hot fat played its part and our sharp-set appetites did the rest.

"A most wonderful and full day."

Such is the entry in my diary at the head of the next day's chronicle. So much, or so little rapture did I allow myself to express over our triumphant arrival on the height of land. For it *was* triumphant, even though we were unwashed and unkempt and our upper garments were still wet and we had slept in our clothes for nine long nights.

"I do believe that you enjoyed pigging it," was the comment of our families when, eventually, we had returned home and were describing the scenery, the beauty, the difficulties and the conditions of our journey up the Rat. The outstanding fact to them was that we could not undress to sleep and how could we ever explain that, in our great enterprise, such discomforts were only a means to an end? We gave up the attempt. We would change the subject and describe the magnificent physique of Lazarus, the satisfying power of small lumps of pemmican, the aspect of the rapids or other such aspects of our journey that would appear to them strange without being squalid.

As a matter of fact we *were* beginning to feel extremely dirty but we had not hitherto found a mosquito-free camp where we could undress, step into the river and begin to remove what we felt was the dirt of ages.

On the morning of our arrival at the summit, clouds were low on the mountains, mosquitoes were more ferocious than ever and after a chilly, wakeful night we were not feeling, physically, at the top of our form. Mentally we were lords of the world, were conquerors, we were unconquerable; or so we felt as we began to repeat the maneuvers of the previous day.

We made four portages. We did our best to help by man-handling the rucksacks and the lighter packages, but we felt weak as straws when we watched Lazarus and Jimmy carrying the heavy stuff. We helped as best we could, to drag the canoe over these longer portages, but it must be confessed that most of our energy was expended on keeping our balance. After the third portage we came to Loon Lake, ringed round by mountains and holding, in utter stillness, their reflections.

There are some feelings too deep for tears, some thoughts that may not endure the captivity of words, some memories that are set apart among life's enduring treasures. I can shut my eyes now, dismiss all that has happened in thirty-five years and recapture the silence of Loon Lake. We were two middle-aged women travelling for pleasure, disheveled and unwashed, with tired feet and tired bodies, but I think as we stood on the shores of that lake, gazing down at the reflected mountains, listening to the silence that was almost audible, we must have experienced what the Saints describe as ecstasy. Gwen said never a word. Nor did I.

Down the Porcupine

If ever two men had earned their wage by faithfulness and labour, those two were Lazarus and Jimmy. It was with real regret that we said good-bye to these two faithful companions.

We were absolutely alone now in this wilderness. If we wanted help, there would be none forthcoming except from our own resourcefulness. If we met with an accident, no one would be any the wiser. If we should encounter rapids, snags or swift water, we should have to call on our own reserves of initiative and skill. I do not think that all these things were clearly in our minds as our guides walked away, but we did feel a queer depth and breadth of solitude. However, instead of dwelling on unknown difficulties ahead, we decided to look upon our solitude as complete freedom and to celebrate this freedom, we undressed completely, stepped into the water, each with a cake of soap, and washed thoroughly from head to toe. While we were soaping ourselves in such a fervour of cleanliness as we had never known before, we discussed the next lap of the journey. . . .

In the early afternoon we came into the Porcupine River and paddled on quietly, taking an hour ashore to build a fire and make tea and then at seven o'clock we found a perfect site for a camp, on a spit of land with a beautiful view of mountains. There, we unpacked all our personal belongings to find that everything in the canvas bags was soaked and mildewed, so we hung up each article one by one on a willow tree to dry. Our camp was on mud and mares' tails but we cut and laid out willow shoots to keep out the damp. Gwen cooked "Puftaloonas" and we turned in under that strange northern light which had kindled the water and all the trees and their reflections to a dull gold.

On the height of land the vastness of the unpeopled country was apparent and at first it was terrifying, it seemed to be a menace to security but after a while the open spaces filled us with exhilaration. This was the country that we had come to see, the land beyond the bounds of civilization, the wild land that had lured us from our homes to cross the Atlantic, to journey across Canada and down the Mackenzie River. There were even moments, each evening, when this new world was bathed in golden light and we would feel that it was our real home, for it held a hitherto unimagined beauty that had always been missing in our lives.

If the true story of our Arctic journey could be recaptured, its main concern would be with enlightened moments when we were face to face with absolute beauty and the tale would be told in winged new words, free from cumbersome associations: but I have no such words at my command. The name of some flower that we found, some bird that we saw, details about camps and bedding and speed of water and weather conditions, such things as these occupy too much space in my diary, but when I write about crossing the rapids and Gwen murmuring "Delicious, delicious," and when I note how the evening sunlight would gild all natural objects from a spruce bough to a wide river, then I am getting near the truth. The truth was that despite a few tremors over snags and currents, during our four and a half days of paddling or drifting from Old Crow we were living an enchanted life. We moved in a golden light down a golden river, free as butterflies, forgetful of all yesterdays, without care for any morrow. That is how I see the journey now, although I know, of course, that we did stop to wash and to eat hearty meals of pork and doughnuts and that we had to watch out for troubled water and snags.

272

Realizing that we had to depend on our own exertions had steadied my nerves. Whenever there were frequent bends in the river, one of us would always be on the look out for snags and boulders while the other paddled. Sometimes there were rough patches of water to negotiate, swift or swirling currents. Once when I was paddling, we passed under a bank hollowed out by fallen lumps of frozen soil and were suddenly confronted with a dead tree branch sticking up in the deep water. "Backwater," shouted Gwen and I failed to respond, as my mind did not work quickly enough. However, we went swirling down and missed the tree by inches. "Land-lubber!" was all that Gwen said and indeed I was surprised that she said nothing worse until I remembered that, to her seafaring mind, there could be nothing worse than a land-lubber.

Soon after that incident the river straightened out and everything around us seemed to have become immeasurably vast. The forest stretched away to the North Pole, the hills were interfolded endlessly and the straight reaches of the river must, in some places, have been six or eight miles long. Sometimes, when looking ahead down one of these reaches of river that were green in the morning, gold under noonday sun and burnished gold in the evening, we felt that the current must be taking us down to bottomless gorges or to cataracts like Niagara. It was like a dream in which everything had begun to swell, to extend and to deepen in all directions.

It was very difficult to judge our speed when traveling downstream. Often we just steered and drifted instead of paddling. We had short hours of travel, we slept long nights, we lingered over meals and sometimes went ashore between meals for Gwen to sketch while I prowled about and collected flowers. Often that glassy water seemed so still that we did not appear to be moving, and only when we looked at the banks did we realize that the current was alive. So we went down, down, on that green or golden river into unknown country. Sometimes there were echoes. A swan would go honking overhead and the trees would echo the sound back again. Or a Northern raven would fly croaking into the forest and once we passed some fine rocky bluffs where peregrine falcons and eagles were screaming overhead but always, when those echoes had died away, the unearthly silence of that country would come flooding back to fill our world. We paddled softly, trying not to break that silence.

Returning and Remembering

When you walk beside a river, following its course from mountain cradle to the sea, or dip your paddle in the water, keeping on the middle downward course, after a while you are carried out of yourself, becoming subject to all the moods of your mighty companion, becoming also aware of a power that is self-sufficient and independent of your friendship, beneficent to the land through which it flows . . .

When we got home no one was really interested in the Rat River. Our friends and families were far more interested in the fact that we had spent nine days and nights without changing our clothes. "Well," they would say, "some people take their pleasures sadly," and they would give a sympathetic sigh over our folly and that would be their final comment on our Arctic journey.

The net result in outward and visible signs was threefold. 267 kinds of pressed wild flowers were sent to Kew Herbarium. 600 dollars worth of Gwen's sketches were sold. We both, in our respective home areas, had many invitations from Women's Institutes to come and talk to them about our travels.

But what of the inward and spiritual grace? For myself, I keep certain pictures indelibly imprinted on my memory. Those pelicans above Fort Smith, ranging to and fro over the troubled waters. The crackling of the Northern Lights. The kindness and hospitality that we received from strangers. Columbia glacier. The hummingbird. The strange clarity of near and far objects and the golden colour of lake and river when lit by Arctic sunlight. Paramount among all these is the memory of those days when we paddled alone down the Porcupine, having achieved absolute freedom in a world of absolute beauty.

Watching the Water: Grand Canyon Journal
MARGIE ERHART

Margie Erhart is a writer, living "as far east as you can in this country, three houses from the tip of Cape Cod." Her first novel, Unusual Company, *will be published by E. P. Dutton in the fall of 1987. She's been on rivers in the Southwest and northern Canada in kayak, raft, and canoe, but right now "my kayak and wetsuit are in a barn in Iowa and my paddle was lost somewhere in Arizona."*

"This is a journal I kept for a 21-day trip through the Grand Canyon in 1979. I traveled with ten or so people, knew none of them ahead of time. Someone had a private permit, and the rest of us were lucky enough to go along. I rowed an inflatable Havasu raft, a boat about 15 feet long and 6 feet wide. I carried both baggage and friends."

9/9/79

Strong with excitement.

Return to the camp where little more than a year ago I watched Mom and Dad sleep. They lay half in half out of their sleeping bags, pale pajamaed ghosts. Austerity and tenderness.

9/10

Being on.

A.M. early: The bats are still out.

House Rock Rapid, pure white-light blue, letting us all go, all boats, one, two, three, four.

Yesterday two airplanes came at us across the water, ducking *under* Navajo Bridge, dipping their wings. Oh, I love it . . . their flight and ours.

Cyril—portrait in European bikini bathing suit.

Catherine—all that blond hair.

Janet singing, "Ladies of the Moose, Ladies of the Canyon," sweet the guitar, sweet the starred sky, opening like a barn door onto white winter when up comes the moon. Up comes the moon and in camp we are all aprowl. Bats are out and the sand is tumbled deep with the weight of our feet—some tracks lead to the water and others to the rock. Don drinks fish from my wooden bowl.

I could put the pen down. I don't have to write this. I don't have to write anything. The days are a comfort. I can do anything I want.

9/12 South Canyon

Deep purple moving across the beach, blond hair in handfuls. Purple in the marbled limestone, climbing through monkey flowers and poison ivy to the top of Vasey's Paradise; to the top where the water surprises the Redwall, shooting out the way it does from nowhere. We take the paddle-boat down at dusk and climb up that waterfall, and fight upstream again singing like madwomen, calling to the flashlights held by our friends.

Redwall Cavern

Four people moving to the center, the cavern like crossed hands above them, a folded wing. Quiet, so quiet—a quiet as clear and calm as the last time I was here when Deedie and I danced and the others played music. The music shone then, as if there were a light inside it. And the time that was passing shone, then turned melancholy, then later lightened again but with something gone out of it. And I welcomed the change, all changes. I had to.

It's like riding a cloud, these days of weightless random. We climbed to Silver Grotto and I ran so lightly along the rock, swam deeply in the pools; as if we are all the most graceful, the most on, unselfconscious, home, when time isn't with us—when time just runs by. The three places where I touch home these days, where I lose that part of me that isn't at all perfect and am left with something entirely whole: boating, writing, sex with people I love.

The nights: I lie down to sleep on the boat, usually the last to come away from Janet's guitar. The shadow of bats frightened by the flashlight, the shadow of insects attracted to it. Watersound (like tide coming in, or if we're camped by a rapid then a sound much harder to sleep to). Oars rubbing. Moon coming up like snow on the opposite rock face; the sudden silhouette of boulders shaped like toys on the canyon's rim. And always the several wakings to check the boats, to watch the light grow; wakings to feel my palms stiff and burnt with blisters, and yesterday's overdose of sun on my back where I can't reach with the tanning goop and am still strangely too shy to ask anyone else to do it for me. Always the intention of visiting some of the friends who aren't with me, by dreaming, or daydreaming in the early morning before I get up. But at night I fall asleep before visiting, and the dreams are so thin that I remember nothing of them; and in the early morning I just want to get up and go see things before breakfast and loading the boat, so there's no visiting then either. And I laugh thinking, Ah well, maybe tomorrow; maybe tomorrow there will be the time and place to consider friends left behind—to not be simply and joyfully present. That's the best here, the language this place knows: be exactly where you are because that's all there is. No need for anything else. No need.

Don after the portopotty lecture: "You are responsible for every inch of the water ahead of you. Play with it. Learn from it. Love it, hate it, let it terrify you." I hear myself: "Austerity and tenderness. Here we come."

9/15

I cry at Unkar. No more river talk. Catherine asks me who I've learned from. I tell her Lew. I tell her the Maine fishermen, my grandmother, anyone with oars and boats and respect for the water. The kingfisher dips wildly above Nevills Rapid. Above that, the angel's window is a fist of light. I love these people. I tend to their afternoon goosebumps like a mother. I listen to them, watch them as if we are together now for the last time. We are. That unmistakable shine of civilization has worn away and we're down to the other layer—my favorite. But nothing will last. It all moves closer and farther and closer and farther. Let it.

9/16 Clear Creek

Our friend flew over this morning. Cyril said, "Oh, that's Michael, he said he might drop by," and I looked up quickly to make the racket of that plane meet the sight of it, though the sight lagged around a curve in the canyon a few seconds longer before we all saw it sweep low, low, much too low across the water, so the narrowest part of the river lay close under the wheels of a rocking plane. As it passed over the boats an arm reached out the window and tossed something—a muffin! A muffin landed in the water a yard from my feet and I jumped for it. Airdrop! I loved it. It came so when I needed a *good* albatross. I loved our friend too, his spirit, whatever it is in him that stands so against fear (or so welcomes it) that everything is available. For an hour before that I listened to the kind of river talk I like the least, the kind that forgets to be light with it and dwells upon terror and gloom. Talk about the boat-eating Inner Gorge – Horn Creek Rapid, then Crystal: water the enemy, water not being benevolent or teaching us or letting us go. As if the water were something to conquer rather than simply be with; the shadow of the gorge instead of the splendor. I so wanted a reminder, a glee-bearing albatross, and then there it was, the arm with the muffin and my heart sailing up to it. I loved it. I carried that with me through Horn and Granite and Hermit, and will tomorrow through Crystal. Something to bounce off of. Something whispering: Go *play* in the water.

Crystal Camp

Below me Janet sits cross-legged on a low water beach, playing the bass recorder. Lorna behind me doesn't hear the recorder, nor the rapid, even though it's low water Crystal and booming. Unless we have a campfire at night it's difficult for her to take part in the conversation because she can't read lips in the dark. What an awesome place, the canyon, in which to be deaf. The light is closing down, bats awake. Kimberly's chicken curry for dinner and the fish that Janet caught, Jeanette cooked. I said it today in my boat and it comes so strongly at times, in flashes that linger: I love these people. They are home to me. The butterflies are gone from my stomach, even in the crazy water they are kinder, their wings are softer. Many are the times I feel graceful.

Sometimes after rowing my hands don't fit the pen.

9/17

If the point were to arrive, we'd have to spend time planning for what next. No matter how well you know the water, how gracefully you row a boat, there is always learning in it for you – something more to see. If you want to be done with it, you'll cause a finishing point and call it "having arrived."

The hole in Crystal: I looked into it, up to it, as if out of some intuitive respect, watching the water pour over and over and over until it took my oar – a split second – and that need for action hit me hard and quick. *Cut free the spare oar? Try to paddle out with this one? Jeanette, Kimberly, stay high side!* Then: *I want not to be here. I want it to be a dream.*

Unusually, there was time enough in the hole to *feel*, which is different

278

than flipping a boat because then, without time having gone anywhere, you're underwater or bobbing up again. But here there were long minutes to feel, yet fear wasn't one of those feelings. Even with the water pouring into the boat and the river sucking us *up*stream, snugging us against the big boulder which formed the back of the hole, I had no thought of drowning. Just a simple longing to go with the other two boats as they stroked by. They had the spirit of a picnic about them and it was that spirit I longed to go with.

It shakes you. For a while you're not on at all. The path of the water isn't as clear to you; people are less of a joy; you stumble in camp or walking the thwarts of the boat. You're not on and then you're less on because you're trying to cover for it. Don't try to cover for it. It will be that way. If hitting the hole in Crystal and being kept by it, a full two, three minutes, didn't shake something in you, you would love the water less. Remember that. It is the reason for doing all this.

North Bass Camp

Fish jumping. Don in sackcloth, bandaging an injured foot. Cyril in sandals and toga. Later, two making silent love as I pass quickly by, not invisible to them against a gray dark. The cup of a hand, this night, this camp, where the Vishnu Schist is going under, the Tapeats descending to water level. The only schist-black we have now is off the wings of the raven.

9/19 Blacktail

Up above the sixth waterfall at Elves' Chasm, up there where the seventh fall stops you and you can just see the shoulder of Royal Arch, monkey flowers playing in the water that spills over, I jumped naked, rock to rock this afternoon and was alone moving through the canyon. The place gave itself to me after twice seeing that I wasn't ready to have it. Twice before, I had climbed into the chasm and had seen nothing because my senses shut down in the face of that abundance. This time I went intending to have nothing again, and accepting that because down here it will happen — it will happen and to not accept it is to not respect the place. But then came this delight above the sixth waterfall, and knowing that I was finally at home with Elves' because I hadn't tried to be — just a half-clad woman who climbed away from river and people and boats to be alone in the canyon, and dropped one more piece of her clothes at every waterfall.

Vital. All of it so simple, so vital – *pieno di vita, full of life.* I love the oars. I'm not yet good with them. I love the signs and secrets in the water. I see the path to take and am not yet good enough, well-timed enough, to take it. Immensely frustrating to be over and over again unclean in a rapid.

The night before running Dubendorff I dreamt of a woman who washed me. Very sensual – a lovely thing, to be washed. I didn't recognize her. We stood in the river and with the greatest care she washed me. Such an abundance and absence of the sexual down here, I love it. The sexual turned sensual. Touch is all things, hands to the oars to the water. And that touching that city people do (is it a way of throwing out an anchor? of grounding?) isn't so urgent here because the place is the anchor. In the airport coffee shop Janet and I talked about passion, and I laugh now because the raven that just flew over knows all of that and nothing and is full.

A day of transition and two bighorn sheep above a horrifying mid-water Dubendorff. Midpoint in the trip. Folks akimbo. We humans are a delight with our lack of clarity, those surprising swatches of gray. Which is why the water and the oars upon it are so essential, so welcome. What an opportunity for balance the river provides, and all ours if we can just see it: that which skips along the surface and that which runs deep; the great and the small; the teller of tales and the listener; the ego and the quiet receiver; soft, hard, impotent, strong; all tension and completely at ease. I stand in such appreciation of the place that at times it nearly breaks my heart. Sweet, soft music of recorder and guitars up Blacktail Canyon, dark, no moon, and the man's voice singing high like a woman's half in half out of my dreams. At times, between a waterfall and the two faithful ravens, or coming through the tail end of Dubendorff, tiny matchstick girl alone in my boat, I blink as if to see better what I'm seeing and then suddenly the tears are all over my cheeks.

Bandit raven making off with four fish and a sack of brown sugar. Cyril in Arabic dress (turban and watercolor blue wrap, sandals) on the beach at Tapeats: "I have good news for you, my friend, there *is* a God!"

At night I lie awake long enough to pick out Aquarius in all that tangle of stars, and I find the water that spills from his jug, the waves of it that drench the far wall of the canyon. In the morning I remind myself of him when I'm up early throwing out the old dishwater. The bucket arches, and with the light coming through it the water hangs like stars before falling flat and slap-sharp to meet the river.

Discipline – the bell. Lightning – the method.

Inside Thunder River

I doused the flashlight and stood with one foot on each limestone wall, straddling an underground river. I listened to the water sing. Like an airplane warming up it sang, and then like the same airplane flying very close overhead, aiming for a tunnel. The water tolled and the water applauded. It jumped up and soaked my legs. It took my voice (but left my breath). There wasn't anything but water, the sound of water, the feel of water. I'm told there's a lake a quarter of a mile in, after the tunnel forks right, then left, then right and left again. You paddle around on the still water where all the ropey waters come together (*Chinle*—"Where the ropey waters come together"— loosely translated), and the Redwall chants, the darkness rings. They say the temptation is to stay there forever, a sort of aural flicker vertigo.

9/22 Camp at Olo, river rising.

Lorna rode in my boat today and asked how loud the rapids were. She saw the curl on the lip of a nasty hole and loved it. "In the East," she says, "you have roots, but here in the West we are wild."

9/24

Ran the hole in Upset Rapid yesterday with Lorna as only passenger. Afterwards I told her it was strange, I had heard nothing in there. She was smiling, a huge smile as if her face, her whole body, would fly up into the air. She said: "I heard it all!"

Don has taken to wearing a gray cashmere sweater-vest (over bare arms) and red sweatpants as camp attire. Mornings and evenings are that kind of weather. People claim their spaces more, scattering through camp at Olo, around the piazza at Matkatamiba, along Last Chance's ledges (people almost indistinguishable from the drying laundry). There's something unmistakably of autumn in the tone of this last week on the river. I wonder if the season dictates that or whether an adventure makes itself into a microcosmic year—the spring of it full of all hope, all possibilities, and then the dragging summer, rich, sober autumn, internal winter. Certainly a relationship does that (flying so fast sometimes through one or the other of the seasons that you have to look quickly to see it at all), and isn't what two people have together an adventure? Yes, if that's another word for ordinary life.

Learning to read people as you would the water. Having enough history with them to read them.

281

9/25

Belly cramps. A long, dull-sided stripe of pain. Fifth day of that kind of subtle hurting, and a new way in which to see the canyon. I speak little of how it disturbs/puzzles me because there is nothing down here to do for it and that drives it underground.

People spread on the night sand like the arms of a star. Lorna sleeps as close as she can to the water. It's teaching her how to hear.

9/26

There's a black dark first, and then a gray dark, and after that comes the blue dark where the clouds begin to show and the stars shine brighter at first, like the tail end of a candle, and then go out. If I wake in the black dark I always go to sleep again, waiting for the gray dark to wake for good. Then I lie with my eyes open, mind loosely dreaming, until the blue dark comes and the sky becomes too busy to think about. The bats are still out and they scatter wildly against the blue. Nothing yet has a shadow but nothing is any longer hidden. I get up then and fill the buckets with water for boiling, or if I need to I walk off what I feel. By the time the water is heating or I'm back from walking, some of the others are up and the shadows are beginning to show. The clouds are more than just wishes then, but there to stay; and in a way I always feel that the day's possibilities are over, that something which in the dark was rich and vague is now unalterably set, and for awhile there's a little bit of mourning in what I do.

9/27

Cove Canyon like a cathedral, like a calm and gracious point of worship. Rock pews and a dripping altar. Jimson flowers at the portopotty!

Stop on the right to look down at Lava Falls, and I hear Catherine behind me saying, "I feel like I'm going to see God." I wear a dress and dedicate the run to Mom, then of course forget to think about her on the way through.

Intensity of canyon — the black lava. Intensity of sun — as strong as summer that sun, and wind upstream against us. White bright light flattening the water ahead, making it impossible to read. Alone in my boat in the afternoon, and I love it, where I am, what I do, whom I miss. Yes they are, some of the finest strokes. Yes, they are.

BIBLIOGRAPHIES

Books By and About Women and Paddling

Aspen, Jean. *Arctic Daughter* 1988, Bergamot Books. Like her mother before her (Constance Helmericks, below), Jean and a companion travel into interior Alaska to live off the land. In spite of good motherly advice, she has a hard time and needs all her resourcefulness.

Broomell, Helen. *Solo on the Yukon and other Alaskan Adventures*, 1982, and *Solo on the Yukon Again*, 1984. Helen Broomell, Minoqua, WI 54548. Collections of articles she sent to her hometown newspaper when at 65 and 67 she paddled alone down the Yukon River and spent many more months in Alaska, meeting and talking with people.

Clark, Georgie, with Duane Newcomb. *Georgie Clark: Thirty Years of River Running*. San Francisco: Chronicle Books, no date. She first ran the rapids of the Grand Canyon in 1946—swimming 125 miles in a life jacket. She then gradually developed a rafting business to make the river accessible to all kinds of people.

Ferrier, Marion and Ben. *God's River Country*. New Jersey: Prentice-Hall, 1956. A boys' adventure book about Ben and Marion taking a crew of teenage boys on the God's and Nelson Rivers in Manitoba.

Fons, Valerie. *Keep It Moving: Baja by Canoe*. Seattle: The Mountaineers, 1986. The story of her 240-mile voyage around Baja, California in a solo canoe, accompanying Verlen Kruger on "The Ultimate Canoe Challenge." This trip began her commitment to canoeing as a career.

Helmericks, Constance. *Down the Wild River North*. Boston: Little & Brown Co. 1968. Abridged version, Bergamot Books, 1989. An experienced outdoorswoman, and author of many books on living in Alaska, she travelled with her two daughters, ages 12 and 14, down the Peace, Slave and MacKenzie Rivers.

Helmericks, Constance and Harmon. *We Live in Alaska*. 1944. The first of several books, this tells of canoeing down the Yukon.

Hubbard, Mina Benson. *A Woman's Way Through Unknown Labrador.* Originally published in 1908, reissued in 1981, Breakwater Books, PO Box 52 Site C, Portugal Cove, Newfoundland A0A 3K0. Mrs. Hubbard organized this trip, with four Indian guides, to map the interior of Labrador, carrying out the plans of her husband, who had died in his attempt. See also:

James Davidson and John Rugge *Great Heart,* 1988, Viking. The story of the Hubbard expeditions, meticulously based on all historic records, but written as vividly as fiction.

Jacques, Florence Page. *Canoe Country.* Minneapolis: University of Minnesota Press, 1938. With illustrations by Francis Lee Jacques. Diary of a three-week trip in Minnesota's border country in 1938.

Johnson, Beth. *Yukon Wild.* Stockbridge, MA: Berkshire Traveller Press, 1984. Four Texas women paddling 2000 miles down the entire Yukon River, with a lot of information on trip planning.

Kerfoot, Justine. *Woman of the Boundary Waters: Canoeing, Guiding, Mushing and Surviving.* Grand Marais, MN: Women's Times Publishing, 1986 (PO Box 215, Grand Marais, MN 55604). Memories of fifty years of running a resort in the border country, learning bush survival skills.

Kerfoot, Justine. *Gunflint: Reflections on the Trail.* 1991, Pfeifer-Hamilton, Duluth. Collected from 30 years of her columns in the Cook County News-Herald, Grand Marais.

Lewis, Linda. *Water's Edge: Women Who Push the Limits in Rowing, Kayaking & Canoeing.* Seattle: Seal Press, 1992. Profiles of ten women who have made their mark in competitive rowing, kayaking or wilderness canoeing—from early pioneers to current Olympic champions.

McGuffin, Brad and Joanie. *Where Rivers Run.* 1988, Stoddard. A young couple on a 6,000-mile exploration of Canada by canoe, over two summers.

Moore, Joanne Ronan. *Nahanni Trailhead: A Year in the Northern Wilderness.* Ottawa: Deneau and Greenberg, 1980. In 1978 Joanne and her husband built a cabin in the Nahanni River valley, Northwest Territories. They wintered there and canoed out down the Nahanni in early spring.

Nickerson. E.B. *Kayaks to the Arctic.* Berkeley, CA: Howell-North Books, 1967. A 25th anniversary trip, 1000 miles down the MacKenzie River with her husband and three sons.

Niemi, Judith and Barbara Wieser, editors. *Rivers Running Free: Canoeing*

Stories by Adventurous Women, originally published by Bergamot Books in 1987, reissued in 1992, Seal Press, 3131 Western Avenue, Suite 410, Seattle, WA 98121. A collection of women's canoe journals and stories, 1900 to the present.

Shepherdson, Carl, Margie, Tina and Rand. *The Family Canoe Trip*. Merrilville, IN: Indiana Camp Supply Books, 1985. The journal of a three-year, 6000-mile trip from New Hampshire to Alaska by two teachers and their two children.

Sumner, Cid Ricketts. *Traveller in the Wilderness*. New York: Harper, 1957. A southern lady, over 60 years old, joins a raft expedition down the Green and Colorado Rivers to photograph the canyons which were to be buried by the Glen Canyon Dam.

Sutherland, Audrey. *Paddling My Own Canoe*. Honolulu: The University of Hawaii Press, 1978. The story of her many trips, always alone, to the uninhabited north coast of Moloka'i, at first swimming and towing a pack, later in a nine-foot inflatable canoe.

Vyvyan, C.C. (Lady Clara Coltman Rogers Vyvyan). *Arctic Adventure*. London: Peter Owen Ltd, 1961. Two Englishwomen with no canoe experience travel to the Arctic to make a trip up the Rat River and down the Porcupine to the Yukon, in 1926. The author has written many other travel books.

Zwinger, Ann *Run, River, Run* 1975, Harper and Row. A naturalist's view of the Green River, travelled by raft and canoe.

Instruction Books

Unlike the previous category, where titles are too few, there is an excess of instruction books available; the following are selected for variety and quality.

Bell, Patricia. *Roughing It Elegantly*. 1987, Cat's Paw Press, Minneapolis. A beginner's guide to canoe camping, especially suited to Minnesota's Boundary Waters.

Conover, Garrett. *Beyond the Paddle*. 1991, Tilbury House, Gardiner ME. A guide to back-country expedition skills: poling, lining, portaging, maneuvering through ice. Excellent teaching style; a thoroughly non-gender-biased book.

Davidson, James West and John Rugge. *The Complete Wilderness Paddler*. New York: Alfred A. Knopf, 1977. Thorough and entertaining, based on all the stages of the authors' trip on the Moise River, Quebec.

Drabik, Harry. *The Spirit of Canoe Camping*, 1981 and *Guide to Wilderness Canoe Camping*, 1987. Minneapolis: Nodin Press. Good handbooks for Boundary Waters Canoe Area camping.

Gullion, Laurie. *Canoeing and Kayaking: The American Canoe Association Instruction Manual*. 1987, American Canoe Association. For training instructors.

Harrison, Dave and Judy. *Canoe Tripping with Kids*. Brattleboro, VT: Stephen Greene Press, 1981. Tells why as well as how.

Jacobson, Cliff. *Canoeing Wild Rivers*. Merrilville, IN: Indiana Camp Supply Books, 1984, new edition, 1989. Very complete guide to planning major canoe expeditions.

Mason, Bill. *The Path of the Paddle*. 1980; NorthWord, 1988. Beautiful and sophisticated presentation of canoe technique and mystique.

Mason, Bill. *The Path of the Paddle (Videos)* Canadian Film Board; North-Word. Two hour-long videos on quietwater and on whitewater, each covering both solo and tandem technique. Very beautiful as well as instructive.

Mason, Bill *The Song of the Paddle: An Illustrated Guide to Wilderness Camping*. 1988, Key Porter Books, NorthWord. Classic (old-style) wilderness camping, with some instruction on canoe technique.

McNair, Robert, Matty L. McNair and Paul Landry, *Basic River Canoeing*, revised edition, 1985, American Camping Association. Inexpensive, accurate, with focus on whitewater technique, not on trips.

Moore, Pat. *Canoeing with Pat Moore: Basic Solo*. (video; 42 mins. VHS) Pat Moore, Stockton WI. Meticulous step-by-step instruction in elegant flatwater paddling.

several titles in the *Basic Essentials* series published by ICS books:

Jacobson, Cliff. *Basic Essentials of Solo Canoeing*. 1991

Niemi, Judith. *Basic Essentials of Women in the Outdoors*. 1990

Roberts, Harry. *Basic Essentials of Canoe Paddling*. 1992

Canoeing History

Adney, Edwin Tappan and Howard I. Chapelle. *The Bark Canoes and Skin Boats of North America*. Smithsonian Bulletin 230, 1964. A beautifully illustrated history of the construction of craft from natural materials.

Hodgins, Bruce and Margaret Hobbs, editors. *Nastawgan: The Canadian*

North by Canoe and Snowshoe. Toronto: Betelgeuse Books, 1985. A collection of historical essays.

Nute, Grace Lee. *The Voyageur,* 1931; *The Voyageur's Highway,* 1941; *Rainy River Country,* 1950. Minnesota Historical Society. Fur trade and logging history along Minnesota border waters.

Raffan, James and Bert Horwood, editors. *Canexus: The Canoe in Canadian Culture.* 1988, Betelgeuse Books, Toronto in cooperation with Queen's University. Scholarly, varied, and entertaining; the outcome of a 1987 conference at Queen's University.

Roberts, Kenneth and Phillip Shackleton. *The Canoe.* Camden, ME: International Marine Publishing Co, 1983. The history, evolution and impact of the canoe in North America.

Tales of the Canadian North, 1984; *Tales of the Canadian Wilderness,* 1985; *Tales of Alaska and the Yukon,* 1986; *Hunting and Fishing in Canada,* 1988, all compiled by Frank Oppel. Castle, a division of Book Sales, Secaucus, NJ. Collections of turn-of-the-century magazine articles, including many on canoeing. No dates, no introductions, sometimes no sources given. Women are scarce in these stories, which generally reflect white tourists, not native people.

Teller, Walter Magnes, editor. *On the River: A Variety of Canoe and Small Boat Voyages.* New Brunswick, NJ: Rutgers University Press, 1976. A collection of writings from 1878 to 1926.

DIRECTORY OF RESOURCES

I. Women's Outdoor Programs and Publications

In the mid-seventies, there were almost no (organized) outdoor programs for adult women—just women canoeing, hiking and climbing on their own. Now for a woman who'd like skilled teaching or connections with other outdoorswomen, there are too many possibilities to list here. Various current lists include over 120 organizations: professionally guided trips by and for women, volunteer associations and (the majority) co-educational education and/or adventure programs who now offer some women-only programs. Publication of outdoor and nature books has also increased in the last decade. Here are some ways to get access to information.

Women in the Wilderness Judith Niemi, 566 Ottawa Avenue South, St. Paul MN 55107 (612) 227-2284. Guided wilderness travels and canoe instruction, in Canada, Minnesota, Wisconsin, Utah. Mail order book service: current women's outdoor books, books on canoe travel, outdoor skills, nature. Free schedule and booklists.

Women Outdoors 55 Talbot Avenue, Medford, MA 02155. Membership address: P. O. Box 655 Amherst, MA 01004-0655. National network of outdoorswomen with chapters in many parts of the country, most active in the Northeast. $15/year. Quarterly magazine, annual gathering, occasional publications.

Women Outdoors Bibliography by Jan Brown. Extensive lists of current and past books on many aspects of women and the outdoors, cross-referenced by location, sport, and topics. The October 1991 list runs over 80 pages, and it is frequently updated. Available for $4.50 from Women Outdoors or Women in the Wilderness.

Women Outdoors publications include: *Getting a Job Out There* Contact addresses and advice on seeking work in the outdoors. Frequently updated. $1 postpaid. *Women's Adventure Skill Programs* compiled for reference only, not endorsement. Most listings are co-ed groups that offer some women's trips; the most up-to-date record of women's programs. Frequently updated. $1 postpaid. Both are available from Women in the Wilderness or Women Outdoors.

Women Outdoors: The Best 1900 Books, Programs and Periodicals by Jennifer Abromowitz. 1990. 179 pages of bibliography (not always annotated or with bibliographic data) of literature, skills books, trail guides, and lists of periodicals and programs. $28, from the author, RD 1 Box 345C, Williamsburg, MA 01096.

Women's Sports and Fitness subscription address P. O. Box 472, Mt. Morris, IL 61054. 8×/year, $19.97/yr. $29.97 for two years; for Canada, add $5/year.

Women's Sports Foundation Information and referral service, (800) 227-3988 may be able to help you locate sports and outdoor organizations in your area.

II. Canoeing Magazines and Organizations

American Canoe Association P. O. Box 1190, Newington, VA 22122 $25/year; $35 voting member. Newsletter, book service.

Canadian Recreational Canoe Association 1029 Hyde Park Road, Suite 5, Hyde Park, Ontario N0M 1Z0. (519) 473-2109. $10/year. Quarterly newsletter *Kanawa Magazine*, book service.

Canoe magazine. Subscription address P. O. Box 7011, Red Oak, IA 51591-4011. 6×/year. $18. (800) 678-5432.

Che-mun: the Newsletter of Canadian Wilderness Canoeing Box 548, Station O, Toronto, Ontario M4A 2P1 Quarterly. One year $10; two years $18.

NORS [National Organization for River Sports] Resource Center, Box 6847, Colorado Springs, CO 80934. (719) 473-2466. Good source of river guidebooks for all parts of U.S. and abroad.

Northern Books P. O. Box 211, Station P, Toronto, Ontario M5S 2S7 (416) 531-8873 A mail-order book service, used and rare books on the Canadian North and canoeing.

Paddler magazine. Subscription address P. O. Box 697, Fallbrook, CA 92028. (619) 723-8155. 6 ×/year. $15, 2 years, $25; Canadian subscribers add $12/year.

Sea Kayaker 6327 Seaview Avenue N.W., Seattle, WA 98107-2664. Quarterly, $13/year U.S.; $15 (U.S.) to Canada.

Wilderness Canoe Association P. O. Box 496, Postal Station K, Toronto, Ontario, M4P 2G9. Membership $15 student, $25 adult, $35 family. Quarterly newsletter, *Nastawgan*, on Canadian wilderness paddling.

Wooden Canoe Heritage Association P. O. Box 226, Blue Mountain NY 12812. Membership $20/year.

ABOUT THE EDITORS

Judith Niemi has been a wilderness guide for twenty-five years and is the director of Women in the Wilderness. She lives in St. Paul.

Barbara Wieser has been a wilderness guide for ten years and currently works at Amazon bookstore in Minneapolis.

SPORTS AND OUTDOORS TITLES FROM SEAL PRESS

DOWN THE WILD RIVER NORTH by Constance Helmericks. $12.95, 1-878067-28-1. In 1965, Connie Helmericks announced to her two teenage daughters: "We are going to make a canoe expedition to the Arctic Ocean." This is their remarkable story of a wilderness adventure down the Peace, Slave and Mackenzie river systems in a sturdy twenty-foot canoe.

WHEN WOMEN PLAYED HARDBALL by Susan E. Johnson. $14.95, 1-878067-43-5. This book is a celebration of the brief yet remarkable era of the All-American Girls Professional Baseball League and a remembrance of a sensational championship series. Filled with colorful stories and anecdotes by the ball players, as well as play-by-play action and insightful commentary exploring League culture, *When Women Played Hardball* honors a unique chapter in sports history.

THE CURVE OF TIME by M. Wylie Blanchet. $12.95, 1-878067-27-3. This is the fascinating true adventure story of a woman who packed her five children onto a twenty-five-foot boat and explored the coastal waters of the Pacific Northwest summer after summer in the late 1920s.

WATER'S EDGE: *Women Who Push the Limits in Rowing, Kayaking and Canoeing* by Linda Lewis. $14.95, 1-878067-18-4. An inspiring book takes us inside the world of competitive rowing, kayaking and wilderness canoeing through ten candid profiles of women who have made their mark in these sports—from pioneering rower Ernestine Bayer to Arctic distance canoer Valerie Fons.

LEADING OUT: *Women Climbers Reaching for the Top* edited by Rachel da Silva. $16.95, 1-878067-20-6. Packed with riveting accounts of high peak ascents and fascinating narratives by some of the world's top climbers, this exciting collection is an inspiring testament to the powers of discipline and desire.

UNCOMMON WATERS: *Women Write About Fishing* edited by Holly Morris. $14.95, 1-878067-10-9. A wonderful anthology that captures the bracing adventure and meditative moments of fishing in the words of thirty-four women anglers—from finessing trout and salmon in the Pacific Northwest to chasing bass and catfish in the Deep South.

SEAL PRESS, founded in 1976 to provide a forum for women writers and feminist issues, has many other books of fiction, non-fiction and poetry. You may order directly from us at 3131 Western Avenue, Suite 410, Seattle, Washington 98121 (add 15% of total book order for shipping and handling). Write to us for a free catalog.